GATHERING POWER

GATHERING POWER
THE FUTURE OF PROGRESSIVE POLITICS IN AMERICA

PAUL OSTERMAN

BEACON PRESS
BOSTON

Beacon Press
25 Beacon Street
Boston, Massachusetts 02108-2892
www.beacon.org

Beacon Press books
are published under the auspices of
the Unitarian Universalist Association of Congregations.

06 05 04 03 02   8 7 6 5 4 3 2 1

This book is printed on acid-free paper that meets the uncoated paper
ANSI/NISO specifications for permanence as revised in 1992.

Composition by Wilsted & Taylor Publishing Services

Library of Congress Cataloging-in-Publication Data

Osterman, Paul.
   Gathering power : the future of progressive politics in America / Paul Osterman.
      p.   cm.
   ISBN 0-8070-4338-9 (cloth : alk. paper)
   1. Political participation—United States.   I. Title.
   JK1764 .O85 2002
   322.4'0973—dc21
                                                        2002006811

For my family:
Susan, Rachel, and Michelle.
And to my parents,
Henry and Esther Osterman.

Contents

1   **Reviving Progressive Politics**   1

2   **Building Organizations**   35

3   **Faith**   88

4   **Practicing a New Politics**   122

5   **Managing Our Economic Destiny**   148

6   **Gathering Power**   171

   Notes   193

   Acknowledgments   210

   Index   212

Chapter 1

Reviving Progressive Politics

These are not happy days for politics in America, or at least so it seems from the perspective of Washington, D.C. The percentage of Americans reporting that they mistrust government is rising while voter turnout is declining. And if this is a bad time for politics in general, it is even worse for progressive politics. Progressive politics is going nowhere at the national level. Democrats have run to the center and will no longer touch issues of power and privilege lest they be accused of class warfare. In Washington, interest groups checkmate each other, and those few that represent progressive causes cannot compete with their opponents in money or influence. The union movement, the traditional backbone of progressives, continues to produce funds and foot soldiers for elections, but its membership base is eroding and its moral claims are unfortunately no longer compelling to most Americans.

The decline in politics has been accelerated by how we have come to think about the economy. The boom of the 1990s brought many benefits, but it was accompanied by a rhetoric that implied that citizens could, and indeed should, have little voice in the trajectory of the economy. The economic difficulties of Germany and Japan, both of which had practiced a form of capitalism that restrained the play of pure market forces, contributed to this trend, but more important, the spread—in reality and in rhetoric—of globalization introduced a new force that seems impossible to control or restrain. Occasional eruptions, such as those at the

1999 World Trade Organization conference in Seattle, testify more to a sense of helplessness than to any ideas about a way forward.

Viewed from Washington, the political scene is indeed discouraging. But if things are so bad, how can we explain what happened in Austin, Texas, on a Sunday and Monday in April 2001? That Sunday the Industrial Areas Foundation (IAF), a network of community organizations in the Southwest (with sister organizations in other cities around the country), convened its annual Human Development Fund and Alliance Schools conference in an Austin hotel. The purpose of the conference was to celebrate the network's achievements, to provide ongoing training to its members, and to lobby the state legislature to pass the network's legislative agenda.

The hotel ballroom filled with fifteen hundred people for the two o'clock Sunday start. Many were active members in IAF organizations from Dallas, Houston, El Paso, San Antonio, Fort Worth, Austin, and the Rio Grande Valley. Also scattered throughout the room were teachers and principals from some of the Texas schools that the IAF has organized through its Alliance School program. Some of these people had gotten on buses at 4:00 A.M. in order to reach Austin on time. The room was bursting with energy, and that energy exploded with the roll call that kicked off the session.

Twenty people stood at the microphones in the front of the room and in turn yelled to the crowd, "I'm from EPISO in El Paso, and we're here 50 strong," "I'm from Dallas Area Interfaith, and we're here 100 strong," "I'm from Valley Interfaith, and we're here 250 strong," "I'm from COPS in San Antonio and we're here 200 strong," and so on through the roll of Southwest organizations that had sent representatives to this meeting.

The meeting then began with opening prayers, led by an African-American Baptist minister from Dallas and a rabbi from Austin. The leadoff speaker, Ernesto Cortes Jr., the supervisor of the IAF network in the Southwest and a member of the IAF National Executive Committee, then rose. Cortes gave a talk that captured the IAF mix of politics, religion, and organizing.

> We have been told we are going through a historic period of prosperity, unprecedented in terms of growth, employment, wealth creation. We are the wonder of the world. Yet if we look at what is happening to the

richest and the poorest, anyone who has a brain and a heart would find it very troubling. . . .

I'm reminded of another time which comes out of our tradition. And our cantor with his beautiful prayer and beautiful song reflected some of that great tradition, which comes out of the Old Testament prophets. I'm in particular struck by the story of a prophet, a fellow called Amos, who considered himself not a prophet but a worker. Not a man of substance but an ordinary fellow who was moved by the great injustice he saw. And Amos was challenged because when he came to the great capital city, when he came to Los Angeles or to Phoenix, when he came to Houston, what he saw was a great disparity between rich and poor. He saw a perversion of the tradition, of the institutions and especially the courts. If Israel was faithful to its tradition, these courts were a critical institution because these courts were the place where everyone had the same status. They were run by the politicos, the men of power and wealth, but these courts were under an obligation to give fair treatment to the widows, the orphans, the elderly, to those on the margin of life. . . . And these courts were not functioning.

So, what Amos says in the great prophetic book is that Israel had strayed, that Israel had wandered off. And he goes after those who are the elders, those who are the rulers, but more importantly he goes after the religious leaders because they too had sold out. Those too had catered to the powerful and the rich and given up their prophetic voices.

So Amos feels this need to say, "I can't stand this situation. I can't stand that kids in Los Angeles go to school every day but are off track and are permanently on vacation, I can't stand that eleven- and twelve-year-olds in Phoenix can't go to school because they have to take care of their little brothers and sisters. . . ."

The only way we are going to be successful, the only way we are going to make it possible for our children to have health care, to make it possible for our children to be well educated, to make it possible for our families to have living wages is to learn to organize.

How do we learn to organize? Organizing means looking for leaders. Organizing means understanding the iron rule "Never do for someone what he or she can do for themselves." Organizing means understanding that power comes in two forms: unilateral, top-down, expert-driven power from organized money. . . . But power also comes from organized people with their institutions. Power can also be not just unilateral but also relational. Relational means when two or more people get together and have a plan and begin to act on that plan. When you put together a house meeting, you are building power. When we build power across our region, then we can have the kinds of initiatives, the kinds of programs we want. We have to remember our mantra "power before program." "Power before program." Got that?

The meeting then broke up into about twenty workshops. Some of the workshops dealt with policy issues confronting the network, and these included topics such as how to create effective job-training programs, how to improve the classroom performance of teachers, how to organize the parents of a school, and how to initiate a living-wage campaign in a community. Other workshops were about organization building: how to conduct one-on-one meetings with prospective members, how to organize house meetings, what the IAF means when it characterizes itself as a broad-based organization, and how to work with congregations to help them increase their membership and encourage them to link with the IAF.

One round of workshops took place after the opening session, another after dinner, and a third early the next morning. People thus attended three workshops, and the enthusiasm never flagged. Some were professionals, accustomed to training but still not having been in school for many years. Many others had less than a high school education. Some spoke only Spanish (each workshop had its own translation setup). Many of the people were well past middle age, and the travel and early morning sessions must have been difficult. But everyone moved from session to session with energy, paid careful attention, asked questions, took notes. The IAF, says Rosa Boden,* an attendee from the Rio Grande Valley, is "my university," and that was never more clear than during this day and a half.

On Monday, at the end of the third workshop, the fifteen hundred people reconvened. Now came the first hint of the political power the IAF wields. The Texas Commissioner of Education, a Bush Republican, addressed the group and complemented them on their Alliance School

---

* I have used, with permission, the real names of virtually all of the IAF leaders and organizers mentioned in this book. The names that are pseudonyms are Manuela and Jaime.

program. Assorted school superintendents from around the state also took the stage to praise the organization. In a hint of what was to come, members of the audience stood to ask very specific questions of these officials and to extract commitments from them. With a closing prayer, the conference came to an end, but a long day was ahead of the group: they climbed into buses for a short ride to a downtown church, where a rally was planned that focused on the IAF legislative agenda. The size of the crowd swelled because conference participants were joined by new members who had traveled to Austin simply to attend the rally. From the Rio Grande Valley, a five-hour bus trip away, another 250 people arrived at the church, and more members came from the other Texas cities organized by the IAF.

What was billed as a rally was really what the IAF calls an accountability session. On the stage stood a half dozen IAF members from different organizations around the state and another dozen or so state representatives and senators. The IAF members systematically worked through their legislative agenda. First, they outlined the legislation the IAF proposed on health issues, a series of measures to ease Medicaid eligibility and to expand the CHIP program for uninsured children. They then turned to each legislator and asked a simple yes or no question: do you support our agenda on this issue? If the legislator equivocated or launched into a campaign speech, the IAF members waited politely for a brief period and then if the speaker wound down returned to the simple question: do you support our agenda? If the speaker seemed to go on too long, he or she was, in a friendly fashion, cut off and then confronted with the question. With the health agenda completed, the accountability session turned, with a similar pattern, to support for the Alliance Schools and for the IAF's job-training and economic development agenda.

Prior to the rally, the IAF organizations had visited the legislature regularly to press these issues and to invite members to the rally/accountability session. However, not everyone they approached agreed to attend. With the accountability session completed, two thousand people marched to the state capitol and broke up into groups from each city. Each group went in search of the legislators who had not attended. Several hundred people from the Rio Grande Valley tracked down Senator Eduardo Lucio, chair of the Subcommittee on Border Affairs, who represents a district in the Valley. Lucio was on the senate floor and refused to come out to meet the group. They waited an hour. When he finally appeared, Rosa Boden and Father Alfonso Guevara, both members of Valley Interfaith—the IAF organization in the Rio Grande Valley—stood on the top of the stairs with him, facing the crowd below, and repeated the same accountability questions that had been put to his colleagues earlier. The senator responded affirmatively.

At the end of the day people boarded their buses and returned home. However, the next day, and every working day thereafter in the spring, smaller numbers returned to work the legislature.

If we juxtapose these two days against the earlier critiques of the health of American democratic processes, something does not compute. We see a cross section of people—professionals and high school dropouts; whites, Hispanics, and African-Americans—working together in a common political enterprise. In the morning of the first day they listened to speeches, but from then on they were active players, not passive members. Partly they were there to learn about issues and about organizing so that they could be more effective political actors. However, they were also there to enforce accountability on the part of their elected representatives. That is, they were unwilling to accept that decision making and politics were beyond their control.

This book is about what is wrong with progressive politics in America and how to fix it. The "how to fix it" ideas draw heavily on the lessons of the IAF, but first we need to explore more deeply what has gone wrong.

The Poverty of (Progressive) Politics

Contemporary debates, at least within the Democratic party, are about how to identify and present the right national message that will attract voters. My argument is that this is the wrong tack. The core problem facing progressives is the declining participation of their constituency: the falling voting rates and declining political activity of people below the median in the income distribution. Politics is increasingly biased toward the better off. The solution lies not in crafting a better message to beam from Washington but rather in effective local mobilization. What is missing are opportunities for poor and working people to participate and learn firsthand about politics and to become connected in an ongoing way to a political organization. Absent such a connection, cynicism and withdrawal will continue, and absent such a connection, it will prove very difficult to build a reliable progressive constituency.

Before turning to the ills that beset politics, a fair question to raise is why should we even care about a progressive agenda. There are two answers to this question. The first is precisely the discussion of politics: progressives believe that citizens should have multiple opportunities and incentives to participate in politics, to help shape what our government does. Yet the trends have pushed away from this. As we will see, politics is increasingly a game played by the economic and political elites operating out of Washington. Fundamental ideas about what it means to be a democracy are violated when few are engaged and when those who do participate are not representative of the citizenry.

Of course, a more open politics need not lead to a substantive set of progressive ideas. The newly involved may have a different agenda. However, as we will see, people who have distanced themselves from politics as practiced today are more sympathetic to progressive concerns than are their wealthier fellow citizens who have managed to remain connected. The substantive core of the progressive agenda is economic inequality.

Not everyone agrees that there really is a potential constituency in America with respect to issues of inequality. A skeptical view was recently put forward persuasively by David Brooks in his comparison of economic attitudes in upper-middle-class Montgomery County, Maryland, and working- to middle-class Franklin County, Pennsylvania.[1] The income disparity between the two areas is substantial, but Brooks reports finding no resentment on the part of the residents of the poorer region. The cost of living is much lower, and according to Brooks, there is nothing for sale in the area that people can't afford. Furthermore, economic concerns are not really all that relevant to people. In the words of one minister he interviewed, "There is nowhere near as much resentment as you might expect. People have come to understand that they will struggle financially. It's part of their identity. But the economy is not their God. People value a sense of community more than they do their portfolio." Brooks concludes that all is pretty much well, and his analogy is to a high school cafeteria in which different subcultures coexist peacefully with no sense of dissatisfaction. In this picture there is no room for a strong progressive political agenda focused in economic inequality.

Is this right? In the year 2000, 22 percent of all American families with children had total incomes of less than twenty-five thousand dollars.[2] To describe these people as functioning on equal terms in a high school cafeteria with the affluent seems a stretch. Even during the expansion of the 1990s, the prosperity was very unevenly shared. A dramatic example comes from tax data collected by the Internal Revenue Service. If we look at the period from 1989, a business cycle peak, to 1997, in the midst of the expansion of the 1990s, the patterns are remarkable.[3] The richest 1 percent of the American people experienced a gain of 36 percent in their income, the next richest 4 percent saw their incomes grow by 16.8 percent, and the next 15 percent enjoyed a 9.7 percent increase. Meanwhile, the bottom 20 percent had a 0.0 percent increase in their income, and the second poorest 20 percent saw their incomes grow by 5.6 percent. To put dollars on this, the top 1 percent saw a $179,000 increase in their annual income, whereas the bottom 20 percent enjoyed no increase. Income inequality exploded in this period, and this was a continuation of the 1979 to 1989 period in which the divergence was even greater. Preliminary IRS data suggest that 1998 and 1999 patterns showed more of the same.

Polling data show the problem quite starkly. A *Business Week* survey done in 1999 showed that 75 percent of Americans believe the benefits of the "New Economy" have been distributed unevenly, and 69 percent said business was doing only a poor or fair job of raising living standards.[4] In the summer of 2001, 44 percent of Americans described the nation as a society divided into haves and have-nots.[5] In the late 1980s, at the end of a previous economic boom, the fraction subscribing to such a description was only 26 percent. In 2001, more than a quarter of Americans reported that they did not have enough money to make ends meet. In stark contrast to Brooks's assertions, only half said that they could afford the things they want.

If progressives can find a credible way to address these issues, and if they can convince people that a fair and open politics is possible, then they will have a strong constituency. The puzzle, of course, is the disconnect between the economics and the politics. Part of the issue is that the rhetoric of national politicians is not consistent with their actions. It was hard to read about Al Gore's fund-raising techniques in the 2000 election and conclude that he stood, as his slogan claimed, for the "people against the powerful." After all, "the powerful" must have expected to receive something for their money.

A deeper explanation is the failure of political institutions to connect with and mobilize people. Political parties, the distinguished political scientist Walter Dean Burnham once optimistically wrote, are "the only device thus far invented by the wit of Western man which with some effectiveness can generate countervailing collective power on behalf of the many individually powerless against the [privileged] few."[6] This is true no longer. The Democrats may be closer to this vision than the Republicans are, but dismal turnout among those at the bottom suggests that their message is not convincing. A recent survey of nonvoters concluded that they "want politicians to engage more directly with them in venues that are closer to their lives; they want more contact."[7] All of the evidence about turnout and mobilization suggests that only via strong local organizing can turnout among nonvoters, particularly nonvoters located at the bottom of the economic distribution, be increased.

The General Contempt for Politics

Alan Wolfe recently interviewed people around the country and, among other topics, asked their opinion of politics and politicians. It seems that nothing positive was said, and a fair sample of their remarks include "Politicians, they never talk straight. They always find an excuse for everything," and "It's all elaborate pretend and deceit," and "There's inherent dishonesty there."[8] These comments are reflected in nationally representative data on political attitudes held by all adults (regardless of whether or not they voted). In 1972, 52 percent of people said that government is run by "a few big interests looking out for themselves," and 25 percent felt that "government pays a good deal of attention to what people think." By 2000, the former sentiment was held by 65 percent of Americans and the latter by 16 percent.[9]

Even in 1972 (toward the end of the Vietnam War but before the Watergate scandal), the level of overall trust in the government was strikingly low, but it has fallen substantially since then. There is nothing in these data that would lead one to think that Americans have a very high opinion of their political system.

Not only are attitudes about politics very much on the negative side, but so is behavior. People are walking the talk. Or, to be more precise, they are sitting on their hands. As is well known, voter turnout has declined. In 1960, 58 percent of the eligible population showed up on election day to vote for a president, but in 2000 it was 51 percent. Turnout in nonpresidential election years is even more dismal. Although there is some debate in the professional literature about how much of this decline is real and how much is due to a miscounting of the potentially eligible population (because of the surge of immigrants), the evidence that voter turnout has genuinely declined is quite strong.[10] Furthermore, elections are only one of the ways in which people can participate politically. They can also write letters to their representatives, attend meetings, sign petitions, and so on. It turns out that there has also been a long-term decline in these forms of governmental participation.[11]

The Tilt to the Top

These attitudes and behaviors have to disturb anyone who believes that a healthy political system is important. It is not hard to think that civic life would be improved if people felt more positively about politics and if politicians earned a better reputation. But for progressives the news is even worse. "The flaw in the pluralist heaven," commented renowned political scientist E. E. Schattschneider in his aptly titled book *The Semi-Sovereign People,* "is that the heavenly chorus sings with a strong upper-class accent."[12] Patterns of political participation have a strong class, or at least income, bias to begin with, and the decline in participation has exacerbated the problem.

The evidence on the tilt in political participation toward those with higher income is quite extensive. In the 2000 election, among the bottom 20 percent of the income distribution, 54 percent voted, whereas among the top 20 percent, 88 percent went to the polls.[13] To pick another example, in their classic quantitative study on political participation Sidney Verba, Kay Lehman Schlozman, and Henry Brady report that participation in political activities is much higher among the better educated and the better off.[14] When the authors do a simple count of the number of political acts people engage in, the figure is 1.3 for people with annual incomes of less than $15,000 and 3.4 for people with annual incomes of more than $125,000, and this pattern holds for all activities, not just campaign contributions.[15] For example, 7 percent of people with annual incomes of more than $75,000 engaged in protest activities, whereas 3 percent of those with annual incomes of less than $15,000 did so.

The tilt toward the top has worsened over time. In the 1972 election, 60 percent of people whose household income was in the bottom quarter of the income distribution voted, but by the 2000 election only 51 percent of people similarly situated went to the polls. Meanwhile, among people whose income was above the median (that is in the top half of the income distribution), turnout actually increased a little bit (from 81 percent to 83 percent) from 1972 to 2000.[16] The consequence of this is easy to see: not only are people in general increasingly turned off from politics, but an important natural constituency of progressives is coming to represent a smaller share of those who remain active.

This bias toward upper-income groups in politics is also reflected in the composition of new national political associations that have emerged in recent years. For example, Theda Skocpol studied members of Common Cause, one of the largest public interest political associations: 42.6 percent of adherents had a graduate or professional degree, 14.5 percent had some graduate training short of a degree, 18.7 percent had a college degree, and average family income was 85 percent above the national median.[17] Comparing new political associations with the earlier groups such as Veterans of Foreign Wars or the Knights of Columbus, Skocpol writes, "Contemporary associations are heavily tilted towards upper-middle class constituencies. . . . The wealthiest and best-educated Americans are much more privileged in the new civic world than their (less numerous) counterparts were in the pre-1960s civic world centered in cross-class membership federations."[18]

The tilt in the electorate away from poor and working people poses a serious problem for progressives, since it robs them of their natural electoral constituency. It creates what voting historian Alex Keyssar characterized as "that most distinctive and paradoxical feature of contemporary American politics: the low, class-correlated turnout of voters."[19] Furthermore, contrary to the assertions of some observers, the political views of those who do not vote are in fact different, and more progressive, than those who do vote.[20]

Although there is a long history of formal restrictions on voting, legal barriers don't explain these dismal patterns. Formal restrictions were gradually eliminated beginning in the 1970s, and in 1993 the National Voter Registration Act, the so-called motor voter bill, eased the remaining registration barriers. This was "the final act [of] removing obstacles to the ballot box."[21] The bill led to a substantial increase in the numbers of the potentially eligible population who registered: within two years an additional 9 million people, 20 percent of the nonregistered population, registered.[22] But consider what happened next: actual turnout among registered voters continued to fall, and the class bias in voting increased.

To explain these patterns, social science tends to focus on the characteristics of individuals, and this proclivity is encouraged by the ready availability of large-scale data sets that permit analysis of the relationship of personal characteristics to behaviors such as voting. However, at least with respect to the class bias in voting, this style of explanation is deficient. In other nations lower-income people vote at much higher rates than in America, and this is true for countries that have winner-take-all systems as well as for those with proportional representation (a system that is more friendly to the emergence of third-party alternatives and therefore is likely to encourage voting by otherwise alienated citizens). The historical record within the United States is also a problem for proponents of explanations on a purely individual level. For example, during the New Deal, when politics clearly mattered and when the Democratic party spoke to people's interests, the rate of voting increased across the board.

The failure to increase voting turnout despite the easing of registration requirements points quite clearly to the inadequacy of politics centered on television, mass mailing, and slogans. It reinforces the importance of building strong local institutions to which people can relate and that can convince them that political participation can have a payoff for them.

It is also important to understand that there is more to politics, and to having a political voice, than voting. It is natural that commentators focus on elections; they are after all the preeminent symbol of American democracy. However, the formulation and implementation of policy typically takes place off the electoral stage. These additional forms of participation are important for several reasons. First, and most directly, they help influence substantive outcomes that are important to people. They also feed back into voting. A major source of political cynicism is the widespread view that politicians make promises at election time and then proceed their own way after the polls have closed. Effective mobilization requires convincing people not only that they can have an impact on who is elected but also that there are mechanisms to ensure that the person they elect is accountable once in office. For local mobilizing institutions to succeed, they must have the capacity to enforce accountability.

How to Fix It (and How Not to Fix It)

In the face of these trends, there have naturally been important debates within the Democratic party and within progressive circles about how to respond. The main line of thinking, which is consistent with what has happened to politics in general, is how to better articulate a message. For example, during the 2000 presidential campaign, Al Gore on occasion used populist language aimed at drug companies, HMOs, and sometimes business in general. After the election was concluded, the centrist and conservative wings within the Democratic party attacked this progressive tinge by claiming that Gore had erred by engaging in "class warfare" and pandering to special interests. The Democratic left replied that Gore's message was popular.[23]

This emphasis on repairing the prospects of progressives by focusing on program and message has been given support by several scholars and policy analysts who are less rooted in the news of the day. Ruy Teixeira and Joel Rogers have forcefully made arguments along these lines.[24] In their view, the greatest loss suffered by the Democratic party is the defection of white voters with less than a college education, who have been under severe economic pressure in the past decade and a half and have concluded that the federal government is ineffective in meeting their needs. These people are not inherently antigovernment; they are simply pragmatic about assessing whether they are benefiting from government policy. To date they have a negative assessment. However, although this group holds conservative cultural values, its members are potentially responsive to a progressive economic agenda. The Democrats have moved toward this group's values—the objective of President Clinton was to moderate the social rhetoric of the Democrats—but they have erred by buying into the conservative economics espoused both by Republicans and by the Democratic Leadership Council. For a progressive agenda to be appealing to this "forgotten majority," it has to include initiatives in areas such as health care, retirement security, and education.

The emphasis on message, whether in ephemeral electoral rhetoric or in the deeper policy commitments of the party, is understandable. Developing a popular program is obviously important. The process of getting this position right—polling, writing policy papers, running conferences, consulting with interest groups, selling the idea to the press—is just the kind of work that is congenial to a political world centered around Washington and to the think-tank and academic establishments. However, the progressive Washington institutions that have emerged in recent years are not friendly to real people participating.

Sidney Tarrow, a leading student of social movements, describes the emerging pattern as "a combination of small professional leadership; large but mainly passive mass support; and impersonal network like connective structures."[25] This approach cannot succeed in mobilizing the missing progressive constituency. As critics such as Marshall Ganz have noted, politics today has come to mean polling, fund-raising, television advertising, and fine-tuning a message.[26] None of this involves people in any real way in practicing and doing politics. Nor can these methods overcome the cynicism created by lack of accountability.

At best, the emphasis on message and advertising creates only ephemeral advantages. Next year, or in the next two years, conservatives will hit upon a more attractive message or slogan or candidate, and voters will defect. Washington-centric politics as practiced today is what prevents the real resurgence of an effective progressive political base. An effective progressive politics has to be built from the ground up by strengthening the local political institutions that connect people to politics and that generate political skills, commitment, and—indeed—optimism that are necessary to create a critical mass of engaged citizenry.

Mobilizing

Increased political commitment flows from two types of local organization. The first are those of everyday life: churches, schools, clubs, and so on. A substantial body of research supports the proposition that being active, even in organizations that are nonpolitical, teaches skills and awakens political interests.[27] Indeed, I will pay a great deal of attention over the course of this book to the role that religion and churches play in fomenting political activism.

The second way in which people become active in politics is when a more explicitly political organization mobilizes them. This can happen when unions organize their members around an issue, when local political parties involve people in a political campaign, or when people get caught up in social movements such as the Civil Rights movement or environmental causes. The point is that people's involvement and commitment are not spontaneous but rather are encouraged by a political organization that reaches out and connects with them.

The evidence that political participation is driven by local mobilization efforts is supported by more than common sense and anecdotal examples. Two scholars, Steven Rosenstone and John Mark Hansen, who carefully studied political participation, were able to compare surveys of political participation undertaken in the 1960s with identical surveys executed in the late 1980s. They ran a horse race between two explanations for the decline of participation: the personal characteristics of individuals and the extent to which the kinds of organizations mentioned above systematically mobilized people. They summarize their findings as follows: "The results . . . are dramatic. . . . The changing patterns of mobilization by parties, campaigns, and social movements account for at least half of the decline of electoral participation since the 1960s."[28]

As we have seen, political participation is low, particularly for the constituency of progressives. The logic just laid out suggests that we first ask about the role, or the failure, of our political parties in organizing people. After all, more than any other institution, we would expect that parties would teach people about the issues, involve them in formulating positions, and mobilize them for elections.

The weakness of parties today as mobilizing institutions can be seen in a variety of ways. One is simply the decline of party identification. Since reliable data were first collected in the early 1950s, there has been a steady fall in the percentage of people who identify themselves are partisans of either party. The leading scholar of this trend writes that "citizens simply see the parties as less relevant than in the past. With the growth of mass media and candidate-centered campaigns, the importance of parties . . . in general has been weakened."[29]

A sign of this trend is how little contact parties have with people (and also that what little contact they do have is income-skewed). For example, when asked about whether they were contacted by either of the political parties in the 1996 presidential election, only 21 percent of those with a high school degree responded affirmatively, whereas 30 percent with some college and 34 percent with a college degree said yes. Among those in the bottom 15 percent of the income distribution, 18 percent responded affirmatively, whereas among those in the top 5 percent, 34 percent said yes.[30]

A vivid description of how parties (don't) function is provided by A. James Reichley for West Los Angeles, where local and state races in the early 1990s were controlled by the "machine" of three congressmen, Howard Berman, Henry Waxman, and Mel Levine. At the center of the operation is a political consulting firm managed by Berman's brother. The firm specializes in direct mail, and it can target the mail to subgroups depending of the ethnicity implied by the surname, whether the names are prefaced with "Ms.," and so on. Each of these is a clue as to which piece of mail to send. The firm also arranges endorsements, raises funds, and so on. What is missing is any involvement by ordinary people. "The alliance places little stock in grassroots organization. . . . It maintains little two-way contact with most local neighborhoods and communities. . . . It operates a form of local politics designed for a society in which localities as organized communities hardly exist and in which voters are represented as identifiers with interest groups."[31]

Political scientist David Mayhew exhaustively examined political systems on a state-by-state basis and concluded that (as of 1980) 37 percent of the nation's population lived in states with strong state political parties.[32] However, this represented a steady decline from earlier years, and the numbers would be even lower today. In Mayhew's words, "Money has been replacing the mobilizing powers of patronage-based and membership organizations."[33]

The current weakness of political parties and the inability of political institutions to mobilize people are not new. The pattern emerged over much of the last century. In the nineteenth century, voting rates, among enfranchised white males, were remarkably high.[34] In every presidential election between 1840 and 1896 national turnout ranged between 69 percent and 82 percent and in the north the rates were even higher.[35] These impressive rates were sustained because voters felt strong attachments to their ethnic group, to their religion, and, in the cities, to their local political machine. Together these mobilizing institutions maintained a high rate of participation. Accounts of this period are full of stories about parades, neighborhood canvassing, and ward bosses who kept people connected to politics. The accounts also suggest that the electorate felt a high degree of passion and commitment to politics.

This system fell apart with the election of 1896, which pitted William Jennings Bryan against William McKinley. Bryan, the nominee of the Populists and the Democrats, represented a protest against the surging industrial capitalism and east coast finance that was reshaping the American economy. McKinley, the Republican nominee, represented the Northeast as well as modern industry and finance. Bryan's decisive defeat forever altered American politics.

The election eliminated vigorous party competition in most regions, with the South becoming overwhelmingly Democratic and the Northeast and Midwest Republican. This not only reduced the incentive to mobilize new voters but actually led to a positive desire not to do so, since with the parties in full control of their territory new voters could spell possible trouble. However, the election, and the events surrounding it, provided other reasons for the political parties to discourage those at the bottom of the social ladder from voting. The contentiousness of the Populist movement, the growth of unrest among industrial workers, an unrest that often resulted in violent labor-management conflicts, and the potential difficulties represented by large urban conglomerations of immigrants all provided incentives for established political power to suppress electoral turnout.

Voting turnout was reduced in a variety of ways. Among the most important were the reforms introduced by the Progressive movement aimed at weakening political machines. Political machines connected to people in a far more personal way than does the modern politics of television, mail, and focus groups. As a result, the machines were effective mobilizing institutions.

Urban reformers aimed at reducing participation by the "masses" and achieved this in a variety of ways. On the basis of her study of reform in the Southwest, political scientist Amy Bridges wrote:

> Reformers' aims of loosening the ties of politicians and their constituents on the one hand, and limiting the number of constituents on the other, informed their designs. To those ends reformers endorsed nonpartisanship, citywide and nonconcurrent elections, selection of the mayor by city council, and a variety of barriers to registration and voting. . . . Reform regimes governed a political life of low participation and little public dissent . . . the exclusion of most urban residents from the political system.[36]

Taken as a whole, the consequence of developments after 1896 was "the secular decline in voting . . . a decline that with relative minor variations has persisted throughout the twentieth century."[37] Historian Robert Wiebe, one of the most perceptive interpreters of twentieth-century American history, wrote that "by and large, America's twentieth-century parties simply shaped their operations to the disappearance of the bottom third."[38] In a world in which incumbents are regularly reelected, it makes little sense to stir the pot by vigorously going after new voters. Nor does it make sense when politicians live or die by how much money they can raise to fashion platforms that appeal to the interest of an inchoate group of nonvoters at the expense of a reliable voting and financial base.

Three Examples

At the start of the twenty-first century we lack a strong system of political mobilization. Political parties have become advertising and fund-raising operations. Although at election time any given candidate may try to contact the slice of voters that he or she feels is sympathetic, there is no ongoing vehicle to connect people to politics on a regular basis. The consequence is that the last-minute appeals and efforts to craft the right message fall short. Washington-centric advertising-mailing list-focus group-message-crafting politics cannot succeed in building the kind of attachment that is necessary to commit progressive constituencies. Local and state political parties lack the ability to do so.

Strong local organizations, political and otherwise, are necessary to teach skills, to educate people about political issues, and to mobilize people. Individuals, for their part, commit when they are active and learn and have a role to play, not simply when they are passively on the receiving end of advertising messages.

Three quite different examples—the Civil Rights movement, the emergence of the Christian Right, and the political work of unions—illustrate the importance of local organizations and institution building for underwriting political activity.

The Civil Rights movement was not the result of clever thinking and strategizing by a national elite, nor did it arise spontaneously from the individual outrage of thousands of citizens who somehow came together to demonstrate. Rather the movement was based on local organization and institution building that taught people skills, connected them to each other, and provided ongoing support. In his history of that movement, Aldon Morris writes that "the basic resources enabling a dominated group to engage in sustained protest are well developed internal social institutions and organizations that provide the community with encompassing communications networks, organized groups, experienced leaders, and social resources including money, labor, and charisma, that can be mobilized to attain collective goals."[39]

At the national level, the only possible entity that could have been considered an elite was the National Association for the Advancement of Colored People (NAACP), but Morris shows (and virtually all historians would agree) that as important as the NAACP was in bringing court cases and representing the Civil Rights movement in Washington, it was out of touch with the grass roots and was too bureaucratic and cautious to claim credit for the events that flowed from the Montgomery Bus Boycott to the Freedom Rides, the Student Nonviolent Coordinating Committee organizing in Mississippi, and the struggle in Birmingham.

Nor was the movement a spontaneous local eruption. Morris shows that local organizing was an essential prerequisite for effective action. The key organizing institutions were what Morris calls Local Movement Centers, which brought together the churches—the key institutions in the African-American community—and other community leaders under a relatively clear leadership structure. The prototype center was the Montgomery Improvement Association (MIA), which was formed as an "organization of organizations" the day after Rosa Parks refused to sit at the rear of the bus. The organizations that underlay the MIA included the African-American churches and the Women's Political Council, a long-standing group that had a history of attacking Jim Crow laws and that had been planning a bus boycott for some time.[40] This planning, and the fact that Rosa Parks had a history of refusing to accept the Jim Crow bus rules, makes it clear that what followed was not a spontaneous explosion. The crucial role of the churches in mobilizing people shows the importance of an underlying local infrastructure. The response of the local NAACP representatives, who, when asked whether the organization would support the boycott, replied that they would "have to wait to talk to New York to find out what they think about it" make it clear that central national planning can claim no credit.[41]

Other Local Movement Centers were created throughout the South, including the Inter Civic Council in Tallahassee, the Alabama Christian Movement for Human Rights in Birmingham, the Nashville Christian Leadership Council, and the United Christian Movement in Shreveport,

Louisiana. These organizations were loosely coordinated by the Southern Christian Leadership Conference and were provided with training by institutions such as the Highlander Folk School. Local institution building and training of citizens, and neither national direction nor spontaneous action, built the Civil Rights movement.

Juxtaposing the emergence of the Christian Right with the Civil Rights movement might seem incongruous. The popular image of the Christian Right is that of a media-based campaign centered in the television ministries of Pat Robertson, Jerry Falwell, and their colleagues. However, this perspective overlooks the history of the Christian Right and how its emergence was underwritten by local institution building. As sociologist of religion Robert Wuthnow notes, evangelicals were "institution builders who were in command of considerable resources such as seminary professorships, journals, and pulpits."[42] The process began with the founding of the National Association of Evangelicals in 1943, the establishment of the Fuller Theological Seminary in Pasadena in 1947, the growth of other seminaries such as the Moody Bible Institute in Chicago and the Dallas Theological Seminary, and the spread of organizations such Youth for Christ, the Voice of Christian Youth, and the High School Evangelical Fellowship. Long before television came to dominate the scene, the evangelical movement created a strong institutional backbone.

The strength of the Christian Right is based in strong, growing, and healthy local institutions: churches. Through these congregations, people are connected to the movement and become committed to it. Evangelical congregations have been the fastest-growing in America—by 1967 Southern Baptists had become the largest denomination in the nation[43]—and the evangelical congregations have continued to grow at the expense of the more traditional denominations.[44] Furthermore, the evangelical churches are healthier than their mainstream competitors. They do better on metrics such as the ratio of both clergy and buildings per parishioner.[45] After it grew strong, based on its roots in communities, the Christian Right successfully turned to the task of mobilization. People were registered to vote in church. In the 1984 election, over three hundred registration training sessions were held in two hundred cities.[46]

The union movement is the third example of the importance of institutions in connecting people to politics. The main business of unions is to bargain with employers on behalf of their members. However, unions also play at least two distinct political roles. First, like churches and clubs, they teach their members how to do politics. Most local unions, for example, have regular elections in which the membership chooses its leaders. What is at stake is not simply the national presidency but also the office of head of the local union. Although the national leadership elections may seem distant and hard to influence, local elections are typically open and democratically run. In addition, when contracts come up for renewal, the local membership is involved in discussions about the nature of the bargaining position the union should take. Through these discussions and political contests, union members learn political skills, and their interest in politics is awakened.

Unions also play a direct role in mobilizing their members to vote in state, local, and national elections. They do so in all the ways in which political parties used to activate people: meetings, phone calls, rallies, and mailings. Typically, but not uniformly, unions have supported the Democratic party and are the backbone of national election campaigns.

What evidence do we have that the organizational activities of unions are actually effective in teaching people politics and in mobilizing them to participate? The answer turns out to be quite clear. Even after taking into account a variety of demographic differences between union and nonunion members and their families, the union members and their families are more likely than their nonunion counterparts to vote. And they are more likely to vote for Democratic candidates.[47]

Unions succeed both in mobilizing their members and in influencing their political attitudes. When this finding is combined with the history of the Civil Rights movement and the emergence of the Christian Right, then there is very substantial support for the core argument that the secret of involving people in politics and mobilizing them is the development of strong local organizations.

Why the IAF?

The key to reviving a vibrant politics and to rebuilding a progressive constituency is founding, strengthening, growing strong local political organizations. These organizations should teach people how to do politics by convincing them to vote and to participate in other ways, and by connecting them to something they believe in enough to stay committed to the political process. Success will reverse the class and income bias in politics by bringing in people whom the current system ignores.

The potential candidates for these local mobilizing organizations include political parties, unions, and community-based organizations. Each has its advantages and drawbacks. Political parties have the advantage of connecting directly to electoral politics and offering the clearest opportunity to influence who takes office and who does not. However, once the members of a given party are in power, the local party apparatus is unlikely to be effective in holding them accountable to their promises. Unions have a long history of being at the center of the progressive agenda, and it is essential that their power be rebuilt if progressive politics is to grow in influence. However, unions by their very nature are centered in the workplace, and this can limit the range of issues that they can address. Unions also face a major challenge in convincing a broad cross-section of people that they are relevant and attractive. Community organizations can address a wide range of concerns and can be effective both in electoral politics and in holding politicians accountable once they are in office. Historically, however, they have suffered from uncertain resources and instability and hence have not provided a long-lasting organizational base. But the IAF is a network of community organizations that overcomes the weaknesses of its genre and possesses the key traits necessary for building a successful progressive politics from the ground up.

Many of the people who attended the IAF meeting in Austin could remember when the first Southwest IAF organization, Communities Organized for Public Service (COPS) was founded in 1974. At that time the poor neighborhoods in San Antonio were regularly flooded when it rained because city development resources were directed to constructing infrastructure for new suburbs on the outskirts of town. When the organization had managed to accumulate sufficient power, it was able to engineer a substantial shift in the city's priorities. Over the years COPS and its fellow organizations in other cities have had numerous other successes.[48] A job-training program begun by COPS in San Antonio, Project QUEST, has been replicated in other IAF cities and has gained national attention. The IAF school reform program, the Alliance Schools, garnered substantial resources from the state government and is implemented in 129 schools throughout the state. The IAF network proposed indigent health care insurance and pushed it through the state legislature, and it was a key player in obtaining school finance equalization legislation. In the Lower Rio Grande Valley, the IAF organization organized a living wage campaign that raised wages for over eighty-five hundred employees. In Dallas in 2002, the IAF organization was essential in obtaining voter approval for a $1.4 billion school bond, the first such bond to pass in nearly a decade. In each of the cities in which the IAF is active, it can claim credit for numerous local successes ranging from libraries to parks to health clinics.

These programmatic achievements are impressive, but perhaps the most important accomplishment of the IAF is to reverse the apathy that characterizes American politics. Over the course of this book, I will introduce many members of IAF organizations, and their stories are compelling. Gilbert Garcia captures how the IAF commits, and recommits, people to politics:

> I was energized. All of a sudden these politicians were there to serve us. Not we serving them. All of a sudden I realized that we had the right to just go into their office and confront, demand, and say what are you doing about this. So, it was, basically, I discovered the power that we had as a people. At the same time, the other realization is that we had allowed, or I had allowed, this to happen for such a long time. It's as if I had a reawakening in that regard. I saw the connection between church, my beliefs, justice, and social justice. It all came together.

Today's Industrial Areas Foundation organizations are successors of the pioneering work of Saul Alinsky, the man who virtually invented community organizing in America.[49] Alinsky, a graduate of the University of Chicago sociology department, began organizing during the 1930s. Closely associated with the union-organizing drives that were exploding during this era, as well as with the Catholic hierarchy in Chicago, Alinsky created a style of organizing that proved remarkably durable. In Chicago he founded the Back of the Yards organization in a white working-class area and the Woodlawn Organization in an African-American community. He sparked organizations in Rochester, New York, New York City, and California and trained several generations of organizers, including Cesar Chavez. Alinsky was famous for his flam-

boyant tactics but also for his tough-minded pragmatism and willingness to accept half a loaf, or "the world as it is, not as it should be." Indeed,
more doctrinaire leftists attacked Alinsky for his lack of ideology.[50]

With Alinsky's death in 1972, his protégé Ed Chambers took over the
national IAF. Chambers was a former seminarian from Iowa who connected to the IAF after coming to Alinsky's notice for organizing tenants
in Harlem. Upon taking over, Chambers undertook a set of organizational reforms. Compared to how it was in Alinsky's time, the IAF today
has a larger and better-trained corps of organizers, is more formally connected to institutions such as churches and schools, takes on more complex issues, and operates at metropolitan and state levels as well as at the
neighborhood level.

Ernie Cortes, who was the keynote speaker at the Austin convention
described earlier, played a key role in revitalizing the IAF. Cortes is the
supervisor of the IAF network in the Southwest and a member of the
IAF National Executive Committee. Cortes was born in San Antonio in
1943, the son of a drugstore manager. He attended Catholic schools in
San Antonio and was the first member of his family to enroll in college,
Texas A&M. Even as a teenager he was an organizer. A frequently told
story is how he organized his cousins to boycott a local swimming pool
that had refused admittance to one of them because her skin was too
dark. While in high school and college, Cortes was involved in student
organizing via the Mexican-American Civil Rights movement and the
United Farm Workers. In 1971 he went to Chicago for IAF training. Cortes organized in Chicago, Milwaukee, and Indiana before returning to
San Antonio in 1974 to build COPS, the first IAF organization in the
Southwest network. From San Antonio, Cortes moved to Los Angeles,
where he put together the first IAF organization in that city, UNO. He
then returned to Texas and established organizations in Houston, Austin, and the Rio Grande Valley, as well as sponsoring committees in a
number of other cities, including Dallas. Cortes is part tough street organizer and part intellectual who has nearly always read more than anyone
in whatever room he happens to be in.

As the vignette at the beginning of this chapter suggests, and as we
will see in greater detail later in this book, the IAF is an organization
whose explicit goal is to teach people how to do politics. It nurtures and
builds an active citizenry that has the skills and commitment to participate effectively in politics. The IAF is the antithesis of a typical staff-

driven membership organization whose only communication with its supporters is via periodic fund-raising letters.

IAF organizations are long-lasting. The IAF distinguishes itself sharply from more ephemeral social movements. The core of the IAF approach is to organize by enrolling institutions—churches, schools, unions, and community groups—rather than by directly signing up individuals. The stable nature of IAF organizations is crucial to their success. Unlike protest movements, which can ignite with great passion but also burn out, the IAF will be there year after year and issue after issue.

A second major strength is that the IAF is broad-based. The people who are active in the organization are drawn from all races and ethnic groups and from different points in the income distribution. The IAF is not plagued by a history of racial tensions weakening the organizational underpinnings. It searches for issues that cut across potential racial divides. Furthermore, unlike many of the Washington-based progressive associations dominated by middle-class staff and advocates, the IAF is heterogeneous. Its political resources are substantially augmented by its ability to speak for different parts of the community.

Finally, the IAF refuses to focus on single issues but rather addresses (successfully) a wide range of concerns from policies to create a more equitable job market to health care to building neighborhoods via school reform, libraries, and parks. By integrating issues of neighborhood, family, and work, the IAF can appeal to a broad and varied constituency. In addition, by addressing multiple issues, the IAF teaches its members the craft of agenda building and compromise but also avoids being pigeonholed as a special-interest, single-purpose organization.

The IAF model has another advantage. It is based on very traditional American values. American history is full of efforts to change politics as usual that have gone nowhere. It seems clear that there is a strong aversion in the broad American public to anything that smacks of radicalism. Why this should be so has been the subject of a great deal of head scratching among social scientists, beginning with Werner Sombart's *Why Is There No Socialism in the United States?*[51] But the fact itself seems clear and explains why the "class warfare" attacks on progressive impulses have been effective.

A sprinkling of comments from the last presidential election illustrates this point. After Al Gore spoke in his acceptance speech at the Democratic convention of supporting "the people, not the powerful,"

George W. Bush charged that Al Gore is "a candidate who will pit one group of people against another, a candidate who wants to wage class warfare to get ahead."[52] When a Gore spokesperson attacked the Bush tax cut proposals suggesting that they would only aid the wealthy, Karen Hughes, the Bush press aide, replied, "There you go again! Class warfare."[53]

The IAF is not vulnerable to these attacks. Despite having a strongly progressive agenda, what is striking about the IAF is how middle-class and mainstream are the values of its members. Of course, there is considerable anger among its members, anger about the unfair distribution of political and economic power and the consequences that flow from this inequity. But this anger, and the solutions that are proposed, is firmly rooted in traditional values and traditional rhetoric. Inflammatory language, arguments about social class, and critiques of capitalism are not part of the IAF repertoire.

The faith-based character of IAF organizations also reflects core American values. Most Americans believe that increased religiosity would improve the quality of American life.[54] In the National Election Surveys people were asked whether they agreed or disagreed with the statement "This country would have many fewer problems if there were more emphasis on traditional family ties," and 52 percent agreed strongly and an additional 33 percent agreed somewhat.

Beginning in the mid-1980s, conservatives and the Republican party worked hard to make this set of issues and emotions their own and in important measure succeeded. Although most religious people do not subscribe to the hard intolerance associated with the Moral Majority,[55] it is also clear that the "values issue" has substantial resonance. The question, then, is whether progressives can take the high ground on values while at the same time maintaining a progressive stance with respect to economic issues. The IAF shows how to do this because it is able to naturally embrace both a progressive programmatic agenda and a very mainstream set of cultural norms.

The Setting

The IAF is a national network, with organizations in cities such as Baltimore, Boston, Chicago, Los Angeles, and New York. In each of these cities, the organizations have enjoyed successes comparable to those described earlier in the Southwest. However, the focus of this book is on the network in the Southwest, with special emphasis on the Rio Grande Valley. This is partly accidental: I began working with the IAF in Texas in 1995 and over the years have come to know the organizations in the Southwest very well. It makes sense to focus in depth on one area because this provides a concrete setting to see how the IAF approaches the challenges posed by a particular political and economic environment. Whatever disadvantages might flow from focusing on one area are in large part mitigated because the central elements of the IAF model are standardized, and organizations in other parts of the country will be easily recognizable from the description of the Southwest. This happens because of the rotation of organizers, because an important piece of IAF training is done nationally and draws upon people from all parts of the country, and because the most senior IAF organizers from around the country frequently meet and share notes.

Much of the material in this book is based on my observation of the IAF over seven years. I closely followed a number of campaigns, and during this time I was present at a great many of the IAF's actions and meetings and I had uncountable conversations with organizers and members. In addition, on several occasions I conducted more formal evaluations and assessments of IAF labor market programs. As I prepared to write this book, I became more systematic in my interviews. Natasha Freidus, my research assistant, and I formally interviewed over fifty organizers and active IAF members. The bulk of the interviews were in the Rio Grande Valley, but a number were elsewhere in the Southwest. These interviews (in both English and Spanish) lasted between two and four hours and were taped, transcribed, and analyzed.

The IAF organizations in the Southwest are not identical; they have somewhat different histories and master narratives. In the Rio Grande Valley, the struggle to improve living conditions in *colonias*, third-world shanty towns along the Mexican border, continues to dominate the organization's oral history and culture. In Dallas, the organization's culture is strongly marked by its efforts to overcome the city's racial divisions. In El Paso, the organization continues to be shaped by its early experience of surviving a severe red-baiting campaign led by the far-right wing of the Texas Republican party and conservative Catholics. However, although these master narratives do differ from city to city, I have chosen not to make very much of them. The book is not intended to be a history of the IAF but rather to draw lessons about American politics from the IAF experience. Given this goal and given the fact that the basic organizing strategies are standardized across cities, I freely draw examples from different cities without paying a great deal of attention to the contextual differences. I am confident that for the purposes of the arguments I make very little is lost by this strategy.

Having said this, it is also the case that more material is taken from the Rio Grande Valley than from elsewhere. Over the past seven years I have spent more time in the Valley than in other parts of the Southwest and have come to know its people and campaigns better. The Valley is a fascinating locus of many of the most dynamic forces in American society—immigration, international trade, and ethnic diversity.

Dallas and Houston need little introduction to most Americans. Large and diversified cities, they thrive on a mixture of finance, oil, shipping, and high technology. Even San Antonio, the gateway to southern Texas, houses a familiar mix of businesses, with the addition of a thriving tourist industry driven by the Alamo, Riverwalk, and its sports stadiums. What is perhaps unusual about these cities is their political history and their surprising levels of poverty and inequality. The disparity of economic outcomes in Texas is stark. The state is the seventh worst in the United States in the level of income inequality among families, and in recent years the income trends have hewed to this pattern. Between the late 1980s and the late 1990s, the family income of the poorest 20 percent grew by 3 percent, whereas for the top 20 percent the growth rate was 17 percent.[56] The political history of the region will be described in some detail in chapter 4, but suffice it to say that until recently it was dominated by an Anglo business elite that saw little reason to open the doors to people outside its circle. The doors have now been forced open, in large measure through the efforts of the IAF.

If the great cities of Texas are familiar to most Americans and would seem much like home, the same cannot be said of southern Texas and the Rio Grande Valley. This is a region that seems neither America nor Mexico, but rather a border zone that is a mixture of two cultures and two economies. Over 80 percent of the population is Mexican-American, and many families travel to Mexico to visit relatives. At the same time, on Friday nights in the fall, North American football (not soccer) is king, and the roads are filled with families traveling to watch their high school team take on a neighboring town's team.

For decades the Rio Grande Valley, anchored at one end by the port city of Brownsville and at the other end by McAllen, was agricultural. The vast majority of people worked part of the year in the fields or the packing houses and then traveled north in the summer to harvest elsewhere. Others found employment in the apparel factories that had moved to the region to take advantage of the cheap labor. The political history of the area reflects this heritage. In the early twentieth century, Texas rangers maintained order through vivid demonstrations: they drove with dead Mexicans lying on the hoods of their cars. Checkpoints throughout the region made sure that Mexican-American agricultural workers stayed on local farms and that recruiters did not tempt workers to leave for slightly better pay up north. As late as the 1960s, Jim Crow laws controlled social and political life in much of southern Texas.[57] For twenty-one years, between 1977 and 1999, the mayoralty of McAllen was held by one man, a grower and owner of packing sheds in the Valley and of agricultural operations in South America.

People still leave the Valley to travel north as migrant workers, but agricultural employment in the Valley itself has shrunk. Damaged by the frost in 1983 and squeezed by competition from Florida and California, agriculture today accounts for 3 percent of Valley employment.[58] The apparel industry, too, has radically diminished, as even the low wages of the Valley cannot compete with those of Haiti and China. The Valley today seems dominated by endless strip malls filled with fast-food restaurants, but the area has benefited from a booming medical establishment, growing government employment (mainly schools), and jobs flowing from trade with Mexico. Between 1990 and 2000, the population of Brownsville grew by a remarkable 41 percent and that of McAllen by 48 percent.[59] The engine of this growth is the interaction between the U.S. side of the border and Mexico.

In the Rio Grande Valley, the ten-thousand-pound gorilla at the core of economic development is Mexico and NAFTA. Whether NAFTA has been a boon or bane to American workers has been the subject of great controversy. Unions fear the flight of work from high-priced U.S. factories to low-wage Mexican ones, and the spread of automobile supply plants all along the Mexican side of the border certainly suggests that these fears are well grounded. Set against this, other American workers benefit from new employment opportunities flowing from trade, and American consumers enjoy lower prices. How the sums add up depends on who is doing the math, although the mainstream view is that the net effect has been positive, albeit modest.[60] However, whatever the impact for the country as a whole, for the Valley NAFTA and the associated growth of the border economy in Mexico has unquestionably brought substantial benefits. The city leaders in McAllen and Brownsville are so convinced that the growth of Mexico drives development on the U.S. side of the border that their economic development staff—people who are paid by American tax dollars—spend most of their time trying to convince firms from around the world to locate their factories in Mexico.

When northern employers think of the Rio Grande Valley, they still focus on cheap labor (and the Valley's economic development authorities still advertise that the labor is cheap[61]), but the industry has changed. What is coming to the Valley, in addition to the suppliers to Mexico's factories, are call centers and a somewhat random collection of labor-intensive low-skill manufacturing. Tourism, health, services, and government are also creating jobs. Each of these sectors is driven by the population growth. The annual influx of winter Texans—older people from the North who come to Texas to escape the cold in a cheaper setting than Florida—as well as the attraction of the beach resort South Padre Island bring tourists to the region. These tourists increase the demand for health care, as do the natural population growth and the influx of new immigrants. Unlike much of the rest of the nation, hospitals in the region are consistently profitable, and doctors have grown rich on Medicaid. Government employment, mainly in schools, has also surged in response to the population growth.

But economic growth in the Rio Grande Valley has not brought prosperity. Although the political violence and grinding poverty of an agricultural regime are mostly in the past, the region is nonetheless among the very poorest in America. In 1999, 39 percent of the population and a whopping 44 percent of children in the Valley lived in poverty, compared with national rates of 14 percent and 19 percent. A full 40 percent of working-age people in the Valley lack health insurance.

The Rio Grande Valley, along with the rest of the border region, also houses a phenomenon found nowhere else in the United States, colonias. Colonias, of which there are fourteen hundred along the border with Mexico, are rural lots sold as residential subdivisions by unscrupulous developers who made promises of paved streets, sewage, and drinkable water but never delivered. Because the colonias are located outside of incorporated towns, no political authority was willing to take responsibility for them. Regulating colonias, forcing towns to take some responsibility, and passing state bonding legislation to fund improvements became the early signature issues of the IAF in Texas. Even today, however, an estimated three hundred thousand people live in colonias, and many still lack the most basic amenities.

The struggle in the Rio Grande Valley puts in the starkest terms the challenge that much of the nation faces. The Valley is growing and in many respects has great opportunities. NAFTA is a spark, and—as in numerous cities elsewhere—the rapid influx of immigration brings energy and vitality to the area. But the challenge is to ensure that growth and opportunity also translate into economic equity and political inclusiveness. The progressive agenda is to create a new politics in which people can have a voice in the economic and social trajectory of their communities. If this can happen in South Texas, and in Dallas and Houston and San Antonio, it can happen in cities and suburbs throughout the nation.

The IAF is building a new politics and a new local economics. It is accomplishing this by organizing and mobilizing the very people who are left out by politics as practiced today. It also manages to build organizations that bring together these forgotten people with a broad cross-section of middle- and working-class individuals and families. My goal is to describe this model and explain how it can be used, by both IAF organizations and by other progressive groups, to rebuild politics in America.

Over the decades the IAF has developed organizing strategies and techniques that have proved very effective. Its philosophy is to organize through institutions (churches and schools), create broad-based inclusive organizations, and emphasize building power before turning to issues. At the core of the model is a recognition of the importance of developing leaders, and a substantial measure of the organizations' impact is the stories of how people developed new conceptions of themselves as active and capable political actors. The next chapter describes how IAF organizing takes place and also describes the kinds of challenges it faces as the organizations become more established and run the risk of becoming rigid.

Chapter 3 takes up the role of religion. At the core of the IAF organizing model are religious congregations. The IAF organizes through churches, and its values and rhetoric are drawn from religious traditions. Many, though not all, of its people are motivated by their religious commitment. The trade between the IAF and the churches is two-way: although the IAF uses congregations as the basis for much of its organizing, it also works with congregations, in a process it calls congregational development, to help them more sharply define their mission, develop new leaders, and grow their membership.

In the communities where it operates, the IAF has taken people who believed that they were powerless and taught them to think of themselves as effective political actors entitled to having their voices heard. The IAF has also transformed how politics is done. Power relationships have changed, and most important, the idea of accountability has been articulated and enforced. Chapter 4 describes how the IAF operates politically and the impact that it has had.

I then turn in chapter 5 to the IAF's economic program. Just as many Americans are unhappy about the health of politics, so too there is widespread dissatisfaction about what is happening in the economy and the job market. It is one thing, however, to be dissatisfied and another to know what to do. It is very hard to think about what works well with respect to shaping the trajectory of local economies. The IAF has put together a package of initiatives—ranging from job training to living wage campaigns to efforts to reform education to campaigns to reshape how cities spend their economic development funds to efforts to build employee associations—that represents the most sophisticated community-level response in the nation to economic distress and inequality. Chapter 5 describes these efforts, discussing both the accomplishments and what remains to be done.

It is clear that the IAF represents an alternative view of how to conduct politics. In the final chapter, I describe this perspective in somewhat more abstract terms, and I also discuss how the IAF approach relates to critiques of American politics that have been developed in recent years by a variety of scholars. The final chapter also takes up the crucial question of whether the IAF model can reach a national scale. What will it take for the IAF model to diffuse, in terms of new organizing by that organization itself as well as by other progressive organizations learning the lessons and absorbing the techniques the IAF has to offer?

It is also important to think through potential limitations of the IAF model. One issue is how the IAF can broaden its attractiveness so that it can penetrate more deeply than it has into middle-class communities. Another concern is that at some point the congregation-based organizing strategy will run up against the fact that a great many members of a potential constituency for progressive politics are not connected to organized religion. In the end, the IAF will need to be part of a coalition. The final chapter considers what that coalition would look like, what its members will bring to the table, and what the prospects are for a new progressive politics in America.

It is not true that Americans are apathetic about politics. In fact, Americans have a strong urge to participate in politics. The newspapers are full of stories about people who confront their schools about high-stakes testing or oppose public subsidies for a sports stadium or fight to clean up a waste site near their home. The problem is not that people do not want to be involved.

Nor is the problem that Americans are opposed to government or that they stand in opposition to the core elements of the progressive agenda. As E. J. Dionne notes, "The current political upheaval can be defined less as a revolt against big government than as a rebellion against bad government —government that has proved ineffectual in grappling with political, economic, and moral crises that have shaken the country."[62] When asked about their views, most Americans support the broad elements of a progressive agenda: economic fairness, more resources into education, equitable access to health care, and so on. So the problem is not that people are unsympathetic or uninterested in the important issues.

What then is the problem? One difficulty is that people are cynical. They believe that politicians and government are outside of their control. Recall that in 2000 only 16 percent of Americans thought that government paid attention to what people wanted. A central IAF ritual is the accountability session, in which politicians are brought in front of IAF members and asked quite specifically about their positions on IAF agenda items. The IAF then follows up with these officials after they are elected and places continuous pressure on them to adhere to their commitments. By placing accountability at the center of its approach to politics, the IAF speaks to a deep need in American politics.

The problem is also that there are no mobilizing institutions that connect with people who are turned off and disconnected from politics.

We lack ongoing organizational forums in which citizens can learn political skills, participate in politics, and build something that is lasting and effective. We also lack organizations that can credibly mobilize the potential voters whose absence tilts the electorate toward the Right. Ultimately this book is about how to move forward on this organization-building agenda, because without an organizational backbone firmly centered in communities, progressive politics will never make it.

Creating these mobilizing institutions rests on two central ideas: agency and community. Agency means giving people the skills to engage in politics and the opportunities to do so in a meaningful way. Community means changing the way politics is conducted. Today's politics is not only passive but also isolated. Individuals do not connect with other people to discuss issues, debate positions, and arrive at agendas. Instead they are limited to being on the receiving end of messages, fund-raising letters, and strategies developed in Washington. We need to create political communities of conversation and learning. Wilson Carey McWilliams captured what is required when he wrote, "Any political renewal for American democracy will have to be founded on a 'host of little democracies,' the revitalization of local parties and civic life."[63]

The ultimate goal of progressive politics is to gather the power necessary to move forward. Gathering this power means creating strong community organizations that teach politics and that are stable and long-lasting. The Industrial Areas Foundation is one model—a powerful and persuasive one—of how to accomplish this. The lessons taught by the IAF are applicable not only to its own practices but also to efforts to revitalize other key elements of a progressive coalition, such as unions, other community groups, and even local political parties. By learning more about the IAF and its people, and by moving back and forth between the story of the IAF in the Southwest and the larger challenges of progressive politics in America, we can begin to see the path toward a new politics in this country.

Chapter 2

Building Organizations

Rosa Gutierrez is a cheerful woman in her mid-forties. She was born in Guanajuato, Mexico, and visited the United States as a child to be with her father, who was a migrant laborer in this country. Rosa moved to the Rio Grande Valley at age thirteen and grew up working in the fields and packing houses. Over the years she traveled from the Valley to harvest in Florida, Delaware, Wisconsin, and Nebraska. Rosa met her husband some twenty years ago while working in Idaho, and they now have four children, with the youngest in kindergarten and the oldest just turning twenty-one. A monolingual Spanish speaker, Rosa left school well before high school graduation. Today she lives in a neighborhood in the south side of McAllen, the poor part of town, and raises her children.

Eight years ago, when Rosa was a member of St. Joseph the Worker Church, her pastor, Father Bart Flaat, began to hold pastoral meetings at the church at which parishioners talked about what was bothering them. There was a great deal bothering Rosa. She described the situation in her neighborhood—unpaved streets, no sewage or running water—and, by telling her story, began the first step in her development as a leader in Valley Interfaith.

In short order, both Father Bart and Elizabeth Valdez, who was the lead organizer of Valley Interfaith at the time, visited with Rosa. They asked her to help organize house meetings at which her neighbors could tell their stories, and they also asked if she would attend IAF training sessions. Rosa recalls that she held back and said to them that "I'm not a good speaker; I'm afraid." She remembers that they responded, "That is because you haven't been given the opportunity." Rosa did begin to organize house meetings at which other people told their stories, and she soon felt comfortable telling hers. "This was a great thing; I was discovering myself," is her memory of this process. She now says of herself, "I've changed a lot; I make myself talk. I'm nervous, but I do it." Rosa sums up the changes as follows:

> I now speak a lot. I have developed in that, and I have learned a lot. I have met people, such as very important politicians, who in spite of their studies are not higher than us, because they are there because of us. I have learned that when there is something in the community that we can do ourselves, we can go and talk with the appropriate persons in order to do it. I have developed a lot in terms of fighting for our own interests, against the injustice in our community.

Elizabeth Valdez, the organizer who recruited Rosa, was herself identified by Ernie Cortes on one of his first visits to the Valley. The child of migrant workers who circulated between the Valley and the harvest fields to the north, Elizabeth, like many Valley youth, had to leave school early to work. When Cortes arrived in 1981, Elizabeth had left the migrant trail, was married to a man who worked in a local vegetable packing shed, had three children, and was working in a Levi Strauss plant.

When Cortes met her, Elizabeth had been elected president of the union in the Levi plant, and she was still working on the shop floor as a trimmer. Explaining how this happened she remembers: "Well, I've always been a fighter, and so, you know, I would not settle for management mistreating me or others or forcing us to work harder or longer hours. So, they started seeing me arguing with supervisors and still there. And so they said, maybe you should represent us. You should run for president." The problem was that the union was able to accomplish very little. When a woman died of heat prostration because the plant air-conditioner was broken, Elizabeth started to look for new ways to organize. She thought about a career as a union organizer, but at one union training session she met Ernie Cortes, who gave a talk on power and the pressures on families. Elizabeth remembers that the union organizers thought this talk irrelevant, but she disagreed and arranged to meet with Ernie and with Jim Drake (the lead organizer at the time). She recalls what happened next:

> I started going to the training sessions that Ernie was doing on a monthly basis with clergy, women, and lay leaders. It began to make sense to me why things never change in the workplace; we were disconnected. I began to become much more interested. At that point, in those conversations, in those small group meetings, I heard people's stories about the conditions in the colonias—not having water and waste water. About the conditions in the fields with pesticides and so forth. So once you hear those stories, you're not the same person going home. At that point Ernie began to agitate us and say, "Look—it is going to be very hard to organize in the valley because there [are] thirty-four municipalities." Each one was fighting for [its] own little project. Well, once we did the individual meetings and heard everybody's pain and struggles, there began to be a connectedness. So we started to work, and we said we can make something happen. So for the first two years of the organization I was involved as a leader. The only actions we did [were] to learn how to do individual meetings and house meetings. By the time we had our founding convention with Governor White, we had five thousand people coming in from all over the valley. It was my first experience—public experience, speaking publicly before then governor. I spoke on the issue on workers' comp and so forth. So I began to see a new person emerge.

Seeing a "new person emerge" is a common experience of people who go through the IAF leadership development process. Elizabeth spent several years as a leader with Valley Interfaith and then decided to try out organizing. Along the way she returned to school and got her GED and then did college work at the University of Texas branch in the Valley. After organizing in the Valley and in El Paso, Elizabeth is now the lead organizer in San Antonio.

People become involved in politics in a wide variety of ways. Sometimes all they do is vote (although, as we have seen, too few people do even this). Many others go beyond voting to engage more deeply. They might write a letter to an elected official or call him or her. They might attend a public hearing. They might get involved in protesting against (or advocating for) a decision, such as whether a local school should be closed or whether to put a stop sign on a corner. Sometimes people engage in bigger issues, such as protests against high-stakes testing in schools or efforts to block public subsidies of sports stadiums. These activities, although not common, are not rare either. About a third of Americans report having signed a petition on a political or governmental issue, and just under 20 percent attended a public meeting on town or school issues.[1]

Participation of this sort is important and valuable. There is too little of it. However, even if there were more, it would not address the key deficiency confronting those interested in rebuilding politics, and progressive politics in particular. As we have seen, those who participate are disproportionately drawn from the upper reaches of society. What is missing are stable organizations that mobilize a broader range of people and provide them with opportunities to grapple with issues and to learn how to give voice—effective voice—to their views. Such an organization should both do politics and teach political skills. It is only through such ongoing mobilizing institutions that a real foundation can be built for a new politics.

There are a great many reasons why building vibrant local political organizations is difficult, indeed unlikely. An impressive array of forces argue against success. The first set of reasons is practical. To build an effective political organization, it is important to deliver the goods, to win some battles. But winning battles requires power, and that power depends on having a strong organization. This chicken-egg problem is made even more difficult if the organization is concerned with problems of economic or political equity, since the opposition is likely to be strong.

Also standing in the way of success are more general dilemmas that confront any organization that asks people to give their time. The first is simple inertia. People are busy with jobs and family, and it is tough to convince a hard-pressed person with children to support and a family to manage that they should devote a substantial amount of their time to an enterprise whose promise is very uncertain. A second difficulty is the free-rider problem. People may ask themselves why should I get involved when I know that if the organization succeeds I will receive the benefits regardless of what I did. If a group of neighbors are fighting for a local park, any resident can use that park, even if he or she never did anything to get it. Thinking of this sort makes it hard to pull together a group of committed people. A final challenge comes from defending against powerful forces that push against the group's ability to continue along the intended path. People get tired and drop out. Leaders emerge who want to monopolize power and who undermine the very purposes of the effort, that is, the goals of educating and involving people in politics.

These difficulties are multiplied when the purpose is to organize poor and working-class communities. People in these communities have limited resources, and hence they have to be even more careful about how they allocate their time. In addition, they have good reason to be skeptical about their power to accomplish anything. There is a major mental hurdle to overcome.

How is it possible to overcome these roadblocks and establish ongoing local political organizations? One of the reasons the IAF model is so important to the broader concerns of progressive politics is that the IAF has succeeded, in the face of these obstacles, in building strong stable political organizations. The IAF is not interested in organizing a protest movement in which a group of people respond to some single burning topic and then return to normal life. Rather the IAF wants to build a long-lasting organization, not tied to any particular issue but rather devoted to accumulating political power that is fungible across a wide range of concerns. Creating an organization with staying power is far more difficult than igniting a short-lived protest.

Over the course of establishing these organizations throughout the nation, the leaders and organizers in the IAF have given a great deal of thought, explicit thought, to how to overcome the challenges of organization building. As a consequence, a well-developed organizing doctrine has emerged and is utilized whether the IAF is coming to a new city or working with established organizations to keep them vibrant. The goal of this chapter is to lay out how the IAF organizes in order to learn some broader lessons about building progressive political organizations in our communities.

IAF Organizations

There are three questions one can ask about IAF organizations. The first is, what does the organization look like? In the language of business, what is its organization chart? The second question is, how does it get there?

What are the techniques or processes that are used to build the organization? Third, how does the IAF maintain its organizational energy and integrity in the face of considerable internal and external pressures? It seems most useful to begin by describing the organization, drawing its organization chart, before turning to the more subtle issues of the actual organizing.

Local IAF organizations are organizations of organizations.* Individuals do not join Valley Interfaith or COPS or any other local IAF organization. Rather, the members of the IAF are institutions such as churches and schools. Churches are the most common organizational affiliate, but increasingly schools are joining and to some extent other organizations, such as labor unions and community groups such as health centers. People get connected to the IAF through their institutions in ways that I will describe shortly. To give a sense of magnitudes, Valley Interfaith has forty-five member churches and sixteen schools as members, and these represent over sixty thousand people. The IAF organization in Chicago, United Power for Action and Justice, has three hundred member institutions. In Los Angeles, LA Metro is building toward a goal of 150 member congregations, 10 member unions, and 50 member schools. When churches or schools or unions affiliate with the IAF organization, they commit to paying dues. The goal varies by organization, but a typical target is that congregations contribute 2 percent of their annual budget to the IAF organization.

The typical political organization goes directly after individuals, therefore the IAF strategy of building through institutions is distinctive. There are several reasons for the IAF approach. Institutions, particularly

* Strictly speaking, the Industrial Areas Foundation itself is a training institute with a national headquarters in Chicago. Local organizations (such as COPS, Valley Interfaith, L.A. Metro, and so on) contract with the IAF for leadership training and development. The IAF has a national staff of men and women who have sufficient experience as lead organizers to be responsible for the recruitment, training, and development of other lead organizers. Hence, to be accurate when describing the nature of local organizations, I should either identify the specific organization ("COPS does such and such") or when making generalizations about the characteristics of all local organizations—it would be more accurate to use the phrase "members of the IAF network do such and such." This, however, is awkward, and so I will use the term "the IAF" when I generalize about local organizations.

churches, are inherently more stable than are individuals. People may leave town, their life circumstances may change, they might lose energy. Churches, by contrast, will always be there, and if a congregation is committed as an institution to the IAF, then as specific people move through life's transitions, new individuals will be available. In addition, since an obvious problem facing any organization is resources—money—by affiliating with institutions and requiring dues the IAF partially solves this concern. This source of "hard money" financing is an important organizational innovation. Valley Interfaith's goal is that two-thirds of its budget come from contributions of member organizations, with the remaining coming from grants from foundations and national church groups.

More substantively, the IAF is explicit about rebuilding connections between people. To accomplish this in a lasting way, it is necessary to revive the institutions that hold neighborhoods together, and by working through these institutions, the IAF takes a big step in this direction. Indeed, as we will see in the next chapter, so-called congregational development is a central activity of IAF organizers.

The other major structural feature of IAF organizations is that they are broad-based. The IAF distinguishes itself from two other types of community groups: civic organizations and movements. Civic organizations might be social (the American Legion), or they might deliver services (the Boys and Girls Club). Movements focus on one specific issue. By contrast, broad-based organizations include a cross-section of people, are concerned with a wide range of issues, and have as their main goal building power, not delivering social services. Unions and political parties are other examples of broad-based organizations.

Being a broad-based organization raises a series of fairly subtle issues. First, to say that the IAF is not in the service delivery business does not mean that the organizations are unconcerned with the quality of the services that flow to its members. Indeed, a great deal of energy is devoted to improving schools, creating job-training programs, improving health care, upgrading water and sewers, and so on. However, the IAF does not want to be in the business of delivering these services. Furthermore, it does not want to be known as an organization that specializes in one particular set of issues. Rather, as a broad-based organization, it moves from issue to issue.

Because the IAF wants to pull together coalitions, it does not focus on the special concerns of more narrow groups. As a practical matter, this means it does not directly address racial issues or gay rights or women's issues. The IAF leadership is diverse, but the IAF does not address these issues explicitly. One reason for this is that the IAF believes that identity politics is divisive. Its unwillingness to directly address topics such as race, gay rights, and women's issues is a strength, at least in some respects, but it does raise difficult questions about how the IAF can relate to groups for whom identity concerns are important. I will discuss this issue with respect to race later in this chapter and return to the broader set of identity concerns in the book's conclusion.

Many commentators believe that single-interest groups have come to dominate the landscape in Washington and that these groups, by their nature, are unable or unwilling to recognize either diverse viewpoints or the legitimate concerns of other interest groups. The result is deadlock. An advantage of being broad-based is that it forces the organization to engage in internal politics to reconcile different interests and different points of view. As we will see, the IAF's internal political process demands that its members be in continual dialogue about various issues and viewpoints and are regularly forced to compromise among them. Being broad-based encourages a healthy style of politics.

What does an IAF organization do? First on the list is leadership development and training. This is at the core of how the IAF defines its mission. Over the course of any week, organizers and many of the primary leaders (the IAF term for the most active members) will hold one-on-one conversations with people whom they contact through their churches or schools or other venues. These conversations are aimed at identifying people who might want to become active in the organization and also at learning what issues people are most concerned about. Ernie Cortes argues that the difference between putting together an organization such as the IAF and mobilizing people for an event or a protest is that organizing is selective in identifying and training leaders, whereas in mobilizing the goal is simply to attract as many people as possible. People who do become connected to the IAF then attend a variety of training programs, ranging from intensive ten-day training to shorter weekend or even evening programs.

The IAF also brings people together. On a regular basis the IAF organization conducts house meetings, attended by ten to twenty neighbors, who are called together to talk about issues that are on their minds. Several times a year there will be conferences that people involved in the organization attend. Some of these are local (e.g., in the Rio Grande Valley), whereas others are statewide. Some conferences focus on specific issues, for example, school reform or voter registration, and others are training sessions in IAF doctrine and organizing strategies.

Parallel to the ongoing work of identifying and training leaders, the local IAF organization works on issues. However, it is important to understand that when a new organization is being built in a city, several years typically pass before the IAF addresses any issues. The time is spent identifying leaders and building relationships among leaders, organizers, and member institutions. This process is slow and can frustrate other activists who are eager to pick their first fight. Progressive organizations, such as unions, sometimes argue that the IAF emphasis on building relationships prior to turning to issues is impossibly slow. However, IAF organizations are long-lasting and have deep ties in their communities. This endurance is obviously related to the effort, put in both at the beginning and then as a routine part of the organization's ongoing life, devoted to leadership development and organization building.

When the IAF does turn to issues, those issues are varied in their nature. Some are very local. For example, a regional subgroup of Valley Interfaith, consisting of half a dozen churches in Brownsville, might be working to convince the city to open a branch library in its area. At the same time, the Valley Interfaith is also continuing its campaign to bring water to several colonias in another part of the Valley. Other issues are broader in scope. Most IAF organizations are active in school reform and work with Alliance Schools throughout their area, and several are involved in living wage campaigns that have implications for their entire community. Finally, the organization is likely working with sister organizations throughout Texas on statewide issues, passing a specific piece of legislation on topics such as child health funding or school reform funds or else a statewide voter registration drive.

This combination of leadership development, internal training, and work on issues is the typical fare of the IAF. The process is managed by two groups: the leaders, who connect to the IAF through their member institutions, and the organizers, who are full-time paid employees of the organization. Who are these people and how do they become connected and committed to the IAF?

The People

Valley Interfaith meetings range from the fifteen leaders who sit on the executive committee to the ten thousand leaders and followers who might attend the annual assembly. A leader, as distinct from a follower, is, in Ernie Cortes's words, "someone who has a following, who can deliver that following, and is relational." The IAF distinguishes among several levels of leaders. Primary leaders are committed to building the organization and their own development and also have a substantial following whom they can deliver. Secondary leaders are committed to raising funds and building the organization but have somewhat less reach, whereas tertiary leaders have smaller followings and work on narrower issues such as local schools, parks, or events at their workplace. Of course, over time many of these people may attend a training session or an issues workshop and deepen their involvement, and so the distinction among levels of leaders is not rigid.

A standard precept of the IAF is that the heart of organizing is developing leaders. When asked about what she saw as her core duties, Sister Judy Donovan, the lead organizer of Valley Interfaith, said:

> What we call looking for talent through individual meetings. We also make the discipline and practice of having individual meetings as part of all of our larger meetings. We hold leaders accountable to [those whom] they are talking to [and ask] what new people they are bringing in. Asking institutions why they are not talking to that Methodist church in your town? Or to the local public school? Who they are meeting in the city that's interesting? [We are] always challenging ourselves and our institutions to be thinking beyond their walls.

This search for talent is systematic. An effective IAF organizer does dozens of one-on-ones every week. The goal of these conversations is to identify people with the talent (even if yet unrealized and perhaps unrecognized) and motivation to engage in political activity. In searching for talent, the organizers typically avoid people who bring with them a preset activist agenda. These people, in the view of the organizers, too frequently act as gatekeepers. Rather, a good potential leader is someone who is "relational," that is, who has a wide network of contacts via a leadership role in a school, a church, a neighborhood club and who has some anger that can be tapped into and channeled into political activities.

The individual meetings that are at the heart of IAF organizing are called "one-on-ones." In these meetings, two leaders, or a leader and an organizer, share their stories and begin to develop trust. What makes the IAF organizations long-lived and durable are the twin foundations of institutional members and the relationships between people. These are connections that survive any particular victory or defeat on an issue.

A good example of a one-on-one is a conversation that took place between Joaquin Sanchez, an organizer, and Maria Lopez. Maria, who had very little prior contact with the organization, had just attended a short IAF training session at the suggestion of her husband, and Joaquin was following up. In response to Joaquin's opening question about how she liked the session, Maria said, "I learned a lot at that three-day training. I was always the type of person that would keep to herself and was kind of selfish." This led Joaquin to ask Maria how she came to be this way, and Maria talked, with evident feeling, about her mother, a person who was very critical of Maria and was also selfish. Maria felt that her own behavior reflected her reaction to her mother. This led to a discussion about anger, where it comes from and how to respond to it. Joaquin talked about his own anger and how he learned to use it:

> Joaquin: You take your private anger, your personal anger, but then you kind of use that anger in a public setting. And I know for a long time one of the things that I didn't want to confront was that at a high school where I was working at while I was in college the students that I was working with were either right on the verge of getting kicked out or dropping out. And so we tried to do all these things to get them involved and get them to graduate, but after three years one of the students that I was working with got killed in a fight, and part of what I didn't want to accept was my responsibility in that process.

> Maria: I see. Very hard.

> Joaquin: And it was and it still is. But part of what I'm doing now, and I think part of the reason I'm doing this work now, is trying to use . . . that sense of powerlessness and build something. I don't know, does that make sense?

This comment led Maria to talk about what she really wanted to do and how she really wanted to act:

> I'm not like my mother. I'm so different from her. I'm a very caring person. And I think I would just love to do stuff for the community and for my children and for people. And to get involved. Because it's something that I never knew when I was growing up. It was never about reading. It was never about watching the news. It was never about helping others. It was always for me. For me. And I think that I learned a lot. I learned a lot in this training. It opened my eyes. Because with my husband, when he started I was upset because I was selfish, because I was thinking that he was giving all the attention to all the other people and that he was going to forget about us. And when I went to training I saw I was wrong. I was very wrong, because you're helping others because of your family, because you love your family and that's why you're out there helping for your family. And it was like my eyes were just shut, and when I went there I got a clear picture of what was going on.

This interchange was followed by a discussion of Maria's life story, and it emerged that she was a radiologist who was very interested in health issues. She also told some stories about how she had struck up conversations with strangers while waiting in lines at banks and so on, and that some of these conversations had touched on public health. Joaquin concluded by pointing out that her ability to talk with these people suggested that she could indeed be a leader and act as a public person and that there was a great deal to do in the Valley around health policy.

The most important result of this one-on-one was that Joaquin and Maria opened themselves up to each other and established at least a modest level of trust. Conversations like this take place frequently between organizers and leaders and among leaders. They constitute the glue that holds the organization together. In addition, several of the themes in this one-on-one, notably the use of anger and the distinction between public and private personas, are also important in IAF organizing theory.

The other basic building block, in addition to one-on-ones, are house meetings. At house meetings small groups of people connect to share stories and to explore what interests they have in common. Father Alfonso Guevara, the priest at the largest Catholic church in the Valley, explains why these stories are so important:

> Their stories make them realize that they have richness of experiences that have formed them. But the story has not ended. It has not ended. You ask where is meaning and significance in your story? What brings meaning to your life? Who are the models? Who are the people who touch you? Who inspires you? What are the significant things that have happened in your life? Those stories are used so that you can connect and listen to other people so that we begin to listen to many people and realize that we're in the same boat. We're experiencing the same frustration. So we begin to share the pain and make the pain public and say, "O.K., now what are we going to do with the pain?" Well, we're going to do something about it by going and speaking and doing research. How is the money available? Who is in power? Who has the decisions to make?

As Father Alfonso's comments suggest, house meetings serve two functions: to some extent they function as one-on-ones, giving people an opportunity to connect with each other and to develop trust. They are also forums through which the organizations develop their agendas. The issues that emerge at house meetings are aggregated and come to set the priorities for the organization.

Signing Up

Becoming active in the IAF does not entail the same kind of physical risks as did joining the Civil Rights movement in the South did during the 1950s and 1960s. Nor is it as risky as union organizing, since people are not threatened with losing their jobs. However, being a leader in an IAF organization entails a very substantial commitment of time, energy, and emotion. Furthermore, Americans are reducing their commitment to civic life. They are also increasingly cynical about politics and are less likely to want to be involved. Yet the IAF organizations swim successfully against this tide. Why do people make this commitment?

People come in contact with the IAF through networks of friends or because their clergy or school principal ask them to come to a meeting or get involved in a simple action. Alicia Alvarez's explanation is typical. A friend who was an active leader nagged her into attending a meeting.

> So, as a result of her pining and pining and telling me to go to the meetings, I said, "OK, I'll go, because she needed to meet her quota." But I kept going, but I wasn't into the organization. I was always marginal, and studying them because I'm not exactly liberal always. Politically I'm not. But a lot of the stuff I was hearing was pretty liberal. But then I started to see things that made a lot of sense that they were working on. And particularly of interest to me was the way that they were doing the accountability sessions with the local legislators, the state legislators that were from the area here and the commissioners and the board members and what have you. So I liked it.

The IAF looks for people who have some personal anger that can be translated into political action. Recall how Joaquin tapped into Maria's anger during their one-on-one. Personal anger can take many forms. For some people the anger is straightforwardly related to politics, as in the experience of many leaders when their neighborhoods flooded or their children attended schools in trailers. Andy Sarabia, the first president of COPS in San Antonio, was born in Chicago and recalls the shock of coming to San Antonio. He and his brother were asked to sit in the back of the bus when they traveled downtown, and in school assemblies all of the students were told that because they were Mexican they would end up working as laborers and hence should not even think about college but instead attend the vocational high school. Andy went to college and landed a good civilian job at the local air force base. Like many IAF leaders, he was active in the church, serving as president of the parish council and Holy Name Society, as well as leading the festival committee. He recalls how his anger was catalyzed in a conversation with Ernie Cortes. Andy lived on the outskirts of a neighborhood that regularly flooded in heavy rains, so much so that the fire department had to bring boats to rescue people. After one such rain, he was talking with Cortes in his driveway and standing in a puddle. Cortes asked him if he liked standing in water, and when Andy said no, Ernie asked, "Well, why are you doing that?"

For others, the anger seems more personal. Joe Hinojosa described to us how IAF training helped him understand the depth of his anger at his absentee father and how he managed to transform this emotion into intense involvement in Valley Interfaith:

> Sister Judy said, "Why are you angry?" And then it finally dawned on me that I was angry at my father, and I was lashing out at everybody else because of him. So I made peace with him. Of course, he's been dead for eighteen years, so it was a one-sided peace. But I still had to do it. It was very painful for me, anyway. But I thought about how to use that anger in a more positive way, instead of the negative way that I [had] been using it before, lashing out at everybody and not using it in a positive way.

In some cases the anger seems to have little to do with politics, but what the IAF looks for is a person's capacity to take that anger and use it. The motivation for using it might be to make sure that the same thing does not happen to another person, where the "same thing" might be a generalization of the personal experience. Joe generalized from his experience with his father, and his activism focuses on preventing other people from being ignored by the powers that be. For many people, political activity is a good way to discharge the energy that the anger triggers. Sister Christine Stephens, a senior organizer who supervises the IAF in Texas and Louisiana, says that politics is a chance to "own the anger, deal with it, use it."

The IAF also recognizes the power of self-interest. The organization frankly accepts self-interest as the driving motivation for all parties involved in politics, members of the IAF as well as possible opponents. Saul Alinsky insisted that the only basis on which long-term stable organizations could be built was to found them on the self-interest of their participants. In ten-day training the IAF spends a substantial amount of time helping trainees learn how to identify people's self-interest and learn to use this knowledge tactically and strategically.

A number of the leaders of Valley Interfaith became active specifically because something was going seriously wrong with their lives and Valley Interfaith offered a path for solving the problem. For Manuela, it was that her children were at school in a temporary building, a trailer, and each year they were moved to another location. The promise of a new school never came true, and Manuela began to talk to her neighbors about contacting a Valley Interfaith organizer.

Today Manuela's children are in a new school, built because of pressure Valley Interfaith put on the authorities. Manuela's comment both documents the success of the effort and hints of its impact on her views of herself:

> This school is ours. We protect it. We fought for it. I go through
> and talk to teachers and say, "What do you need?" and the principal
> doesn't like that. She calls me into her office, and she says "I opened
> my doors to you." And that really burned my ears. I said, "You didn't
> open your doors. These are not your doors." Going through the organi-
> zation process helped me know how to respond. Because a bashful lady
> would never have said that. She never would hear about me again. But
> this organization has brought out the rights of a person. These are not
> your doors. You didn't open any doors. This is not your school. Let's
> get this plain understanding that this is not your school.

The self-interest of Manuela, Rosa Gutierrez, and many others is direct and tangible. Another form of self-interest is social. Many IAF leaders report feeling isolated in their communities, that they lacked meaningful connections to people and to institutions. This isolation, part of which is loneliness in the simplest sense of the word, but part of which also reflects the deterioration of civic networks, led these leaders to connect to the IAF. The story that Yolanda tells is typical:

> When I got here I was afraid because I didn't know anybody. When
> I started going to the church of San Jose, I realized that something
> called base communities existed, which are groups of people that live
> nearby that get together to share their problems, their happiness, every-
> thing, and they also shared the word of God. And I said I want to have
> such a community in my neighborhood. There had never been some-
> thing like that here, because here people do not know each other. And
> so the priest told me you have to go and knock on people's doors and
> invite them to your own house to ask them if they want to build this
> community.
>
> And it was very, very hard for me. With my husband we did it,
> and we thank God that the doors opened to us and people were happy

that we had invited them, and this is how I started to get involved with the church. And now, thanks to God, I can organize by myself more communities in other areas. I can help them out. And this is what motivates me the most, to form new communities, and not only mine, because they gave me the training to do it.

The isolation Yolanda felt seems partly a function of her relatively recent arrival to the Valley. However, some leaders recall a different kind of isolation. Noelia Espinoza, a teacher in one of the school systems in the Valley, felt trapped in a narrow world:

I would not have had an opportunity to meet people from across the Valley because I was, you know, closed in my city. I would go from my home to the job. I had my friends from college, but I really did not know other people. And with the organization we would get together, and we would hear about their experiences and what we needed to do, how we could change things, and getting to know them. And to me that was attractive. Because they came from all parts of the Valley, from Brownsville, from La Joya, from Pharr, from all over, and they were interesting. They had interesting stories, and they had this positive thing about them, that they were willing to work for change.

Comments of this sort speak directly to the lack of networks that connect people from different areas and different social strata to each other. The broad-based character of the IAF meets this need. But Noelia's observation highlights another motivation for involvement, an urge to "do good."

Doing good is held in poor regard by IAF doctrine. There are two reasons for this. It is seen as a weak foundation upon which to build an organization. Self-interest is much more reliable. In addition, doing good has a flavor of middle-class noblesse oblige, but the IAF believes (based on its experience) that people living in relatively comfortable circumstances still have issues in their lives that can be effectively addressed through a broad-based organization and that speak to their self-interest. They may feel cut off, as Noelia did, from the broader community in which they live. Their schools, while not housed in trailers, certainly leave a lot to be desired. Be this as it may, it is also the case that the motive to "do good" is widely shared and is not limited to middle-class people or communities. In my interviews, people in very poor circumstances spoke of their urge to work for Valley Interfaith because of their outrage about what was happening to other people in their communities. Although it may be true that people whose initial motivation has the tinge of charity frequently come to see their own self-interest, the urge to "do good" cannot be ignored as a potent initial motivator.

Training the Leaders

The IAF approach to organizing is centered on identifying and training leaders. Carmen Anaya's comment is representative: the IAF is "a university that educates us. We're prepared for any event." This training takes place via the individual relational meetings and through seminars and workshops. At a typical training session, organizers or outside experts run small-group workshops on particular topics, both substantive (e.g., new ideas about school curriculum or water law or the economics of living wage campaigns) and organizational (e.g., how to run a house meeting or social doctrine in the Bible or voter registration strategies). In addition, IAF leaders read material ranging from economics to theology. Several small groups often read a common set of articles and one group then summarizes the material for the entire assembly while another discusses how the readings relate to ongoing concerns in their lives, neighborhoods, and cities. These workshops take place every several months, and the more committed leaders go to national ten-day training that is an extended introduction to the IAF's philosophy of organizing and personal development.

The organizers are constantly prodding leaders to try new activities and to gain new skills. In the formal training sessions, leaders role-play core IAF activities, ranging from recruiting other leaders to talking with politicians and government officials. Prior to public actions, ranging from simple meetings with politicians to full-blown accountability sessions, leaders often practice and rehearse. In addition, the public activities are routinely followed by evaluation and feedback.

A description of this process is provided by Gilbert Garcia, a leader in the Rio Grande Valley:

> Judy Donovan has been instrumental in helping me keep the fire lit
> and challenging me and putting me in situations where I can apply

what I've learned, putting me in leadership positions. She would say, "I need some help. I need a co-chair. I need somebody to run this meeting, and I need you to say a little bit about this. Talk about what you learned in training, and share it with the other people." She would ask me to attend state rallies where we were focusing on a variety of issues and then come back and report to the group. Basically it was through action, putting me in situations where I had to apply what I had learned. It has become very comfortable for me because I've done it so many times, and it's become part of the fiber of who I am.

And another leader, Joe Hinojosa, provides a similar story:

I think a turning point was a time Carissa [an organizer] confronted me. She said, "What have you learned? You've been with us for a year, a year and a half. What have you learned?" And I had never thought about it, about myself. No, you don't just know how to run a meeting, not just about how to talk to people. What have you learned about yourself? And that's when I just had to sit down and say, "Oh, okay, this is what I've actually learned, what I've changed." But it was her confrontation with me that made me dig deeper inside myself and find that spot. She gave me a couple of books to read, and that helped also.

In emphasizing individual development, the IAF is drawing upon a rich organizing tradition. Charles Payne's powerful history of the activities of the Student Nonviolent Coordinating Committee (SNCC), a civil rights organization of the 1960s, describes how organizers would go into isolated Mississippi communities and identify and train local leaders who would be responsible for pushing the movement forward.[2] This approach was consciously contrasted with the top-down charismatic leadership style associated with Dr. Martin Luther King's Southern Christian Leadership Conference. Payne characterizes the SNCC philosophy as "developing leadership in others" based on ideas of community organizing that emphasized "the developmental perspective, an emphasis on building relationships, respect for collective leadership."[3] During this period the Highlander Folk School in Tennessee, founded by Myles Horton, was an important training institution for these local leaders. Septima Clark of SNCC, the founder of the Citizenship School located at Highlander, commented that "the basic purpose of the Citizenship School is discovering local community leaders."[4] Payne describes the Highlander philosophy as follows:

> Workshops at Highlander brought local leaders together to share experiences and to develop techniques that would, in ideal cases, allow them to return home and develop the leadership potential of others. The emphasis on developing others was crucial to Highlander's conception of leadership. According to Horton, "We debunk the leadership role of going back and telling people and providing the thinking for them. We aren't into that. We're into people who can help other people develop and provide educational leadership and ideas, but at the same time, bring people along."[5]

Organizing by emphasizing the development of leaders has even deeper roots. In the *Pedagogy of the Oppressed*, Paulo Freire developed an influential argument about the relationship between teaching style and political organizing. He argued that education as it is typically structured—with a teacher in charge and with the material having little to do with the realities of ordinary lives—renders learners passive and reinforces lack of power. Instead, teaching should be based on the actual experience of people, they should be encouraged to draw on materials that enable them to identify the sources of their oppression, and the style of teaching should be open and participatory. The IAF's use of readings and how it involves leaders in grappling with the material clearly has its roots in Freirian practice.

In identifying and developing local leaders, the IAF draws upon a rich set of traditions and then adds a sophisticated set of techniques and strategies. What is distinctive, however, is how the IAF has gone beyond these foundations by grafting individual leadership development to a strategy for creating stable long-lasting organizations. The interaction of leadership development and organization building is what makes the IAF unique.

The Organizers

In any IAF public function the leaders are in the foreground. They run the meeting, ask the questions at the accountability session, and speak to the press. But there is another group of people without whom the organization could not succeed: the organizers. The organizers work full-time (actually, more like double time) and provide training, strategic direction, and continuity. Indeed, the interaction and relative power of the organizers and leaders is an important theme that I will return to.

The IAF network in the Southwest employs roughly forty organizers. Each individual organization—for example, Valley Interfaith or COPS—employs between two and five organizers, one of whom is the lead, or senior, organizer. The organizers range from relatively new recruits to people who have been with the network since the founding of COPS in 1975. They are a diverse group. The lead organizer in Houston, Joe Higgs, is a relatively young Anglo man. Joe Rubio in El Paso is half Anglo and half Mexican. Willie Bennett, the lead organizer in Fort Worth, is an African-American ordained minister. Several of the most senior organizers are nuns,[6] whereas others are lay men and women drawn to the work because they had been leaders in the one of the organizations somewhere in the Southwest. In sharp contrast to Alinsky, who thought that women had no place in organizing, at least half of the organizers are female.[7]

One of the distinctive characteristics of the IAF is that organizing is treated as a professional career. Organizers are paid respectable wages, with starting annual salaries about thirty thousand dollars, and pay for the most senior organizers ranges between fifty-five thousand and eighty-five thousand dollars. There are frequent opportunities for professional development. The organizers are rotated on a fairly regular basis across different cities. Although the pay is decent and the work stimulating, finding an adequate number of organizers is difficult, and the relative scarcity of organizing talent is seen by senior IAF staff as one of the major constraints on the growth of the network.

Sister Pearl Ceasar is one of the most senior organizers in Texas. Born in Louisiana and descended from Lebanese immigrants, she entered religious life in 1961, attended college in San Antonio, and then embarked upon a teaching career in parochial schools. After some time working in Oklahoma, she ended up back in Louisiana. When she arrived, she had no interest in politics, but this was a time when the public schools were integrating and the Catholic schools were being used as a refuge for whites fleeing the public system. Eventually Pearl (along with Christine Stephens, who was a member of Pearl's religious order and who also went on to organize for the IAF) refused to teach under those circumstances. The local Catholic hierarchy responded by simply firing the nuns. After teaching briefly in another school, Pearl returned to San Antonio to get a master's degree in social work and then traveled to Washington, D.C., to work for a Catholic Sisters lobbying group. While in Washington, she read about COPS in San Antonio and decided to return to Texas. She began working in a local parish and trained under Arnie Graf, then the lead organizer of COPS in the city.

> I started work on a Thursday. I'll never forget October 1, and Arnie told me that I needed to do fifty individual meetings a week, just an outlandish number. And I did. I didn't do all of them that weekend, but I did about twenty that weekend, went back and met him on Monday. And I knew then that's what I wanted to do. It was an incredible experience. It all came together: the experience in Louisiana, where people had no voice, no power in terms of their school, and then seeing in the poorest area of San Antonio that they had some kind of dignity and respect because they belonged to COPS. And they understood what they could do. So I decided that's what I wanted to do. So I've been doing this since 1976.

When Pearl talks about the skills that are required she makes a sharp distinction between the practical skills of organizing and the deeper mind-set.

> When I started organizing, I thought all I needed to do was take the skills I had and put [them] into organizing. What I did not understand, and I think what a lot of people don't understand, is that organizing is not about skills. You can learn the skills of organizing in about a year or two. But I had to understand how I had to be different and remake myself. I needed to relate to people differently. I needed to think of power differently in terms of myself. It wasn't just a question of becoming more assertive. It was a question of becoming truly political in terms of what relationships needed to be leveraged—or not leveraged—how to understand people's interest, how to become very strategic in what I did, said, and acted. All that to me is remaking myself. Because I never had to deal with myself in terms of fears, in

terms of how at different times in those different periods of my life I would act like a victim. I had all kinds of skills, but I would still let myself be victimized but never understood that what was happening. I didn't know how to deal with power. So, it's all of the above in terms of remaking yourself. And most people don't understand that. They think that all you need to do is learn a set of skills.

In fact, the substance of organizing is an unusual combination of politics and psychology and the daily routine a mix of stimulation and tedium. The politics is inherent in the task, and the psychology flows from the IAF emphasis on identifying and developing leaders. The work can be stimulating, since organizers need to learn about topics as diverse as water systems, health care financing, and school reform, and they find themselves in the midst of frequent political campaigns and public actions. However, much of the work of organizing involves worrying about how many people will turn out to such and such a meeting, why someone didn't show up when she said she would, whether the signs have been made and properly placed, who will do the translation, and so on. After a while, these kinds of concerns are both boring and exhausting. One of the major tasks of the IAF network is to find ways to maintain the morale of the organizers and to keep them engaged.

Just as leaders describe the IAF as "my university," the network's strategy for engaging organizers and for keeping their thinking fresh is very much based on an educational model. Roughly every four to six weeks the Southwest network sponsors a seminar built around a set of readings. The author, most typically a university professor, is invited to Texas and has the very unusual experience of interacting over two days with a group of people who have carefully read his or her work and have tried to find ways to relate it to their daily activities. This, in fact, was how I first connected with the IAF, and I still remember how surprising it was to find myself in a group of people who had carefully read what I had written and seemed to be more conscientiously dealing with it than most of my colleagues in Cambridge.

The organizers also engage in considerable peer support via regularly scheduled meetings in which they come together to discuss each other's work. At these sessions the conversation is organized around topics such as "If you were going to leave this work, what would be the most likely reason?" or "What are you doing to keep yourself agitated and how are you mentoring junior organizers?" Christine Stephens describes her colleagues as a "guild of organizers." Between the academic seminars, the support sessions, and the more informal communication, a strong peer network is developed to help the organizers keep up their morale and deal with the sometimes tedious nature of the work.

This strong peer network also has the effect of reinforcing a certain psychological distance between the organizers and the leaders. Although the organizers are deeply committed to their work, it is important that they not become too committed to any particular individual or group. To do otherwise would be an invitation to rapid burnout. There are too many leaders, their lives are too complicated, and there is too much movement of people in and out of the leadership role. It is not uncommon to hear organizers speak of leaders with a measure of detachment that is often surprising given the basic fact that the organizers are devoting their lives to the welfare of these people and their communities. The leaders and their communities are not faceless abstractions—as might be the case with a politician who speaks of "the people" or "the nation." Rather, organizers have to find a balance between committing to people as individuals, and treating them with the decency this implies, and yet maintaining the distance required to survive emotionally. This is a difficult line to walk, but the network works hard to provide a variety of supports.

Maintaining the Organization

It is not easy to build a strong organization, but neither is it a simple matter to keep the organization on track once it is in place. There are strong pressures that threaten to undermine what has been created. These include loss of purpose and mission, loss of energy, and the tendency for those at the top to take over and exclude the majority from meaningful participation. Many seemingly successful progressive organizations, from some civil rights groups of the 1960s to some unions, have succumbed to these pressures. Some have gone out of business, whereas others have become ineffective. The IAF is very self-conscious about these dangers and employs a variety of stratagems to avoid them.

Culture

Academics who study organizations have become very focused on the idea of culture, and for good reason. Any organization—be it a firm, a government agency, or a political organization—has a culture that is at least as important as its formal structure. Culture includes the norms, values, climate, and rules of the game that together constitute what the organization is about and how it operates. Culture develops over time, and those features that endure add up to a coherent whole or pattern.[8]

In the business world, culture is treated as a critical contributor to (or a detractor from) a firm's success. The culture of IBM used to be that decisions were made by committees, peopled by men uniformly dressed in blue suits and white shirts. These committees reported to other committees, and decisions required consensus. This culture conveyed something about the firm: that it was a formal bureaucracy that relied on procedures and rules and that individualism was discouraged. This was a successful organizational culture in the world in which large mainframe computers were sold to customers who centralized all their purchasing in an information technology department. The organizational culture quickly became dysfunctional in a world that placed a premium on fast decision making and in which smaller computers were sold to a diverse and noncentralized customer base. The formal atmosphere was also a problem when talent had to be recruited from a generation more accustomed to the college campus atmosphere of Silicon Valley.

The issue of culture frequently comes up when two companies merge. In recent years, blue-blood investment banking firms on Wall Street joined with hard-scrambling, much less polite retail brokerage firms. Which culture wins out, and how the winners and losers feel, makes a great difference to the success of the merger.[9]

Culture shapes how people think about what they do. It is simply impossible to have a manual of procedures that describes what action an individual or group should take in all circumstances. The world is too complicated and uncertain for such a recipe book to have any chance of success. As a consequence, people have to be inculcated with values, attitudes, and rules of thumb to help them figure out what do to and how to act.[10] If successful, the culture shapes how people act with respect to the world outside the organization and also how they collaborate with their colleagues.

There is considerable variation in how attentive companies are to organizational culture and how extensively it is elaborated. When an organization is aware of the importance of culture, it is likely to put considerable effort into training and socializing its members. Indeed, in the corporate world a considerable fraction of firms' training budgets is devoted to teaching employees about the organization's goals, values, and norms.

Outsiders are likely to be struck by the strong culture of the IAF and by how much effort is put into teaching and maintaining it. New IAF leaders attend either three-day or ten-day training sessions during which they are involved in workshops, skits, and lectures. These are meant to introduce them to the IAF's approach toward organizing and to convey the norms that govern how the organizations operate. In addition, there are frequent shorter training sessions, on weekend afternoons and evenings, some of which are devoted to issues (such as education reform or job training) and some of which are devoted to organizing techniques. But even in the issues workshops, the IAF culture is constantly reinforced as organizers and senior leaders make presentations and lead discussions. This teaching of culture is a central and self-conscious element of the IAF's mode of operation.

The very fact that these workshops and seminars exist is one element of the IAF culture. The organization places enormous value on training, and both leaders and organizers come to expect that they will be learning something new as a result of their involvement. This expectation is useful in a variety of ways. Learning helps organizers cope with the tedious aspects of their work. It is their payoff. Leaders, many of whom are people with little education, gain a different kind of benefit. The fact that they find themselves reading and discussing college-level material, and sometimes interacting on equal terms with the authors, teaches them an important lesson about their own capacities. Not only is their self-esteem enhanced, but the experience enables the leaders to operate effectively in the political arena, researching issues and confronting politicians in ways that would seem an insurmountable stretch if they judged their own capacities by their formal schooling.

The IAF culture is relentlessly pragmatic and nonideological. Ask any IAF leader or organizer to expound their theory of capitalism and the response will be short. At most they will say that everyone, themselves as well as firms and politicians, operate from self-interest. Grand theories are not very interesting and are seen as obstacles to getting something done. Although values, religious and otherwise, play an important role in IAF thinking, the dominant attitude is a pragmatic assessment of the possible. This view of how to operate is hammered home in one of the central readings in IAF training, the Melian Debate, taken from Thucydides' *History of the Peloponnesian War.*

The Melian Debate takes place during the sixteenth year of the war. The Athenians, with overwhelming power, led an expedition against the island of Melos, a colony of Sparta that had refused to join the Athenian empire. Before attacking, the Athenians sent a delegation to negotiate. The Melians refused to let this delegation speak to the people of the island but did agree that their leadership would meet with the Athenians. The Athenians began by asking the islanders to set aside any discussion of right and wrong and of fine principles. Instead, they should focus simply on their self-interest and make a clear assessment of the situation, which was hopeless. The Athenians offered a deal, that they would refrain from attacking if the Melians would agree to accept Athenian sovereignty. Both sides' self-interest, weighted by the relative power relationships, would determine the outcome. "We recommend that you should try to get what it is possible for you to get. . . . The standard of justice depends on the equality of power to compel and that in fact the strong do what they have the power to do and the weak accept what they have to accept. . . . You, by giving in, would save yourselves from disaster; we, by not destroying you, would be able to profit from you."

The Melians clung to principle. "We are standing," they said, "for what is right against what is wrong." They also insisted that the situation was not as hopeless as the Athenians implied. The Melians believed that Sparta would come to their aid, and they also believed in good luck: "We put our trust in the fortune that the gods will send and which has saved us up to now." The Athenians explained why Sparta would not assist them and added that they themselves had just as much reason as the Melians to expect that the gods and luck would be on their side. The Melians refused to budge.

The Athenians left with the comment that "judging from this decision of yours, you seem to us quite unique in your ability to consider the future as something more certain than what it is before your eyes, and to see uncertainties as realities, simply because you would like them to be so. As you have staked most on and trusted most in Spartans, luck, and hopes so in all these you will find yourselves completely deluded." The Athenians negotiators withdrew, and their compatriots launched the attack. Sparta did nothing, the Melians were forced to surrender, all the men were killed, and the women and children sent into slavery.

This story can be read in more than one way. For some people it is very hard to accept the notion that right and wrong should play no role in decisions and that all that counts is an accurate appraisal of power, of allies, and an assessment of self-interest. After all, values—religious and otherwise—suffuse IAF culture and rhetoric, and the IAF organizers and leaders have a sharp sense of justice and injustice in the world. To pick another ancient story, Jews celebrate the defenders of Masada who, facing impossible odds, nonetheless accepted death rather than surrender. In a similar vein, when the story of the Alamo is told, few ask why the Texans did not negotiate and surrender to Santa Ana.

For the IAF, however, the central lesson is that the Melians failed to engage effectively in politics. The Melians may have had virtue on their side, and if they had made an accurate assessment of the situation, it was perhaps their right to die if they wished. Even this is not clear, since the leadership refused to permit the people to participate in this fateful decision. But, more to the point from the IAF perspective, the Melians failed to accurately judge the power relationships, and they also failed to assess their allies accurately. They did not engage in a clear-eyed weighing of reality and a judgment about what was possible. They were not pragmatic politicians, and they and their people paid a terrible price for this failure. The better course, from the IAF's perspective, would have been to enter into a relationship with the Athenians, to "do politics" with them, and over time to get the most that was possible from the interaction.

The IAF makes the Melian Debate a centerpiece in order to teach its people to respond to the world as it is, not to the world as it should be. This very practical political pragmatism is reflected on a daily basis in the organization's business-like dealings with the powers that be. It is also continually reflected in internal discussions when, for example, choices have to be made about what standard should be set in a living wage campaign or how quickly some colonia should be cleaned up.

If political pragmatism and realpolitik are one core element of IAF culture, another is a distrust of established authority and experts. This lesson is driven home in training through two devices: a training exercise and another reading drawn from classic literature. The exercise is simple: in the middle of a talk the speaker asks one or more of the attendees to leave the room and then goes on with the presentation. The departed trainees are simply ignored. Eventually they may peek back in the room, or else they may not be seen until the next break. At this point their behavior is examined. Why, the trainer wants to know, did these people so willingly accept orders? Under what conditions do we, and should we, simply accept authority?

The reading is a chapter in the Dostoyevsky's *Brothers Karamazov* called "The Grand Inquisitor." The story is a parable told by one brother to another. Christ, it seems, decided to return to earth, and he did so in Seville at the height of the Spanish Inquisition. Heretics were burned by the hundreds, and the terrified and passive citizenry was under the control of priests led by the ninety-year-old Grand Inquisitor. Christ is recognized as he walks the streets, and people flock to him. But the Grand Inquisitor is furious and has Christ arrested and thrown into prison. The chapter replays the Grand Inquisitor's monologue defending the dictatorship of the priests to a silent Jesus.

In the ultimate irony, it turns out that the priests are unhappy that Christ returned. "Why did You come back here, to interfere and make things difficult for us?" The original promise of Christ to mankind was freedom, but, the Inquisitor asserts, this has not worked. When men have freedom they cannot manage it. The consequence is chaos and religious strife. "Freedom, free-thinking, and science will lead men into such confusion and confront them with such dilemmas and insoluble riddles that the fierce and rebellious will destroy one another; others who are rebellious but weaker will destroy themselves, while the weakest and most miserable will crawl to our feet and cry out to us." People realize this. "So, in the end, they will lay their freedom at our feet and say to us 'enslave us, but feed us.' And they will finally understand that freedom and assurance of daily bread for everyone are two incompatible notions." There are one hundred thousand people who are capable of governing the millions, and these leaders, the priests, have "corrected Your work," they have improved on what Christ taught, and they now provide "miracles, mystery, and authority." These are the ingredients for the successful management of the world, because "we shall solve all their problems, and they will trust to our solutions completely." The reappearance of Christ is nothing but a recipe for another millennium of disorder.

The Inquisitor, despite his strong statements and terrible deeds, is not painted by Dostoyevsky as an evil man. Rather, he devoted his life to thinking through how best to help mankind and came to these conclusions only at the end. He is tormented and, in fact, backs off from his original intention to kill Christ. He releases Him with the admonition to never again return to earth.

There is, of course, a certain irony in the IAF's use of this parable. The story is suffused with anticlericalism, yet the IAF works closely with the church hierarchy. But the IAF uses the story to teach about how power operates. The Grand Inquisitor is a story about the risk of unilateral power and about the dangers of passiveness and learned helplessness. When the local water authority tells the residents of the colonia Las Milipas that they should be silent and let the authority go about its business because the residents do not really understand the complexities of drainage systems and water tables, the authority is acting like the Grand Inquisitor. When the McAllen business community tells Valley Interfaith that it is okay to involve themselves in citizenship projects but they should be silent about living wage issues because the workings of the economic system are too complex for a community group to comprehend, then the business community is behaving like the Grand Inquisitor.

The IAF also has cultural norms about how people behave toward each other that taken together might be described as "tough love." One norm is the so-called iron rule: "never do for people what they can do for themselves." People need to learn to act on their own behalf, and if organizers or other leaders are too interventionist, this learning won't happen. In a similar spirit, groups of people—be they employees who are paid too little or disgruntled residents of a colonia—need to do the hard work of organizing to change their circumstances. Obviously this rule does not imply that no assistance will be rendered, since the IAF exists to help individuals and groups move forward, but it does imply that people have to make an effort. There is also internal political content to this norm: the organization has to choose what battles to undertake, and if affected parties are not willing to make a significant effort, then that particular issue is unlikely to be on the agenda. Of course, the iron rule, like other such norms, is an ideal and is not necessarily an accurate description of reality. I have observed organizers doing far too much work in helping leaders think through a set of readings and planning presentations. On the other hand, there have been times I've tried to intervene on behalf of people I thought were getting too little credit for their work, only to be told quite clearly to back off; if these people wanted more credit, they could speak up on their own behalf.

Another "tough love" norm is constant evaluation. After every activity, the leaders and organizers will come together to talk about what went wrong and what went right. These conversations can be quite direct. At one evaluation I attended, the event (a rally combined with a meeting with state representatives) was evaluated by out-of-town organizers and with the local organizer on several criteria: how many people attended, the diversity of attendees, whether the leaders took ownership of the event, whether it was clear that the leaders represented specific institutions, and whether the event articulated issues that the politicians in attendance could be pressed to act upon (as opposed to problems that are not actionable). Even at the conclusion of one-on-one conversations, there will be an evaluation of the experience.

Finally, the IAF makes a clear distinction between public and private relationships. Private relationships are those among family and friends. They are governed by a set of emotions—love, loyalty, desire to be accepted—that are widely understood. It is a mistake, however, to expect that these kinds of relationships should be extended to the world of organizing and work. Public relationships are those among colleagues and also between IAF members and public officials. These are governed by power rather than love, by the desire to be respected not by the desire to be accepted, and by self-interest.

Taken as a collection of norms, what the iron rule, the evaluation ritual, and the public/private distinction add up to is a certain distancing or toughness in interpersonal relationships within the IAF. To a newcomer, interpersonal relations within the IAF can sometimes seem manipulative or at the minimum cold. This, however, is a misreading of what is going on. Even a casual perusal of the business press makes it clear that people who work together closely nonetheless govern their relationships by norms that are not those of friends or family. Sandy Weil and John Reed merged Citicorp and for some time acted like the closest of partners. Weil, however, eventually turned on Reed and pushed him out. This story can be multiplied many times, and to it could be added the polite, but still intense, competition among peers within a firm for promotion. Similarly, politicians—including those of the same party who are allies on many issues—are nonetheless competitors for higher office, for committee assignments, for access to donors, and so on. The IAF wants to operate in this world effectively on behalf of its constituency. Given the relational nature of its organizing, and given its base in churches and schools and communities, it would be easy and natural to try to function in the external world according to the norms of family. But the organization would be eaten alive. To avoid this fate, the culture strongly pushes people to understand the distinction between public and private and to operate accordingly.

Along with regular training, periodically an IAF organization decides to systematically reinvigorate through an organizational learning strategy called institutional development. Valley Interfaith undertook such a process beginning in the fall of 2001. Valley Interfaith, like the other organizations in the Texas IAF network, was gearing up for a large voter registration drive aimed at the 2002 state elections, a drive that in IAF parlance is called "sign up and take charge." This involves a door-to-door campaign with each contact consisting of not merely signing forms but also a fifteen- to twenty-minute conversation. As such, it demands a great deal of organizational energy, and the institutional development campaign was intended to set the stage.

Valley Interfaith's institutional development proceeds in three stages. It starts with a training program—covering relational culture, mission, leadership, individual meetings, pressures on the family, and house meetings—that lasts several months in churches and schools that are members of the organization. The training is done by primary leaders who themselves have spent several weeks in training-the-trainer workshops and in developing the curriculum. Following this, a large house meeting campaign discusses particular issues. During this particular round of institutional development, the theme of the house meetings was jobs. This was chosen in anticipation of the drive to build a workers' association (an effort that will be described in chapter 5). In the final phase, the leaders come together to develop an action plan, in this case focused on the "sign-up and take charge" campaign. As a result of this process, thousands of Valley Interfaith leaders are trained, or retrained, in the basic principles of the organization's operating procedures and culture.

Many of the elements of IAF culture originated with Saul Alinsky.

His biographer describes the "iron rule," the admonition to work with the "world as it is, not the world as it should be," and the view that power comes in two forms: "organized money and organized people."[11] Alinsky taught pragmatism through the Melian Debate, and he stressed the importance of identifying and organizing around people's self-interest. Since Alinsky, the IAF has evolved in a variety of ways, most notably through a stronger emphasis on signing up institutions as members and on professionalizing the corps of organizers. There are very few comparable organizations on the American landscape that have had as long a run as the IAF has, and this durability testifies to the power of these core cultural ideas. How has the IAF avoided the traps into which most other organizations fall?

The Dilemmas of Organization

The instinct of scholars who study organizations is not to take at face value organizations' professions of purpose nor the degree to which their members really have a voice in how they operate. There is a long tradition of research that seeks to get behind the facade and understand how organizations actually operate.

A standard finding is that organizations that purport to be open and democratic are in fact dominated by a self-perpetuating elite. This pattern was identified and given a label—the "iron law of oligarchy"—early in the twentieth century by Robert Michels, who studied the German Social-Democratic party and labor movement. Although ostensibly committed to democracy, both organizations were in fact dominated by small groups.

Leaders want to maintain power, and the complexity of large organizations offers them the opportunity to do so. To the natural complexity of large organizations, the elite adds a degree of mystification that makes it appear that only they can manage the organization's tasks. The leadership also maintains a monopoly on political skill, dominates the channels of communication, and controls resources. Over time these tactics lead to low membership participation, which simply reinforces the pattern. These tendencies have been documented in a wide variety of settings, although they are not inevitable.[12] Exceptions aside, there are nonetheless very good reasons to be concerned about elite domination.

According to the iron law of oligarchy, an internal elite comes to dominate organizations even when the original intent was that organization members have a real voice. In this story, people go about augmenting their power, and the nature of modern large-scale organizations gives them the opportunity to do so. There is, however, another pattern characteristic of organizations that is not about people operating in their own interest but rather a story about how the needs of the organization itself come to divert the enterprise from its original purpose. The sociological classic that first forcefully raised this issue is Philip Selznick's study *The TVA and the Grass Roots*.[13]

The Tennessee Valley Authority (TVA) was established during the New Deal to develop—via electricity, agricultural policies, conservation, and economic development—a vast region that had hitherto been poor and isolated. The director of the authority, David Lilienthal, was committed to undertaking these activities democratically, by involving the grass roots in planning. Selznick set out to learn whether this ideal was achieved and found that it was not: "Ideals go quickly by the board when the compelling realities of organizational life are permitted to run their natural course."[14] In this case what undermined the good intentions was not the machinations of an elite trying to maintain its power but rather the processes by which the organization sought to survive and grow in a complicated environment.

Organizations exist in an environment populated by other organizations that are both resources and threats. Survival requires finding ways to draw on those resources and deflect the threats. In the case of the TVA, the problem was the numerous other government agencies who felt that the TVA was intruding on their turf. In addition, the TVA had to cope with political actors in the affected communities who were eager to shape what the TVA did and had the capacity to have their voice heard in Washington. All organizations face similar challenges, and they, like the TVA, act in predictable ways to cope with them. They adopt formal bureaucratic operating procedures that convey the appearance of responsibility and legitimacy to their actions. They try to blend in by mimicking the behaviors, rules, and procedures of the more powerful organizations in their environment. They find ways to include their potential rivals in the organization's decision making, and this co-optation provides a measure of security, although it also diverts the organization from its goals. In short, organizations take actions and adopt policies that, although not necessarily consistent with their original ideals and goals, seem to provide a measure of financial or political security and stability. The logic of the organization and its survival and growth takes precedence over the logic of the founding ideals.

These concerns about the reality, as opposed to the rhetoric, continue to dominate the thinking of many students of organizations.[15] How does the IAF stack up?

There is, in fact, some reason to worry. There are two ways in which the iron law of oligarchy could play out in the context of the IAF. First, the full-time organizers may come to dominate, despite the doctrine that puts leaders at the core of the model. Second, even among leaders an established in-crowd might hold on to power, making it difficult for new leaders to emerge. There are at least hints of both processes in action. For example, although leaders are virtually always the public face of the IAF in meetings, it is not unusual to see an organizer in the background whispering stage directions in the leader's ear. More substantively, it sometimes appears as if the big decisions about the IAF's direction and strategy are made by organizers and then sold to leaders. At Valley Interfaith an example is the recent decision to work with the Service Employees International Union (SEIU) in building an employees' association in the Valley. The idea for the workers' association emerged when individuals approached Valley Interfaith for help with their employment problems. They came to the organization because of its success with its Living Wage Campaign. However, the decision to invite the SEIU to participate was made by senior organizers, who then brought the union to the Valley to meet with leaders. By the same token, it is not only the organizers that we have to worry about. In most cities a group of core leaders have continued to be active in the organization, and one might worry that they constitute a self-perpetuating elite.

There is no reason to expect the IAF to be immune to these threats. What is remarkable is the degree to which the IAF has avoided problems common to most organizations. At the end of the day, the IAF has found a strategy for maintaining the integrity of its original mission and in doing so provides a lesson from which other political organizations should learn. Although the IAF employs specific mechanisms to prevent organizational sclerosis, at the core of its success is its remarkable degree of self-awareness about these dangers. The IAF doctrine and culture is in part specifically aimed at these concerns. As Ernie Cortes frequently comments, "All organizing is reorganizing," and the IAF is vigilant about breaking up patterns that can cause problems.

To avoid domination by a self-perpetuating elite, the IAF constantly recruits new leadership. When new institutions join the organization, for example when a new congregation is signed up, new leaders naturally emerge. Both because it is in their self-interest and because it is part of their mission, local IAF organizations expend a great deal of energy working to gain these new member institutions. Sometimes this is simply part of the day-to-day activities of the organization, and sometimes a special effort is made, as, for example, when Pearl Ceasar recently returned to San Antonio to head up an organizing drive among the congregations in the fast-growing suburbs. In addition, experienced leaders are continually pushed to recruit new ones; recall Noelia's story of how she was nagged into attending her first meeting. The circulation of new leaders prevents the more long-standing ones from dominating the organization.

The relationship of organizers to leaders is more complex. There is no question that organizers are central to the operation. They work full-time for the IAF, whereas most of the leaders hold jobs outside the organization and are available to the IAF only for limited hours. And the organizers are, on average, better trained and more sophisticated about politics than the leaders are. Political intelligence and knowledge about what works and what doesn't move through the network of organizers. For all of these reasons, it is to be expected that the organizers are powerful players.

The question, however, is whether the organizers dominate to such an extent that the idea that leaders have a voice is really a sham. One piece of evidence on this is that over the life of the IAF network in the Southwest there have been several occasions when the leaders in a particular city fired the lead organizer. Beyond these dramatic events, there are other mechanisms by which leaders maintain their power. Organizers are evaluated in the network by their ability to establish a stable dues structure, which requires that the leaders be committed.

The best way to think about the balance between organizers and leaders is by asking how issues are developed. One important source is house meetings, where problems of concern to the leaders surface. This is as "open" and democratic a way of developing an agenda as is possible to imagine. The organizers also contribute to the agenda, and their ideas may emerge from their own observation or because of a larger agenda in the IAF network.

The early days of Valley Interfaith illustrates how this interaction works. Ernie Cortes and Jim Drake had identified equalizing school finance and cleaning up Brownsville harbor as the two key issues. COPS and the other IAF organizations had been very involved in school finance for several years, and the harbor was of considerable concern to some of the more middle-class parishes in Brownsville. In preparing for a visit by the governor to the Valley, Cortes and Drake were surprised to discover that the energy in house meetings was mostly about conditions in the colonias. As a result, the IAF decided to make this issue the centerpiece of the governor's visit.

Whether issues emerge from house meetings or are defined by organizers, what is decisive in determining which ones get the organization's attention is the willingness of the leaders to work. The most common sentiment about the decision-making process has to do with energy. Father Alfonso commented:

> [What] . . . plays into what we're going to do is where's the energy and who has the energy? Because you may identify many issues, but you have to identify what are the issues where more people have energy, and who has the energy to work with them.

Decisions in Valley Interfaith are made via a representational structure that aggregates upward from house meetings through an intermediate body (the regional representatives) to the executive committee. This means, of course, that the broad base of the organization speaks its voice either in house meetings or via representatives; this is not an organization in which plebiscites or large assemblies make decisions. There is, in the end, a decision-making elite, but the structure of the organization forces that elite to listen to the opinions of the base, and, as noted above, the membership of the elite is fluid.

Are debates genuine? The answer seems to be yes. One type of debate has to do with what is in effect horse trading within the organization. Each area might want the organization to go to bat for some particular local project, and the leaders have to sort this out. As Father Bart describes it,

North McAllen and South McAllen IAF leaders negotiate. For example, at a certain moment we had to talk about a north side and a south side library, and because both want one. We have public transportation system here. The north side wanted an extension of that. We said, fine.

Another kind of debate has to do with overall priorities. Recently Valley Interfaith had to decide whether it would get involved in helping people obtain their citizenship papers. As Noelia tells the story,

There was a discussion: is it something that we want to do? This is more in the line of social work. We normally do more building, working with people and educating and identifying leaders. It took a lot of energy and time to work with citizenship. And we decided we wanted to because there were people in our community that were afraid of losing benefits, because they were elderly and if they had worked in the fields there was no record of them ever working, and their only source of money was a check that they got. So there was an interest. But there was some discussion on that.

In these debates about the broader mission of the organization, the voices of the organizers are heard, for example, when they push local organizations to get involved in statewide issues. As Father Alfonso comments, "Sometimes from the perspective of a leader of a local region, there are periods when there's a lot of time and energy that's taken out by the statewide network." And Noelia, in describing the system, notes, "Well, there's a lot of studies. There's study. There's discussion. There's recommendations by the organizers, and then the committee that is in charge looks at the situation."

In short, decision making within the IAF is complex. The ideas of the broad membership are voiced in house meetings. There is a process of voting "by energy," there are different levels of decision-making committees of leaders, and there is the role of the organizers. In the end, the broad membership and the leaders all feel that they are fully involved in the decisions that are made. In none of our interviews did leaders express serious dissatisfaction about the nature or openness of the decision-making process. The IAF's training in self-assertiveness and skepticism toward authority provides a strong foundation for the leaders to be sure that their voices are heard.

The reason the decision-making process is important to understand is that without this broad sense of participation the energy of the members would flag. This loss of energy lies at the heart of the problems facing other nominally membership-based organizations.

Getting Stale

If the IAF has found a way around the iron law of oligarchy, there still remains the question of whether it can avoid the traps described by Selznick. In his account, organizations fall into a set of routines, which, although designed to protect them and enable them to grow, in fact divert them from their original mission.

Over the course of its twenty-five years in San Antonio, COPS has evolved from an organization of outsiders challenging the established structure to a part of that structure. It essentially controls the elections in a number of city counsel districts and plays a very aggressive role in the annual city budgeting process. As a result, it is able to ensure that there is a flow of services into the neighborhoods where it has a strong presence, and it is also able to obtain funding for larger-scale initiatives in job training or housing. In short, as I will discuss at greater length in chapter 4, COPS has come to resemble the classic big-city political machine. The danger, of course, is that its success in building a strong niche for itself in city politics and in securing resources for its programs and neighborhoods will lead the organization away from its mission of agitating for social change. The organization will be secure but will no longer be what it was.

In fact, in recent years COPS seemed to be heading in this direction. It was so caught up in budget cycles and operating service programs that it was forgetting how to organize. But the IAF leadership demonstrated a high degree of self-awareness and took action to intervene. Elizabeth Valdez described the problem:

> Sister Christine did a training session with the leadership. She said COPS and Metro Alliance can become this super civic organization that does a lot of good for a lot of people on health care and housing and infrastructure, fixing all the ills and needs of the community; you can become that if you're not careful. Or you can continue to challenge yourself and agitate yourselves to become a broad-based powerful orga-

nization. And if you're about building power, then your question for the leadership is, who are you identifying and developing as leaders? Because for a broad-based organization the primary concern is what leaders are you developing. How are you developing other leaders and identifying other leaders?

In order to return to the organization's mission, COPS took a numbers of steps. First, it began a series of workshops to help leaders identify the problem. Some of these workshops were led by Christine Stephens and other senior organizers, but others were led by leaders from Valley Interfaith. In addition, COPS pulled back from the business of providing services. Linda Ortega, a COPS leader, describes what happened:

> We had established a housing alliance. We identified families in the community that wanted to be homeowners and helped them through that process. But it was eating up the talent. It was eating up the leadership. We came to the realization that while housing was needed in San Antonio, COPS and Metro Alliance were not about providing services. We've never been about that. And we shut down the housing alliance. Now that was very painful to do. But they understood the role of COPS and Metro was to organize this power organization and identify leaders. There was no debate about where we needed to cut the line.

COPS has also pulled back from its involvement in the allocation of Community Development Block Grant funds (Federal money that flows to cities for local projects) and, over the past year, rededicated itself to a project much more in the original spirit of the organization, a drive to divert sales tax revenue away from physical infrastructure and toward education and job-training projects. Developing the support for this has meant promotion of voter registration, identification of new leaders with energy around the issue, training sessions in congregations—in short, all of the traditional organizing and power-building work that lies at the core of the model.

What is striking about this story is not that COPS, and by extension other IAF organizations, teetered on the edge of settling into routines that diverted the organization from its mission. This is, as Selznick and other scholars remind us, not just a constant danger but a typical path.

The IAF is remarkably sensitive to this danger and has built a self-repair kit into its culture. This achievement distinguishes it from the vast majority of organizations, political and otherwise.

Race: An Ongoing Organizational Dilemma

Race has always been a challenge for American progressive social movements. Sometimes race has been utilized by the opponents of progressive politics to keep potential allies apart. For example, during some organizing drives, firms imported African-Americans as strike breakers. William Julius Wilson catalogs twenty-five such situations during labor strikes between 1916 and 1934, and the pattern continued much later.[16]

Even if we put such episodes aside, it has proved hard to build broad-based progressive movements that include different races. Although the rhetoric of a "rainbow coalition" is attractive, bringing it to fruition for more than brief moments of a particular political campaign has not proved easy. Outside of unions, which by and large have been successful in uniting workers of different races in a common cause, it is very hard to think of progressive movements that have overcome racial barriers to build on common interest. The American legacy of division and distrust is strong and pervasive. Yet creating such a long-term broad-based organization is precisely the aim of the IAF.

Race has been a theme in IAF organizing since the very beginning. A Methodist minister who worked with Alinsky in a mixed neighborhood commented, "You know how the south side was then. I mean the race thing was like grit, it was in everything. You could never wash it out of your food. It impregnated everything."[17]

When Alinsky put together his first effort, the Back of the Yards (BOY) organization in the packing yard area made famous by Upton Sinclair, he faced a difficult racial problem. A central element of the organization was the CIO Packing Workers Organizing Committee. This union had a substantial representation of black workers, and one of the key organizers was black. The union was central to Back of the Yards, since a great many residents worked in the packing industry and were members of the union. Yet the neighborhood itself was rigidly segregated, closed off to blacks via covenants and straightforward discrimination. There were racial incidents when black organizers or union members visited churches and families in the Back of the Yards area.

BOY explicitly included language calling for unity regardless of race. Alinsky and a number of priest/organizers worked hard to reduce incidents and help blacks and whites work together. They had success during the early years of the organization, but eventually the legacy of racial hostility proved too much to overcome. The Back of the Yards organization eventually became a stalwart in the effort by the neighborhood to prevent housing integration in Chicago, and its reputation as segregationist threw Alinsky on the defensive.[18]

The difficulties continued. Alinsky's Temporary Woodlawn Organization in Chicago gained national recognition in the mid-1960s when Charles Silberman wrote about it in *Crisis in Black and White*.[19] But this was fundamentally an African-American organization (albeit with white organizers, notably Nicholas Von Hoffman) and failed to achieve the broad-based nature that is the aim of IAF organizing. Similarly, when Ernie Cortes put together COPS in San Antonio in 1972, it was overwhelmingly Hispanic. Members of the African-American community resisted joining COPS, doubting it would reflect their interests. In part, these concerns were based in race, but they also reflected the geographic fact that the Hispanic community was concentrated in a few neighborhoods, whereas the African-American community was spread out and hence might get lost in any neighborhood-based organization. The IAF responded by building a distinct organization in San Antonio, Metro-Alliance, that contained the African-American churches.

This history suggests that race has not been an easy issue for the IAF. This should be no surprise given that the IAF swims in the current of American history, a history replete with racial tension. Yet the IAF has made more progress than might have been expected. Today COPS and Metro-Alliance share an office and organizers and are, for all intents and purposes, one organization. Carmen Anaya attributes success to the fact that "in the organization there are blacks, rich people, whites, people of all colors and religions." At a typical IAF statewide convention, African-Americans are prominent as speakers, organizers, and leaders. Anyone attending such a meeting would conclude that the IAF has moved a substantial way toward its objective of being broad-based. The IAF has made this progress by being sensitive to racial concerns and possible tensions yet sticking to its commitment to being broad-based by refusing to organize explicitly around racial issues.

The IAF experience in Dallas, which unlike the heavily Hispanic Rio

Grande Valley is racially diverse, is illustrative. From the very beginning Dallas Area Interfaith (DAI), the IAF organization, worked in Anglo, African-American, and Hispanic communities. Indeed, the sponsoring committee (the group of ministers and other leaders who worked together to establish DAI) was led by an African-American Baptist minister, a Hispanic Methodist minister who had previously worked in the Valley, and an Anglo Catholic priest who had worked with COPS in San Antonio. Race was not ignored—people were very aware of it—but the effort was to treat race in a way that unified rather than divided. As Gerald Britt, one of the founding pastors of the organization, commented, "Race is both the strength and the struggle of the organization." The signature piece of the organization was that it was racially diverse, so much so that leaders would refuse to meet unless members of all three ethnic groups were present. When I asked Christine Stephens, who was the first organizer of DAI, why race was a positive in DAI when it is so divisive in other settings, she answered in terms of another IAF idea, focusing on the real interests of people:

> Because [in other settings] people are organized around their anxieties and their fears. And when you're organized around your anxieties and your fears it's always dangerous. If you're organized around your interest, you begin to see that there could be some common interest. When I was organizing in Dallas, I was doing some individual meetings out of Temple Shalom, which was the Jewish temple that was part of Dallas Area Interfaith. And I went to see this young man, and I was asking him about his concerns. And he said, "I have a new son, and now I'm going to have to be concerned about my neighborhood. The crime in this area is beginning to increase." And he said, "I don't like the schools. I'm really thinking of moving out." And then he said, "I just don't understand how in Dallas you're going to pull together any kind of diversity." And I had just been doing some individual meetings in an African-American church, and I'd just been talking to a couple about the crime in their area and their school and I said to him, "I was just talking to Mr. and Mrs. Jones in the south part of the city, and their concerns are crime and school. Now that's how we're going to bring them together. That's your concern. That's their concern. We take a lot of pains to make sure that people do individual meetings and share their stories with one another and learn how to think about inter-

ests. That's the glue that holds things together. If it ever ceases to be in people's interest, then they're not going to stick with it. That's the way we design it."

DAI has attacked efforts by public officials to play on racial divisions. They succeeded in breaking up a political coalition on the Dallas school board organized by Sandy Kress (now President Bush's education staffer) and Bill Kevers, Kress's successor. Known as the slam-dunk group, Hispanics and Anglos on the board operated as a bloc in opposition to the African-Americans. DAI mobilized large numbers of leaders to attend board meetings and convinced the Hispanic school board members to join with the African-Americans to support an after-school program that Kress and Kevers opposed. The school board ended up appropriating even more money than DAI had requested, and this signaled the demise of the racial coalition.

DAI's success with the after-school programs presaged an even larger victory with regard to both education and the troubled racial politics in Dallas. By 2001 the Dallas Independent School District had one-quarter of its students in portable or temporary buildings yet for the past decade had been unable to pass a bond initiative. The superintendent, Mike Moses, was determined to make an effort but was unsure of his political support. The turning point was an assembly organized by DAI with sixteen hundred people and Mike Moses attending. The success of the assembly preempted opposition to the bond, and following the assembly Moses not only proposed one but increased the amount from $900 million to $1.4 billion. DAI participated in the campaign via a get-out-the-vote effort aimed at the Hispanic community, and the bond overwhelmingly passed. In an education conference in the winter of 2002, Superintendent Moses publicly credited DAI for the success of the bond election.

The IAF has made considerable progress on race, avoiding the tendency of most progressive movements to be uniracial. Indeed, in cities such as Baltimore, Chicago, and Los Angeles the IAF organizations include large numbers of African-Americans as well as whites and Hispanics. The IAF has also avoided making itself vulnerable to efforts by its opponents to use race as a wedge issue. But although the IAF has achieved more than any other progressive effort along these lines, it remains the case that race is a tough issue for the network in the Southwest. Organizing in the African-American community has proved more difficult. It is very likely that a smaller fraction of low-income African-Americans in the Southwest are affiliated with an IAF organization than is the case for Hispanics.

For many African-Americans the IAF appears to be a somewhat foreign institution—Hispanic and Catholic—trying to organize in an African-American and Baptist context. As one black minister, who is committed to the IAF, commented:

> The obstacle with the African-American congregation is that it is difficult to identify with this culture. And so we tend to stay away. We tend to feel that it's a threat to our culture or our surroundings, infiltrating our camp so to speak. And so we are very hesitant to get involved, and because it's from a Catholic background and we are not in a heavily Catholic area. We are the Bible Belt, very traditional-based religion—and heavily saturated with Baptists, southern Baptists. This challenges us to be more diverse, and we are not openly willing to do that because we feel like it's a threat to our territory. And in saying that, I'm saying that it's not a religious drawback, it's just that we don't understand, and so that frightens us.

An even more direct statement came from another pastor:

> You have the Baptist Minister's Union, you have the Baptist Minister's Conference, you have the IMA, Ecumenical group. We have the Afro American Pastor's coalition. We have about six or seven major players in the city that is predominantly Afro-American. And to have what they perceive as someone else of a different persuasion, different ethnic group coming into our community trying to dictate what we ought to be about, they won't entertain that. And rather than trying to find out what it's all about, they just pushed them down.

Some pastors are reluctant to join the IAF for fear of losing their identity and power. It is hard to persuade some pastors to go from being the head of their congregation to being one leader among many in an IAF organization. This is particularly an issue in the African-American community, where churches have long been the most important social, political, and in some respects economic, institution. This is a problem in organizing any church, but it may be especially difficult given the special role the church has played in African-American communities.

Most IAF organizations are reluctant to discuss race directly as an issue. The organizers recognize that it is impossible to understand a community without taking into account the history of race in that community. However, they are focused on finding issues that cut across diverse groups. Thus, since blacks, Anglos, and Hispanics all share a self-interest in improving education, this is a core issue for the organization. However, race per se and issues that emerge specifically from the black experience are avoided. The classic reaction of an IAF organizer to the question of whether it is wise to avoid race in this sense is to ask "Well, what are the questions that are issue-able?" That is, beyond saying that race is a concern, what concretely can we organize around?

This view is not fully accepted among African-Americans. In the words of Reverend Britt:

> You can't look at the history of African-Americans in this country and say you all need to get over it. I am the first generation in my family to attend legally desegregated schools. You cannot draw a line in the sand and say, "let's start evenly, and you all forget all that stuff." It doesn't work like that. Just like there are particulars when it comes to Hispanic culture that you have to pay attention to, which means there are things that you can't say, things that you can say one way that'll be taken a different way, things that you do that they don't understand. The same is true in the African-American community, and I think we don't pay attention to that because it makes predominantly white organizers uncomfortable.

This perspective is shared by other African-American leaders involved in IAF organizations. They believe that the IAF needs at the minimum to be willing to talk about race explicitly as an issue. Being willing to talk about it is an important signal of respect, even if it is hard to identify issues that are actionable. According to the mainstream IAF philosophy, this runs the risk of betraying the organization's commitment to being broad-based and in doing so weakening it by creating more narrow constituencies with more narrowly defined interests.

Race, then, continues to be "like grit" in IAF organizing. From Alinsky in Chicago to today in the Southwest, it has posed difficult challenges.

On the other hand, IAF organizations are genuinely more "rainbow-like" than any other comparable effort. Furthermore, the IAF has succeeded in preventing the use of race as a wedge issue against it, as the Dallas school board story illustrates. The IAF has not solved the problems of race and, given the weight of American history, this is far from surprising. It has, however, made considerable progress.

The Suburbs

The suburbs have emerged as the great battleground of American politics. In recent election cycles there has been much learned discussion about the interests and proclivities of "Soccer Moms." Both political parties have shaped their message to appeal to the suburbs, and this goes far to explain the "newness" in the appeal of Bill Clinton's New Democratic platform and style.

In reality, of course, the suburbs are more complicated and diverse that the Soccer Mom imagery suggests. In recent years not only have suburbs become more diverse but poverty rates have increased faster in the suburbs than in central cities.[20] This more textured view of the suburbs notwithstanding, it is worth asking about the possibilities of organizing in the Soccer Mom world. A substantial fraction of population, and population growth, resides in this slice of suburbia, and certainly a great deal of power—political and financial—resides there too. In Texas, for example, as many, if not more, votes come from the affluent suburbs north of Dallas as from the Rio Grande Valley.

Accounts of suburban views of politics provide, at first blush, some reason for optimism. Despite the assumption many observers share about conservatism in the suburbs, Alan Wolfe, who interviewed suburbanites throughout the nation, found that the people he talked to evinced broad support for programs that help poor people. Their view of the economy does not glorify the unfettered market but instead supports what Wolfe terms "balanced capitalism," which implies limits on profits in return for more equitable treatment of employees.[21]

This is all to the good. But the main thrust of what Wolfe found is less hopeful about activism. The people he talked to betrayed no strong dissatisfaction with their own circumstances, and Wolfe describes their interest in politics and social action as "modest." Their political and social aspirations are limited, typically to small acts of charity and goodwill. Exactly the same conclusion was reached a decade earlier by Robert Bellah and his colleagues when they interviewed suburbanites in California. In the words of the authors of *Habits of the Heart,*

> When they think of the kind of generosity that might redeem the individualistic pursuit of economic success, they often imagine voluntary involvements in local, small-scale activities such as a family, club, or idealized community in which individual initiatives interrelated to improve the life of all. They have difficulty relating this ideal image to the large-scale forces and institutions shaping their lives.[22]

The problem, however, is not simply intellectual. If it were, then a good dose of IAF training could overcome it. Rather, these people seem to lack any driving self-interest or anger, which are the two motivating factors for the IAF. I interviewed pastors in suburban churches outside of Dallas, and their impressions were quite consistent. One pastor, when asked what issue might drive his parishioners in the direction of the IAF, responded, "I can't find it yet." A more complete answer was provided by a member of a suburban congregation that is affiliated with the IAF (because of the commitment of the priest) but that turns out very few active leaders. "Well, honestly, I'm not sure that there are issues in their lives. It's a matter of helping them understand that . . . everyone is not okay, that there are neighbors that have issues." Getting involved because neighbors have issues comes very close to charity. The same congregation that can only generate a handful of IAF leaders sponsors outreach days when five or six hundred people turn out to volunteer at social service agencies, staff food banks, and the like. This is all to the good, but it does not build the IAF organization.

There are two other obstacles to successful suburban organizing. One is simply that people are too busy. The pastors constantly described congregations in which parents work sixty-hour weeks and travel a great deal, and when they are in town, they shuttle their children from one activity to another. "When they are at home, they'd like to stay at home just a little bit." Asking these people to come to weekend and evening meetings, particularly when self-interest is hard to identify, is difficult.

The second obstacle is more subtle. The language of power turns off many middle-class people. As another suburban leader commented, "Power terrifies people in the suburbs. Every time somebody brings up that word, power, we get some kind of reaction to it. . . . I think they have images of swarming City Hall or an unruly crowd or something like that." Another leader added, "I really don't like to use the word *power*. I really feel like it puts people off. They are not in this thing for power."

When I describe the IAF to my (mostly middle-class) students, they too react against the idea of power and immediately want to know why the issues raised by the IAF can't be worked out through some kind of consensus or mediation process. Alan Wolfe concludes, "What I heard when I talked to Americans from all walks of the middle class . . . was a distaste for conflict, a sense that ideas should never be taken so seriously that they lead people into uncivil . . . courses of action."[23] Wolfe is describing his interviewees' reactions to conflict among intellectuals, but he may as well have been describing people's attitudes toward the conduct of politics.

The easy reply is to point out that when people already have power (even if they do not fully recognize it), and when they are comfortable and have few difficult issues to confront them, it is easy to abhor contestation and, in fact, it is in their self-interest to take this position. Dislike of confrontation seems to tap into deeper attitudes, too. It is a close cousin of the dislike of "special-interest" groups and reveals an underlying position many middle-class Americans take toward the conduct of politics.

The suburbs thus pose a difficult challenge for the IAF. But the cause is not hopeless. Ernie Cortes says that "we are still in the process of figuring this out," but he goes on to argue that there are issues in the suburbs, ranging from mediocre schools to pension security to environmental concerns. My interviews also reveal a consistent theme: that people feel isolated and yearn for a deeper and broader community than they have. One suburban leader commented, "There was passion and energy around some of the issues, which are the issues of isolation and alienation. . . . [People] don't want to be disconnected, . . . they want to build a social fabric in their city like they had when they were growing up." In Alan Wolfe's interviews, people expressed the same concerns: "People are a lot more isolated," and "There's absolutely no sense of community here," and "I am unbelievably and sadly disconnected from the community that I live in."[24] Bellah and his colleagues also detected a sense of loss and a nostalgia for the unitary life of small-town America.[25]

The challenge for the IAF is how to identify the more concrete issues and also to tap into the desire for community. The IAF is well positioned to respond, since the essence of its organizing strategy is to make connections between people and to build community. But the idiom of the suburbs, particularly the aversion to conflict, is a problem. So too is an underlying impulse to remain separate from the city. In the Dallas region, the suburban churches in Plano are a cluster of the larger Dallas organization but insist on maintaining some distance from the downtown cluster. The Plano leaders believe that their issues have little to do with the downtown itself. Building metropolitan power in these circumstances is not easy. As we will see, the IAF is addressing this in Los Angeles, Chicago, and Boston. But at the end of the day, America's suburbs represent a formidable challenge.

Leaders in Action: The Milagro Health Clinic

Estela Soza Garza was born in McAllen, Texas, the eighth of thirteen children. Her father was a truck driver, earning decent money because his job was unionized, and the family supplemented its income by migrating north in the summer to work the harvest. Estela managed to graduate from high school and attended college in the Valley. Today she is department chair of a human services program at a local community college and lives in the north side of McAllen, the more prosperous neighborhood.

Two experiences dramatically shaped Estela's outlook: her family has a long history of diabetes that has taken a toll on her parents and siblings, and her brother was killed in Vietnam. She recalls her brother's death: "I was maybe about twelve or thirteen at the time. . . . And I did not realize the helplessness that I felt. He was injured . . . [and] in the hospital for two weeks, and I just remember my mom going through that time. . . . You know, my brother was dying alone. . . . If only someone had given my mother some money to visit. Seventeen years later, I realized how angry I really was. I guess that's when I recognized the injustice that exists in life."

Estela connected to Valley Interfaith when her priest announced that the organization was working on health care. Given her family history, this captured her attention. What changed Estela—what got her in touch with her anger and helped her channel it—was IAF ten-day training. "It was the one-on-ones. I had never, ever in my life made the connection.

But I know that since then I had this whole sense of helplessness and anger, and so I think it's just getting to learn where our anger comes from. Part of the whole process of organizing is learning about ourselves." When asked how she is different, Estela says, "I lost that feeling of help-lessness. . . . You begin to see that you can change things. . . . You become a different person, and that begins to spill over into every bit of your life, . . . I mean asserting yourself."

Asserting herself was an important step for Estela but perhaps not a radical one, given her education and job. As we have seen, for Rosa Gu-tierrez, asserting herself represented a total transformation. But Rosa shared with Estela anger about the health insurance system in the Valley. Rosa explains her involvement in the health care issues by telling a story of an emergency in which her daughter became dehydrated and then fainted, how she tried to take her across the border to Reynosa because she couldn't afford care in the United States, couldn't make the crossing because the lines were too long, and how the McAllen hospital then re-fused to treat the child until Rosa could provide evidence of how she would pay:

> But I say, why, why? This was an emergency, it was my daughter.
> And there are many others like me in the colonia, and I convinced
> them to tell their stories. A woman that was losing her leg and that
> was rejected here. She was going to Reynosa too, because here she did
> not have money to pay, and this is how the idea of the clinic "El
> Milagro" appeared.

Although for Estela there was no self-interest in creating the Milagro clinic—her drive to work on it came from her family's poor health his-tory, but not from any immediate need. For Rosa, having a health clinic in her neighborhood took on a sense of urgency.

These two leaders, one with a college degree holding a middle-class job and the other with no English and little formal education, joined with other leaders to create the Milagro clinic. The story of this clinic shows the degree of effectiveness and political sophistication the lead-ers achieve.

The drive to create a free clinic in McAllen's south side emerged out of house meetings in which people recounted experiences similar to Rosa's. First a group of leaders began a "research action." Rosa and Estela were part of a group that set out to learn what they could about the structure and financing of the health care system in the Valley. Their first success came when they contacted the State Department of Health and learned that there was an advocate in that organization for local primary care clinics and that the state would provide some funding. The next task was to raise additional money and to find a suitable location.

In the course of looking for funds for the primary care clinic, the leaders learned that the county was planning to close five clinics where people went for shots and other preventive treatment. The clinics were being closed in part because the providers were not being paid. The leaders visited these clinics, where they were stunned to see students sitting on the floor surrounded by boxes of paper bills from providers, some several years old. These part-time students were trying to generate payments to the providers. The leaders were determined to save these clinics, and they researched the budget, trying to understand just what was needed and where the money might come from. They then attended a meeting of the county commissioners. Estela describes what ensued:

> We remembered that one of the commissioners had made a promise that he would commit money if the other commissioners did the same. So we asked for permission to speak again and said, "Well, we want you to ask Commissioner so-and so whether he was going to honor his commitment." So finally all of them committed. We started negotiating the budget right then and there. And we're going back and forth. Not only did we get the five clinics to stay open, but we got them to modernize. We wanted them to get more computerized, and we wanted them to hire an extra secretary, because we knew that there was no way that it was going to be done unless that happened. This is politics, right?

With this victory in hand, the team of leaders returned to the main issue of establishing the primary health care clinic. Although they had achieved a commitment for state funding, they faced other obstacles. The health care establishment in the region opposed the clinic, fearing it would undermine their plan to fund a research facility in the area. The leaders negotiated for another six months with the leaders of the local medical society, city officials, and the business community and resolved the issue via mediation by a local banker. In addition, the city of McAllen had difficulty deciding what physical facility they would donate to the clinic. The final obstacle was identifying a nonprofit corporation that would manage the center. With respect to each of these issues the leaders—Estela, Rosa, Maria Sanchez, and a few others—were the key negotiators on behalf of Valley Interfaith. The clinic, named the Milagro (Miracle) Clinic, opened in McAllen on December 12, 1996, the day for the Feast of Our Lady of Guadalupe, the dark-skinned Mexican Madonna.

The core difficulty faced by progressives is that the public has lost enthusiasm for political organizations and institutions. There are a variety of reasons why parties, unions, and other organizations have lost hold on their members. It might be, for example, that the positions these organizations take are unattractive or that the organizations cannot deliver what they promise. However, another possibility, indeed likelihood, is that people who are considering whether to be active do not believe that they could be genuinely influential members who have an opportunity to participate and shape the organization's behavior and agenda. There is something about how the organizations are structured that forecloses participation and hence commitment.

The IAF is different. It maintains involvement, enthusiasm, and commitment from its base. Understanding how it manages to cope with the common maladies that infect most political membership-based organizations has broad relevance to a wide range of progressive organizations. As we have seen, the IAF has created a particular strategy for organizing, working through member institutions, with a strong emphasis on leadership development. The culture of the IAF reinforces its strategy, and that culture is taught and reinforced in a variety of settings. The issues that the IAF addresses are generated by leaders through the one-on-ones and house meetings that are so central to IAF organizing.

This is progressive politics built from the ground up. IAF members share a sense of agency, of personal power and capacity. For half a century the IAF has built strong organizations and altered people's views of themselves and their possibilities. The kind of transformations happening today in the IAF are mirrored in a comment made forty years ago by a member of the Temporary Woodlawn Organization in Chicago: "This has been the most satisfying and rewarding period of my life. The organization has given me a real sense of accomplishing something—the only time in my life that I've had that feeling."[26]

Chapter 3

Faith

The Pledge of Allegiance describes us as "one nation under God," and this is not far off as a description of how most Americans feel. Nearly two-thirds of American citizens say that religion is very important in their lives. Americans have more confidence in organized religion than in other public institutions. Twice the number of people report a "great deal" or "a lot" of confidence in the church than in Congress or in organized labor, and the number is also well above the presidency, the Supreme Court, and banks.[1]

Although Americans report that they are religious, it is not always clear just what this means. There is certainly no uniformity of doctrine or practice among the nation's churchgoers. For some, church attendance is simply another social obligation, perhaps more serious than attending children's soccer games but not much more. For others, what counts is not the formal institution of organized religion but rather personal spiritual development not tightly tied to institutions or rituals. And yet for others, the Bible represents the literal word of God, and the only path that makes sense is to organize life strictly around religious principles.

What is clear is that religion is central to politics. This might seem paradoxical in a nation based upon the principle of separation of church and state, but it is nonetheless true. Politics and religion are intertwined and, unfortunately for progressives, in a way that has not worked to their advantage in recent years.

The nature of the problem is seen quickly by considering the term *Religious Right*. The difficulty is that although this phrase describes a recognized phenomenon (though not necessarily uniform or well understood), there is little modern sense to the expression *Religious Left*. The latter does not exist in any significant way, and the consequences are serious. Among regular church attendees, 45 percent voted for the Democratic candidate, Al Gore, in the 2000 election, compared with 57 percent of those who did not attend regularly.[2] Surveys suggest that people who identify themselves as liberal are much less likely than other Americans to report that they are religious.[3]

The problem is not simply the mechanical one of an unfortunate relationship between religion and voting patterns. Religion is a cultural phenomenon that encompasses views about right and wrong, about ethics, and about the values that should underlie society. Sometime in the late 1970s or early 1980s progressives, and the Democrats, lost control of these concerns, and people who took them seriously shifted allegiance to conservatism and to Republicans.[4] Progressives have suffered since then by being on the wrong side of religion and values. Bill Clinton sought to rectify this with his support of welfare reform (in its Republican version) and the death penalty, but these positions simply served to make it even harder for progressives within and without the Democratic party to take values and religion seriously.

In the past few years, the Right has sought to solidify the link between religion and their version of politics by pressing for what they term "faith-based" social policy or charitable choice. The policy, first enacted in the 1996 welfare reform legislation, is meant to encourage religious organizations to operate social programs. Although there is some social science research that suggests that service delivery by religious groups can be efficacious,[5] the real reason for President Bush's vigorous support of the idea is to symbolically deepen his party's identification with religion and to convey the message that the Republicans are the party of morality.

Although religiosity seems these days to be cutting the wrong way for progressives, this need not be the case. First, religious social teachings provide a strong moral and ethical basis for attention to social justice and inequality. The central role of the church, both north and south, in the Civil Rights movement is evidence enough of the power of this tradition, but these foundations go beyond civil rights to economic justice.

Second, churches provide ample opportunities for people to learn and practice political skills. Although these skills can be utilized by the Right as well as by the Left, learning them leads to the natural question of why people seem foreclosed from real political participation. This is a question that is congenial to progressive concerns.

Religion and the correlation between religious participation and political views are too important for progressives to cede the religious arena to the Right. The IAF is working against this tendency by organizing via congregations and by making great use of religious language, symbols, and values. Faith and religion can be turned to progressive purposes. The trade is two-way, and IAF's organizing strategies and techniques help address some dilemmas that currently bedevil the religious community, such as how to maintain membership and energy in the face of a welter of competing demands from the secular world.

The Progressive Potential of Religion

Religion and politics have always been intertwined. From the Crusades to *Roe v. Wade,* religious passions have driven political action. Indeed, fear of sectarian violence helps to explain the deep ambivalence American culture bears toward the mixture of political and religious passions. But although this ambivalence is real, it is inescapable that religious ideas and religious institutions interact with American politics.

Under the radar screen of public attention, and with far less fanfare than the great controversies spawned by religious dispute might suggest, one far-reaching political consequence of religion is that it teaches political skills. This is one of the major findings of Sidney Verba and his colleagues in their exhaustive study of the determinants of political activity.[6]

The distribution of political and civic skills is very unequal in America. The better-educated and the more wealthy citizens have more opportunities (on the job for example) and more time (because of their resources) to learn and practice. The great exception to this pattern is the church. Church members have a chance to learn skills—leading a meeting, giving a talk, arranging an event—and these opportunities are distributed far more equitably than in the rest of society. As a dramatic example, Verba and his colleagues found that among people in high-status jobs 73 percent of blacks and 65 percent of whites report having had an opportunity to plan a meeting. But if job status is low, then these numbers plunge to 7 percent of blacks and 6 percent of whites. By sharp contrast, not only do churches provide all citizens the opportunity to plan meetings, but these opportunities are much more evenly distributed by social class: around 40 percent of blacks and whites, regardless of whether they are in high- or low-skill jobs, get to learn this skill in church. Low-skill workers get to do in church what they cannot on the job.[7] The researchers then go on to show that the civics skills that are learned in church (and elsewhere) are positively related to the propensity of people to participate in politics.

Religious ideals and the more practical importance of the church in teaching political skills came together dramatically in the Civil Rights movement. In the American South, the African-American church was the very center of organizing.[8] The power of faith inspired personal political courage. A black student who was chased by a white mob while trying to integrate the University of Alabama gives this account:

> I was very much afraid at this time. I sat there and tried to compose by myself, and naturally the next thing I thought of doing was saying a prayer. . . . I asked to be able to see the time when I was able to complete my work on the campus, but that if it was not the will of God that I do this, that He gave me the courage to accept the fact that I would lose my life there, and to help me to accept it, because this was a time when I really felt that I might not get out of it alive.[9]

As important as the sheer bravery that religion imparted were the organizational resources that the African-American church provided in both the South and the North. Churches formed a network that provided support, communications channels, and skilled activists (who had, as Verba implies, learned their skills in more prosaic religious activities). The story of the Civil Rights movement is in large measure the story of the African-American church.

What Is Possible Today

There is much in religious social doctrine and in the history of religion in social movements to suggest that progressives would be wise to take it seriously. However, given the discouraging voting patterns and the rise of the Christian Right, a fair question is whether there is in fact any reasonable basis for proceeding in the current climate.

In part, the source of the energy of the Christian Right came from the shifting nature of denominational patterns in America's Christian community. Evangelical and born-again denominations have grown, whereas mainline denominations have declined.[10] The growing groups came to be seen as tied to the Christian Right and simply beyond any redemption by progressives. The sharp emotions of the abortion debate and the role played by both the Catholic Church and the Christian Right in this debate have only served to reinforce this estrangement.

Although it might seem logical for progressives to walk away from religion, in fact to do so would be a serious mistake. Robert Wuthnow has shown that the Christian Right never penetrated very deeply into its natural constituency of evangelicals.[11] This assertion is supported by Alan Wolfe's interviews in the mid-1990s with deeply religious and largely conservative white Christians. These people showed a great deal more tolerance toward the views of others than media accounts would suggest. As one of Wolfe's interviewees commented, "Most religions share the same basic values. . . . I don't feel good about one church coming out and saying 'You're all wrong and you're all bad.' I don't believe in telling everyone else that they are wrong."[12]

More quantitative data also point in the same direction. The National Election Survey polled Americans, voters and nonvoters, in each election year between 1996 and 2000 and asked them about their degree of religious commitment and their positions on questions such as whether the government should spend more resources on education, on aid to the poor, and on child care. It is only among born-again Christians that religious belief is correlated with reluctance to spend government resources for these purposes. Among people who are not born-again believers, those who express strong religious commitments are just as likely as the less religiously committed to support government spending.[13]

Religion certainly poses a complicated challenge for progressives. On the one hand, as Wuthnow, Wolfe, and the survey data suggest, there is more play than progressives might believe. However, it is also apparent that the power of religious values has not been well understood by progressives and, as a consequence, on balance religion today is not the friend of progressive politics. The question is how to turn that around.

The IAF and the Church

The IAF has always been linked to churches, even though founder Saul Alinsky was personally hostile to religious doctrine, showing great even-handedness by refusing to kneel in prayer at Catholic Mass and mocking Jewish rituals at Passover.[14] In spite of that, he drew upon the institutional support of the church. His first efforts in building the Back of the Yards Organization were endorsed by Auxiliary Bishop Bernard J. Sheil, who also helped with fund-raising, and local clergy were leaders in the organization. Alinsky's subsequent efforts in other cities were supported by the National Conference of Catholic Charities.[15]

Ed Chambers and Ernie Cortes put the church at the center of the contemporary IAF model. They conceived of building a local IAF organization as a confederation of institutions (an "organization of organizations") rather than as a collection of individuals. This strategy, as we saw in chapter 2, is at the core of the IAF approach to organizing. The candidates for constituent organizations include schools, unions, community groups, and fraternal societies. These institutions are in fact members of the IAF in one city or another, and the IAF now is pushing particularly hard to organize schools and unions. However, at the center of every organization is the church.

Churches are a natural choice because, as Ernie Cortes wrote, "They are virtually the only institutions in society that are fundamentally concerned with the nurture and well-being of families and communities."[16] Churches are often neighborhood-based and hence can be the meeting ground where people address the wide range of concerns in their lives. They are stable and therefore provide a long-lasting foundation for building an organization. They have resources, another obvious prerequisite for organization building. And, of course, religious social doctrine supplies a rich basis for organizing and motivating political action.

The Role of Religion in the IAF

Attend any IAF meeting, be it a training workshop of twenty people or an annual assembly of five thousand, and it will begin with an opening prayer. Clergy will be prominent among the leaders up front or on the platform. If there is speech to be given by an organizer or leader, it will be full of biblical references, and almost certainly a Bible story will be used to illustrate a point about contemporary politics or organizing. At a large meeting of leaders to discuss voter registration, much of which was devoted to hardheaded analysis of the money and time that would be required to run a statewide effort, the rationale was explained in religious terms. New people were running for state office in Texas, people with whom the IAF had little prior relationship, and the organization needed to impress these new politicians with its ability to turn out votes. The analogy, expounded by the opening speakers at the meeting, was from Exodus: "And then came a Pharaoh who knew not Joseph."

Robert Bellah had this sort of display of religion in mind when he coined the term *civil religion*.[17] He was referring to how religious imagery and symbols are used in public discourse and public education to explain the American past and future. More crudely, in political campaigns all kinds of candidates rush to make clear their commitment to God and to deploy religious language whenever possible. Religion is a big part of American public culture, and in this sense America practices a civic religion.

One might accept this use of religion on face value and applaud the effort to base public life in Judeo-Christian values. It is also possible to be cynical and to wonder how politicians who have no religious commitment in their private lives nonetheless find opportunities to attend church on Sunday (provided that cameras are present). But whether the spin is positive or negative, this use of religion seems somewhat superficial, operating at the level of symbols and rhetoric and not necessarily shaping behavior.

The IAF also consciously uses religious symbols in presenting its public face. For good reason, the IAF works hard to be perceived as mainstream and in line with core American values, and drawing upon religious language and imagery is one way of accomplishing this. Furthermore, this kind of language resonates well with the membership and hence is an effective way to frame ideas.

Be that as it may, to stop at this point would miss most of what is important about religion in the IAF. Religion penetrates more deeply into the organization than either its use as a symbol or an organizing strategy would imply.

Many of the organizers are deeply religious and view their work as a way of expressing this commitment. Some are ordained clergy or members of religious orders, whereas others simply take their religion seriously. Of the roughly forty organizers in the Southwest, six are nuns and several of the men are ordained ministers. One of these is Judy Donovan, the lead organizer of Valley Interfaith. Donovan is a native of Maine who traveled to Brazil as a missionary and got involved in teaching liberation theology to small rural communities. She found herself teaching abstract principles about social justice, but in the end the people in her village were arrested for standing up to the local landowners:

> That was a real epiphany for me in thinking our analysis is wonderful and our theology is beautiful and, you know, we're on the side of goodness and right. But so what? Goodness and right fail all the time. You know, what does it take? So I think when I saw organizing happening, it seemed like that was in the right direction of giving people power.

Out of this came a determination to combine religious commitment with more practical skills. As Donovan says,

> I think for me, I think it's a particularly American form of spirituality, that spirituality needs to be pragmatic. It needs to go somewhere. Something needs to happen with it. I see organizing as a way of living spiritually. From my perspective it's a job and it's also kind of a vocation for me. And it's a way of taking all that idealism and ideological bent and actually testing it and being able to do something with it and directing it and having a community that holds me accountable to doing that. So that, you know, being smart and being around smart people and having great ideas and thinking the right things isn't enough. It doesn't matter if it can't go someplace.

Religion motivates many of the IAF organizers, but it is also deeply integrated into the organization's day-to-day activities and how the leaders think about their politics. To understand the practical role of religion in the IAF, it is necessary to see how it operates on the ground, in communities.

Pastors and Parishioners

At one end of the Valley, in the south side of McAllen, is Saint Joseph the Worker Church. The south side is the poor Hispanic part of town, and according to Father Bart Flaat, the pastor, Saint Joseph was built in the 1960s to minister to the Mexican-Americans so that the Anglos could have their own church. Today five thousand families are members, and on a typical Sunday two to three thousand people attend one of five services. Father Bart, sixty-two years old, is a Dutch citizen and a member of a missionary order. Like Valley Interfaith's lead organizer, Judy Donovan, he spent a number of years in South America and arrived in South Texas in 1977. He worked first in San Antonio and then came to the Valley.

When Father Bart arrived, Saint Joseph was already a member of Valley Interfaith but was inactive and behind on its dues. The Valley Interfaith lead organizer at the time, Tim McCluskey, forgave the dues but suggested that Bart begin by spending his first three or four months in house meetings in the parish. It was at one of these meetings in a colonia that he first met Rosa Gutierrez.

Because of Father Bart's work, the connection with Valley Interfaith deepened, and it was given a big push by what happened the night of a school dance held at the church. A gang whose members had earlier been denied admission returned to attack the dance, destroy property, and beat up some kids. It took thirty minutes for the police to respond. The chief of police explained at a meeting with church leaders that of his two hundred officers only eight were assigned to the south part of town, an area that included a quarter of McAllen's population. As Bart recalls, "We said, 'who makes the decision?' He said, 'well, that's a political decision.' That's when we started our process of Congregational Development. That's when we started looking seriously at how we can make an impact and . . . who can give us power."

Today Saint Joseph is indeed a powerhouse. It was, for example, at the center of the successful effort to redraw city council districts in McAllen, and it can claim numerous other victories ranging from a new library to the Milagro Health Clinic to the living wage campaign in the McAllen schools. What makes the church so powerful is how religion and politics are interwoven, and at the core of this are the *communidades de base* (base communities) that Father Bart organized.

The idea of *communidades de base* comes from the practice of liberation theology in Latin America. Faced with repressive right-wing regimes and a generally unsympathetic church hierarchy, radical priests organized communities into small prayer groups that became the building blocks of opposition organizations. The idea spread into South Texas via the experience of priests who had worked in South America and via the culture of the people themselves. These groups meet not only to pray but explicitly to mix religion and politics. Whereas in Latin America the *communidades* often stood in opposition to the established church, in Texas they are very much a part of the ongoing practice of the parishes.

I attended one such meeting in a small house on the outskirts of Mc-Allen. *Communidades* are neighborhood-based, and this one pulled people from a two-block area. About fifteen people gathered in the living room, including Rosa Gutierrez, who does not live in the neighborhood but who coordinates the *communidades* across the area. It was a smallish space whose sheetrock walls were unfinished and filled with a mixed collection of secondhand furniture. Small children ran in and out of the house and played in one corner. The adults in the room ranged from old women to young mothers. Three of the fifteen were men. One of the young mothers had just moved into a house in the neighborhood. It turned out that she was a recent migrant from Mexico with three children and had been making a living of sorts by collecting old clothes, repairing them, and selling them on the highway and at flea markets. She had been living in a cardboard shack in the area. The members of this particular *communidad de base* had decided as a group to build her a house. Somehow (I was never sure how) they acquired some land and constructed a new home within the two-block area.

We began the meeting by standing in a circle, holding hands, and singing religious songs. This was followed by prayer and then questions based on the Bible selections of the forthcoming Sunday service. That week the sermon was about why people opposed Christ. A passage from the Bible was read, and then the group discussed questions such as whether people resisted Christ because of the kind of man he was or because of his message. There was a debate about this, but the general conclusion was that Christ's message about how to treat people is what led the powerful to resist him. This particular topic and discussion had a clear political edge to it, and although some of the other questions were more purely religious, on balance the Bible discussion was an intermingling of religious doctrine and political beliefs.

The politics was even more explicit in the next stage of the meeting, a discussion of news in the neighborhood and the city. The big event of the week was that the new branch library, for which Valley Interfaith had fought, had just opened. There was also considerable discussion of plans for the upcoming council election, the first to follow the redistricting campaign, and people were encouraged to participate in accountability sessions with candidates. The meeting closed with a prayer, and people stayed for food and conversation.

The *communidades de base* represent Valley Interfaith's view of what religion is about. Previously the groups that came together at Saint Joseph were larger and were purely prayer groups with a strong charismatic flavor. Now the turnout has gone down for the Thursday charismatic service, only two purely prayer groups remain, and Father Bart comments with a laugh, "I think the 'me and Jesus' element has gone down."

Saint Joseph has forty of these *communidades,* and it is quite clear that they are a very powerful resource for organizing. They provide a communications network and a way of motivating people by embedding them in groups of neighbors. But more to the point here, the *communidades* mix religion and politics in a powerful brew. It is clear that for these people religion has much more than a superficial or symbolic link to their political activities.

The only parish in the Valley that rivals Saint Joseph in size is Christ the King, seventy miles away in Brownsville. The pastor at Christ the King is Father Alfonso Guevara, fifty-two years old and a native of Brownsville. Alfonso's parents left Mexico to find work and to escape religious persecution (Mexico, particularly during the revolution and the years following, was anti-Catholic as a matter of public policy). They eventually settled in Brownsville, and Alfonso's father managed a small hospital laundry while his mother raised four children. His parents were deeply religious, and his father, an accomplished carpenter, built a desk in the Catholic school so that it would be possible for his son to attend. Alfonso is quiet but has a wicked, dry sense of humor. He recalls that in his first parish, as an assistant priest, "I got scared because all I was doing was burying people or baptizing children. Most of the people I dealt with were either unconscious or dead."

While in college in a small town in rural Texas, Alfonso became involved in the Mexican American Youth Movement (MAYO), a Hispanic youth organization that in the late 1960s and early 1970s led demonstrations in various high schools around the state. As Alfonso recalls, "We gave life to that little hick town. We are always talking about our rights on this or that." After college, Alfonso taught in public schools for a while, but what was most significant was his exposure to charismatic Catholicism. Unlike the mainline Protestant churches, the Catholic hierarchy, particularly in South Texas, has worked hard to keep Pentecostal urges within the established church, and when Alfonso was born again in 1972 he felt no tension about remaining within the Catholic church.

Alfonso entered seminary in San Antonio and became more involved in politics. In the summers he worked with migrants as far north as Minnesota, and in San Antonio he attended the founding assembly of COPS: "All these people and all these priests and sisters were joining the people. And the enthusiasm and the power that they had was very edifying and inspiring. It was something that I wanted to be part of, however inexperienced I was in that kind of work." Alfonso was also motivated by a history a racism in the church:

> Well, you know, very few Mexican-Americans were ordained priests, because it was a fact that the church was bigoted in the past. They didn't think we could be celibate. They didn't think we could really be good ministers. Most Mexican-Americans didn't have a good education, although I have found lots of very intelligent people who have no education, but they have never had that opportunity. Working here with migrants and working at the parish level, being a schoolteacher in a poor school district, seeing their pain, their frustration was something that I was able to empathize with.

As eager as Alfonso was, organizing a parish did not come easily. Alfonso was, and still is, quiet and shy. He attributes these qualities to being the youngest of four children and to the fact that when he was young his mother was sick and away in the hospital a good deal. At the core of IAF training is teaching leaders how to assert themselves as public figures. Alfonso went through the same process as any other leader.

> Well, theologically I knew that it was something that made a lot of sense, and I preached it. But me involved? I was threatened by it. I was threatened by it because it was putting me in a situation that was foreign to me, which was being a public person. That had never been talked about in seminary, being a public person. Whether you want it or not, a priest is a public person, and has a lot of power. But they don't teach you that. So gradually, I gradually became aware. I wanted

to stand with the people. And at first I was scared and I was hesitant and I was resistant, because I just couldn't see myself speaking publicly with anybody, or going to a politician or going to a meeting. . . . I had seen some of those priests in San Antonio, and some of them were raging extroverts or I don't know what. Or they had a lot of passion, and I had always been a quiet, introverted person. It still costs me, but now I am very convinced that what I do is something that is right.

Today, Alfonso and the leadership at Christ the King are deeply involved in the whole gamut of Valley Interfaith issues, ranging from neighborhood improvement to living wage campaigns to statewide legislative campaigns. Alfonso has organized *communidades de base* and is continuously trying to introduce political concerns into what happens in the church. Alfonso is very critical of what Robert Bellah calls the "caucus church," a feel-good organization that offers a little something for everyone. Instead, Alfonso very explicitly links his faith to his work with Valley Interfaith

Well, I think that there is a great danger of not connecting your faith, your religion to your public life or your life as a citizen. Because I think that what happens is that churches that are not involved in participation in their schools and their public affairs become private clubs, and feel-good places. And that's very sad. And they may have a lot of money. They're very concerned about their parking lot, or they're very concerned about their carpet. Or they're very concerned about this or that, but they're not concerned about their neighborhood. They're not concerned about the quality of the neighborhood across town or beyond your town. They're not concerned about anybody else. Very myopic. Very selfish. Very narcissistic. When you really say I want to do Your will, just go out and look at people. Visit people. And visit the poor. They will convert you. You will want to do something about what has happened.

For Alfonso it is clear that religion and the political work of Valley Interfaith are tightly intertwined. There is no sense in which religion is simply a rhetorical device trotted out on public occasions.

What the Leaders Think

Not all of the IAF leaders are connected to the organization through the church. Manuela sought out an organizer to help her resist the frequent transfer of her children from one temporary school to another. Other IAF leaders can discuss at great length their involvement in the organization without once mentioning religion. However, many of the leaders in the Valley first made contact with Valley Interfaith through their congregation. For those whose connection and motivation is based in religion, a complicated set of intellectual and theological challenges emerges.

At first glance the link between people's religious ideas and their involvement in the IAF seems straightforward. After all, a fundamental element of any set of religious principles is charity and good works. This idea comes up repeatedly when IAF leaders talk about their religious motivation. As Carmen Anaya says,

> I think that the Lord is going to judge us, and he is not only going to judge us for what we have done. He will also judge us for what we haven't done, and that we could have done. I will always, until the day I die, as long as I can walk and have good health, as long as I can, I will work for others.

Although religious teachings can provide a basis for social action, there is a deeply ingrained view that religion and politics should not mix. A common refrain among IAF opponents, in the Valley and elsewhere, is that the organization inappropriately brings politics inside church walls.

The question of politics and religion obviously has a long pedigree in American political discourse. In recent years, however, Americans seem increasingly tolerant of some softening of the boundaries. President Bush's charitable choice or faith-based initiative is one illustration of this, and in the 2000 campaign Al Gore also endorsed something very much along these lines. Polls suggest that many Americans are willing to let politics and religion mix, at least to some degree. For example, in a recent poll 51 percent agreed that churches should express their political views.[18]

IAF leaders describe struggling with this issue, and one of the personal transformations they frequently remark upon is a new view of how religion and politics can come together. Gilbert Garcia comments that "I've learned that Jesus Christ was a political figure," and Tomasita continues:

> In the past they taught us that politics should not be related to religion or to the church, and I always thought of it in that way. But now, since I have realized that it is for the well-being of everybody, I think that we were wrong. Because they have read us some passages from the Bible in which politics and the church were involved.

Another struggle that concerns many members involves the distinction between charity and justice. It is easy to draw from religious convictions the view that God commands us to do good works. What is less clear, and more controversial, is whether God also commands us to try to change the underlying poltical and economic system that creates the need for good works in the first place. The nation is replete with congregations who pride themselves (properly) on doing good works but who also resist the intrusion of anything more challenging or political within church walls. When Valley Interfaith leaders talk about the relationship beween their religion and political action, they often point out that their initial conceptions of religious commandments regarding social action were very limited:

> Before, it used to be very different. For me the church was made up of those who visit the sick, those who care about the families that are suffering, who care for those who are in jail, for all these things. For me this is what religion was about. But as I gave myself the opportunity to learn more about Valley Interfaith, to learn what it is about, I realized that I was limiting my religion too much. Because my religion can't be based only on the sick or the dead, but also it has to be based on the existing world, on those who live, those who are suffering, those who are unemployed, those who are being mistreated, those who are being humiliated, those who are sick. To give them hope of love and peace, of comfort, on God's behalf, which is very important, but it is also important to give them hope where there is some type of benefit for them, of the fight.

For many of the leaders, this new view also represents a rejection of the club or caucus approach to religion, criticized by Father Alfonso, as well as a purely privatized relationship with God. Chayo describes how her thinking has changed:

> I used to think that when I came to church I needed to leave feeling good. You know? Gee, I'm so happy I came. That was just a wonderful sermon. The songs were really great. It was such a happy time. I think we need to feel—we need to leave church sometimes feeling angry, sometimes feeling sad about the situation. When Father Jerry's homily touches us in such a way that we get angry about whatever it is that he's talking about—the situation—and then we leave church angry enough to try to make a difference. And not say, "Gee, I can't believe he did that. You know. There was nothing inspiring. I didn't feel good. He has not made me feel good today. And you know I don't know if I want to come back to this church because it was not a happy church." And now it's like, I came here to hear about God's message. Well, hello. What is God's message? What is really God calling us to do? To only think about myself versus, Oh, I know Jesus loves me. Thank God he loves me. I'm so happy. Thank you so much. Good-bye. As opposed to God wants you to do something. Jesus challenges you. I challenge you to make a difference in your life.

Together these attitudes reveal a transformed conception of what religion is about and the role of the church as an institution. The nature of the transformation is summed up by Rosa Gutierrez as she talks about one of the main religious symbols of the Catholic culture among the poor of Mexico, the Virgin of Guadalupe, a brown-skinned manifestation of the Madonna:

> We used to be different. The activities inside the church were the Christmas celebrations, the Holy Week, and that was it, that was it. Many see the church like I used to see it: as a place where you go for your baptism, your first Holy Communion, where you go to pray to God, to Mass, and that's it. But, thank God, there have been many changes in this community. People are starting to awake to reality; they are realizing that if the church doesn't fight, we don't fight for ourselves.

In the celebration of the Virgin of Guadalupe it is mentioned that the Virgin appeared in front of an Indian man, but a man who had no education . . . but a lot of willingness to fight. And many of us, who are uneducated and come from other countries, but who want to succeed, we want to be heard, to live without oppression, just like those Indians used to be. We are royalty, we can be very big if they give us the opportunity.

Joining (or Not)

Visiting Saint Joseph the Worker in McAllen or Christ the King in Brownsville is seductive. The commitment of the priests and the congregations to Valley Interfaith is apparent and it is deep. The parishes integrate their religious life and spirituality with their political commitment in a seamless way. The language they use to describe their religious beliefs points directly toward political action. This progression seems so logical and obvious. It is hard not to visit these congregations and come away assuming that it is natural for the religious community to be committed, if not to the IAF, then at least to some form of overt agitation for social justice. But, of course, this is naïve. By far the majority of congregations do not engage in the kind of political action that the IAF represents. Why do some congregations join the IAF, or engage in a similar sort of politics, and others do not?

Diversity of views within the church is nothing new in social movements. Not all black ministers supported the Civil Rights movement, and Septima Clark, founder of the Highlander citizenship schools, once observed,

> I understand those preachers. I know they were dependent on white people's approval. Even with their congregation's support, they could be run out of town if the white power structure decided they ought to go. Often they weren't against the Movement; they were just afraid to join it openly. It's simply a contradiction: so many preachers supported the Movement that we can say it was based in churches, yet many preachers couldn't take sides because they thought they had too much to lose.[19]

Political activism cannot be taken for granted. However, most congregations do engage social issues in some way. In her ethnography of

twenty-three congregations from across the nation, Nancy Tatom Ammerman describes an impressive array of genuinely important commitments such as soup kitchens, food pantries, clothing drives, marches on
hunger, AIDS walks, help for the homeless, participation in Habitat for
Humanity, and the like.[20] National surveys show that church members
are more likely than nonmembers to contribute to charities in various
ways.[21] But doing charity is not the same as working for justice. As one
church staffer I interviewed commented, "How many clothes drives and
food drives do you think we ought to have? I mean when is it going to
end?" Only two of Ammerman's twenty-three congregations were "activist," which she defined as working for change.[22]

A useful first step in thinking about congregational participation in
the IAF is to ask what religious teachings have to say about such activities.
In Catholic, Protestant, and Jewish doctrine there is ample support for
social justice work, although most observers believe that the orientation
toward economic justice is somewhat deeper in the Catholic than in the
Protestant traditions.

From Pope Leo XIII's encyclical *Rerum Novarum* in 1891 to the Catholic bishops' statement on economic justice in 1986, the church hierarchy
has consistently supported both the rights of workers and ideas of economic equity. At the core of Catholic social teaching has been an explicit
rejection of unbridled capitalism and a strong statement about the importance of living wages and a fair distribution of economic resources.
These views have been put in practice by both the Catholic hierarchy and
parishioners. The American Catholic church has supported unions since
its leading bishops assisted the Knights of Labor late in the nineteenth
century.[23] The Association of Catholic Trade Unionists played an important organizing role during the New Deal. Dorothy Day's Catholic
Worker movement inspired thousands of citizens to work for social justice. Today in Catholic parishes a visitor is very likely to see a poster on
the wall listing the twelve main points of Catholic social teaching.

There is, of course, also a tradition of concern for social justice in
Protestant and Jewish traditions. Early in the twentieth century, Protestant intellectuals, notably Walter Rauschenbusch, developed the doctrine of the Social Gospel, a set of ideas regarding social reform that was
taught in seminaries and that inspired political action ranging from early
campaigns against child labor to the anti–Vietnam War movement in the
1960s. The national bodies of various Protestant denominations have is-

sued far-reaching statements on social justice.[24] For example, the Social Principles of the United Methodist Church says, "We claim all economic systems to be under the judgment of God no less than other facets of the created order," and it goes on to speak strongly about economic equity. The General Assembly of the Presbyterian Church USA annually issues strong statements regarding economic policy, as does the General Convention of the Episcopal Church. The United Church of Christ in 1989 issued a document called "Pronouncement on Christian Faith: Economic Life and Justice," which states that "there is a sickness in the soul that infects both the poor and the affluent in our nation," and then it goes on to lay out a set of very progressive proposals. The African-American Protestant churches have a long tradition of social activism, and W. E. B. DuBois's comment in 1899 that "all movements for social betterment are apt to center in the churches" is still largely true.[25]

Jewish traditions are also supportive of social action. There are numerous Jewish social service and political action organizations. The phrase *tikkun olam* is about repairing the world, and the American Jewish World Service quotes the Torah as commanding "Justice, justice shalt thou pursue, and Love the stranger for you were once strangers in the Land of Egypt."

There is clearly ample doctrinal material to justify any congregation's decision to be active with respect to social justice. Indeed, some might argue that doctrine demands such a commitment. Yet most parishes and congregations do not pick up on this. There is also considerable reason to believe that the progressive pronouncements of national religious bodies, particularly the National Council of Churches, which represents mainline Protestant denominations, do not accurately reflect the views of congregations.[26]

A useful place to begin to understand why some congregations are activist while others are not is with the differences in IAF success among Catholics and Protestants. It is important to understand that the IAF itself is aggressive in making clear that it does not want to be considered a Catholic, or for that matter a Christian, organization. This would violate the fundamental idea of being broad-based. The organization's aggressiveness along these lines extends even to opening prayers. On two occasions at different assemblies I have witnessed a minister or priest open with a prayer that mentioned Jesus Christ. On both occasions an organizer immediately intervened at the conclusion of the prayer to make the point that "we honor all faith traditions."

The effort to be broad-based with respect to religion extends beyond ideology and beyond the symbolism of prayers and into the reality of organizing. In Dallas, Houston, and other IAF cities in the Southwest, a significant number of Protestant churches, white and African-American, are members of the organization. Outside of the Southwest, in cities such as Baltimore, Protestants are the majority of members. In Los Angles, five Jewish synagogues have joined the IAF organization. Just to pound the point home, consider church funding provided for a new IAF organization in Nashville, TNT (Tying Nashville Together). Resources were provided by the Catholic Campaign for Human Development, the Board of Global Ministries of United Methodist Church, the Southeast Conference of United Church of Christ, the Presbyterian Church USA, the Jewish Fund for Justice, Episcopal Diocese of Tennessee, and the First Unitarian Universalist Church.[27]

Nonetheless, a good starting point for understanding why some congregations pick up on social justice and choose to affiliate with the IAF while others do not is the observation that although the IAF certainly has organized a substantial number of Protestant and Jewish congregations, and although many of the IAF's most committed leaders come from these congregations, it is nonetheless true that on balance the IAF seems to have had more success with Catholic parishes. Put differently, the fraction of IAF leaders who are Catholic exceeds the fraction of Catholics in America, and the financial support the IAF receives from national religious groups is similarly overweighted toward Catholics.

An obvious piece of the puzzle lies in self-interest. In the Southwest and in California, the Catholic Church is heavily Hispanic, and Hispanics tend to be poorer and hence a more ready constituency. Yet this answer, although part of the story, is incomplete. When I visited Plano, Texas—an upper-middle-class suburb north of Dallas—the strongest of the IAF churches was a solidly middle-class Catholic church, St. Elizabeth Ann Seton. Several Protestant churches were also part of the organization, but penetration into the Protestant community was much shallower. Social science research using national data supports this observation: even after controlling for social class considerations such as education and income, Catholics are more liberal than white Protestants on economic issues.[28]

Part of the explanation lies in historical differences. The Catholic Church in America has been urban and rooted in immigration, whereas Protestant churches have been rural. As one Protestant minister said to me, "we don't have a theology of the city." This comment mirrors the analysis of Will Herberg forty years ago. Herberg traces the origins of modern Protestantism from the frontier rural fervor of the Great Awakening to its maturation as the church of middle-class America. The frontier, the small town, and the suburb are all remote from the struggles of urban life, and as America industrialized, Protestantism "grew increasingly remote from the outlooks and hopes of the urban industrial masses."[29] Herberg goes on to observe that "the Protestant approach to the urban-industrial frontier has been, and very largely remains, the approach of morally sensitive middle-class people striving to do something for the 'underprivileged.'"[30]

There are also theological subtleties that tend to bias Catholics more than Protestants in the direction of IAF-style political action. Catholic doctrine gives an important role to the church as a mediating institution between the worshiper and God, whereas Protestant theology tends to place greater emphasis on the direct relationship between the individual and God. In addition, Catholics are more likely to think of their church as being part of a larger community of churches. As a result Catholics are more oriented toward institutions, and that translates into greater tendency to political action.

Catholic churches are also neighborhood-based, whereas a typical Protestant church might draw parishioners from all over the city. This may be because the Protestant church started off as a neighborhood institution but members of the congregation moved elsewhere and maintained their connection to their church. The Catholic parish structure, by contrast, is strictly based on geography: you belong to the parish that is located where you live. This can make an important difference, because many of the issues around which the IAF organizes are rooted in neighborhood concerns. One Protestant minister commented, "That is a big drawback because the people in this community are not necessarily a part of this church. When people come from all areas, it is tough getting them to come to work in an area where really there is no other true interest there."

In sum, a Protestant minister I interviewed, speaking with some irony, noted that if there were a problem with hunger in his community Protestants would likely organize Christmas food baskets whereas Catholics would probably go after city hall.

The Protestant/Catholic distinction is important, but it is only part of the story. After all, the Catholic tradition itself is mixed. The New Deal witnessed the two sides of the church, with John Augustine Ryan representing in the U.S. Catholic hierarchy support for the social reform, whereas Father Coughlin, the radio priest, stood for anti-Semitism and reaction. Ryan's successor in the social action department of the Catholic hierarchy, Monsignor George Higgins, spent a career working with American unions, whereas many Catholic priests in Saul Alinsky's Chicago supported their congregations' militant, and sometimes violent, opposition to racial integration. An observer of the Catholic Church in California wrote that "Catholic charity demonstrated a notable lack of enthusiasm for structural reform until the 1960s. . . . Catholics observed that 'poverty as an unavoidable part of the human condition.'"[31] In Los Angeles in the 1960s, Cardinal McIntyre opposed the participation of priests in the Civil Rights movement and in the growing wave of Hispanic activism. He was an obstacle to IAF organizing, and his career effectively ended when his home was picketed by Catholic supporters of La Raza, the leading Hispanic civil rights group.[32] Unfortunately for the IAF, McIntyre's successor, Archbishop Timothy Manning, was hardly more friendly.[33] In 1992 the Cardinal of Philadelphia forbade parishes under his jurisdiction from joining Philadelphia Interfaith Action, the local IAF organization. Writing of present-day parishes, Andrew Greeley, a leading commentator on Catholic matters, has bemoaned the limited degree to which Catholic social teachings have penetrated to the parish level.[34]

There is enough variation across all congregations, Protestant and Catholic and Jewish, that we need to ask what other factors influence involvement. Part of the explanation obviously lies in the kind of self-interest considerations that are the bread and butter of IAF analysis. The members of more comfortable congregations have little interest in supporting political activity that might undermine their position.

Organizing in wealthier congregations is more difficult. As Judy Donovan observed, "class trumps race" in the Valley (and perhaps elsewhere), and in the Valley several of the wealthier parishes have chosen not to join Valley Interfaith. However, there are exceptions. On the north side of McAllen, Holy Spirit is a member of Valley Interfaith, largely owing to the force of personality of Father Jerry Frank. As one member of the congregation commented, "A more political person than Jesus I don't know. Maybe Father Jerry." Father Jerry describes his sermons:

> Each will get its tone from scripture passages for that particular Sunday as a takeoff. What we're trying to do is go back to the time of the Scriptures and show that Moses and the prophets and Jesus were dealing with socioeconomic situations of economic slavery—what their reaction was, how Christ reacted to that, and then try to update that in terms of what's happening today.

Several of Valley Interfaith's key leaders—Estela, Noelia, Joe—come from Holy Spirit, but the link to Valley Interfaith has been a source of conflict. A number of parishioners left and others complained that when they come to church on Sunday they want to pray and to leave the world of business and politics at the door.

Variation in self-interest, as important as it is, cannot be the whole story, since some congregations whose members earn well below average incomes participate while others do not. The attitudes of the pastor are central. Without the support of the pastor, the IAF can get nowhere in organizing a church. An African-American minister in a poor church said that "people follow their preachers," and the minister in a wealthy Lutheran congregation concurred: "The pastor is the gatekeeper. If you don't work with the pastor, and don't get the pastor on board, you are not going to get anywhere with the congregation." This power of pastors to shape the actions of their congregations is affirmed in academic research. In her study of how congregations adapt to changes in their environment (e.g., shifting demographics in their neighborhoods) Ammerman found that the key variable was the leadership of the pastor.[35]

Applying to churches and pastors the kind of analysis that social scientists conventionally use to understand organizations and their employees reveals that most clergy face a complicated set of incentives and constraints. Even among those who are sympathetic to the IAF cause, political organizing and social justice may not end up very high on their list of priorities. Higher on the list are the financial and physical health of the congregation and the pastor's views about the central priorities of a religious institution. Also important are more personal concerns about the impact of political activism on the pastor's career and job security.

A sense of the complications can be gained by examining the priorities of several pastors whose congregations are already members of the IAF in Dallas. One is working hard to build up his congregation, and he comments, "When I came three years ago, it was about thirty members, and now we are over three hundred in three years. I'm doing some other pastoral things internally that I feel are more essential right now as opposed to externally, outreach. The IAF would be considered outreach." Another minister, a pastor of a wealthy Lutheran church, is deeply involved in managing a church construction campaign. Although the IAF is important to him, it has taken a backseat. A third minister's church is rapidly losing members to the suburbs, and his focus is on survival.

The central focus of most clergy is growing and maintaining their congregation and providing the fundamental religious services that parishioners expect. From the perspective of the clergy, key concerns are both maintaining numbers of members and keeping up their enthusiasm. Enthusiasm, after all, translates into Sunday collections. Churches have a variety of ways of achieving these goals, and sociologist Robert Wuthnow attributes the proliferation of special-interest groups—from athletics to social service to (even) the Fellowship of Christian Magicians—to the need to find some activity that rings a bell with members and keeps them involved.[36] Working with the IAF is rarely seen as central and frequently is interpreted as one in a list of activities, each of which might attract a slice of the congregation.

It is doubtless the case that for some clergy the IAF is just one choice on a list of activities they can offer their parishioners, whereas for others the IAF is at the core of what they take to be the mission of their faith. The problem from the IAF perspective is that participation requires a much deeper commitment of time and energy than will be available if the IAF is just one item on a menu. The tendency of even sympathetic clergy to see the IAF as peripheral to their main duties and concerns is a real problem. As one minister says about his colleagues, "they are running a huge organization, and they are kind of maintaining, and they don't have time for that." A Catholic layperson who has worked to organize priests for the IAF reports that "clergy are overworked. . . . I've been thrown out of pastors' offices because they don't want to do this. 'Leave me alone, I'm too busy.'"

Ministerial reluctance also comes from what might be termed career concerns. Pastors are authority figures in their own congregations, yet in the context of the IAF they are asked to engage in more collaboration than they might be used to. As one African-American minister said in talking about his colleagues, "And if I'm not going to get the credit, then I'm not going. And that view is very prevalent." Another minister notes that it can be threatening for a pastor to sit down at a table as one of many IAF leaders, essentially as an equal along with some of his parishioners, when he wants to return to his church later that day and continue in his role as an authority figure and leader.

There are also career risks associated with affiliating with the IAF. Some members of the congregation may strongly disagree with IAF positions on issues, and others may not believe that their church should be involved in politics. In either case, the pastor risks rocking the boat. Musing about which clergy are willing to affiliate and which are not, one pastor commented:

> It's real safe in a congregation to stick to your own work and be successful. This is a totally voluntary association in a congregation, and anything you do to disturb that is a threat to you, to your family, and it really depends upon the relationship the pastor has with the leaders of the congregation—whether the pastor is a leader and is willing to train people and move people, to take those chances, whether you're willing to take those risks and move beyond congregational life.

Since the Catholic Church is hierarchical internally, if the higher authorities—a bishop or a cardinal—support the organization, that support provides an important opening for the parish priest. In San Antonio, Archbishop Patricio Flores, who was appointed the nation's first Mexican-American bishop in 1970, played a central role in supporting COPS during its early years. Flores would routinely appear at COPS events, publicized COPS in the diocesan newspaper, and provided financial support for organizing.[37] Archbishop Flores hired staff in his chancery who were in effect IAF organizers. He protected, and indeed promoted, priests who worked with COPS. This protection is important; a priest who works to bring his flock into the IAF organization cannot be fired by angry congregants. Only the bishop can do the firing.

Bishop Fitzpatrick played a comparable role in the Valley. In another Valley church Father Bart led before moving to McAllen, he faced opposition from parishioners to his efforts to have that parish join Valley Interfaith. Some members of the congregation went so far as to confront him noisily after mass one Sunday. Bart stood his ground, and the next day "I talked to Bishop Fitzpatrick, and he said you should have told them, 'Hey I'm not running a country, I'm running a church. If you don't like it get out.'"

Although priests cannot be fired by their congregation, they can see their collections decline and the participation of their membership in parish activities subside. That is, they too face the problem of keeping on the good side of their parishioners. Furthermore, although it is true that bishops can encourage priests to support the IAF (and Cardinal Cushing once made a famous remark that every bishop in America came from a union household, a statement that would no longer be true), the fact is that bishops normally limit their strict instructions to matters of doctrine. The actions of the individual clergy still are what matters.

What the pastor does is driven by his or her vision of the role of the church. Father Alfonso and Father Bart see social action as central to their mission, but this view is not widely shared. More common is the perspective of a Protestant minister interviewed by Robert Bellah and his colleagues: "The central issues in Christ's church are, first of all, worship, praising God and joining together in God's love; second, evangelism, winning people to Jesus Christ . . . ; and third, having won them, disciplining them in the faith so that they won't remain baby Christians, so that they can grow in their understanding."[38] In Catholic seminaries, a growing fraction of new priests have turned away from what they perceive as the failed social activism of the 1960s and are in its place embracing a return to a more narrow religious interpretation of their mission.[39]

Whether the social doctrine is adopted or not will depend in part on the how the congregants think about their own self-interest and on the pastor's views of his or her mission as well as his or her assessment of personal gains and risks associated with the IAF. Having said this, it is also the case that the IAF has something to offer the pastor and the congregation that may weigh heavily in the decision. Sometimes the skills of the organizers can tip the balance, as illustrated by a vignette told by Pearl Ceasar:

> The pastor said he had wanted COPS, but in reality he didn't. In fact, at one point he said, "Why would I? I can call the mayor at any time, she's a personal friend of mine—she will do whatever I ask her to do. So I don't need COPS to come in and do housing and streets." What organizing taught me was you can't always be moving around, leaving situations. So what I learned was how to take him on. And how to take him on based on what he wanted to do. I would sit down and have these conversations with him in terms of what he wanted. How did he want to lead that parish?
>
> And what I came to learn was it was the poorest parish. They had the worst housing in the whole city, the lowest income. He wanted to be able to show that there was some change that had taken place there and that he had done it. And so what we eventually came around to was that he was not going to be able to do that by himself. No matter how good of a relationship he had with the mayor, he was not going to be able to do that. So he began to work with COPS. If you go back to that parish today, they have something like ten, maybe twelve blocks of new housing. They have a forty-unit senior citizen housing complex two blocks from the parish. The hospital which was closed was rebuilt as a world-class diabetes center.

Beyond the skills of individual organizers in sizing up what pastors will respond to, the IAF also systematically works with congregations to strengthen their membership base and to build up a committed cadre of internal leaders. This process, termed Congregational Development, can be an attractive inducement to pastors who are weighing whether affiliating with the IAF is in their, and their congregation's, interest.

Building the Religious Community

The terms of trade between the IAF and the religious community are not one-way. Churches have needs that the IAF helps to meet. Congregational Development is a process through which the IAF applies its organizing skills and techniques to the needs and concerns of a congregation.

In good IAF fashion, the self-interest of each party is respected. The goals of the congregation, or the clergy, typically include revitalizing the church, attracting new members, or dealing with internal conflicts that might be beyond the capacity of the congregation to resolve on its own. For the IAF, Congregational Development is a chance to strengthen one of the institutions that constitute its membership and to meet people who are active in the church and who have the potential of being new IAF leaders.

Our Lady of Queen of Angels, a Catholic parish, is located in a rapidly growing rural area where Valley Interfaith manages the largest IAF colonia project in Texas. Because of the history of the parish, it was divided into five smaller missions in different towns, and there was a great deal of tension among these missions. People would not go to one another's churches, the churches maintained separate financial accounts, and members of the different churches were barely speaking to one another. Valley Interfaith was invited to work with them to develop one unified parish.

Valley Interfaith proceeded by utilizing its standard organizing techniques, techniques that would not seem foreign to a management consulting firm called in to solve the problems of a dysfunctional industrial company. Organizers met separately with each mission and then arranged a meeting of fifty people from throughout the parish. They then launched a house meeting campaign of three hundred meetings at which people talked about how they saw their community and what relationship they had with their church. This campaign had the side benefit of increasing the church's membership base, because new families with no prior connection to the church were invited to the house meetings. Following this campaign, a community assembly was convened at which six hundred people laid out the issues that had surfaced in the house meetings. This was followed by the formation of research teams. A year later, all of this work led to a parish convention that created a single unified parish council, a common financial structure, and so forth. In addition, the parish organized a social action team—a Valley Interfaith core team—who became the Valley Interfaith leaders in that particular parish and cemented the relationship between the church and the IAF organization.

Other stories of Congregational Development have different plot lines, but the underlying idea is the same. Every several years Valley Interfaith does Congregational Development at Christ the King Church in Brownsville. Although the church is in good shape, Father Alfonso believes that the congregation benefits from this regular "tune-up." As Judy Donovan describes the process,

> Every two or three years we go through an institutional development process where we bring together not just the Valley Interfaith leaders, but all the folks that are really involved in the church or school. They go through a process looking hard at what they're doing, who are they doing it with, what are they learning? What kind of impact are they having? We then do a house meeting campaign to look for new talent and to listen to what's happening in the community. We come back to do a prioritizing process, asking what do we really want to be about? What do we want to slough off? That leads into research actions about different issues, both internal to the institutions and external. So, for example, after that whole process a church may have a parish convention to set priorities, like reorganizing their youth ministry, reorganizing how they were doing training for different ministries, focusing on neighborhood development or public education in schools and the relationship with their neighborhood schools. Then we go into action. So, some of the issues are internal to the parish life, and some of them are part of a larger community agenda.

One of the core challenges facing most clergy is maintaining their membership, and Father Bart testifies to how Congregational Development can help: "When the church starts getting involved in things that affect families, that are important to families, then families get interested in what the church is doing. And so it's reciprocal. We do things that are for the good of families. And so these families say 'Hey, maybe this church has something for me' and start coming to church. The relationship is built once you start working together."

Denominational Dilemmas

Although religious institutions provide a strong foundation for the IAF, and for other progressive efforts, the base they provide is not as solid as might appear at first glance. It is true that most Americans believe that religion is an important part of their lives, but the actual connection of individuals to their churches may be weaker than surveys suggest. Roughly 40 percent of American adults report to pollsters that they attended church at least once in a typical week. However, when researchers go into the field to tally actual church attendance, the numbers are substantially lower. Although there is some debate about just how much the surveys exaggerate reality, one credible estimate is that actual church attendance is only half of that reported.[40] Low or falling attendance is a problem, since the IAF reaches people who are actually in attendance. Merely appearing on the membership rolls is not enough. To the extent that smaller numbers are in church—talking to pastors, meeting fellow parishioners, participating in church activities, and perhaps playing leadership roles—the prospects for organizing are weaker.

The shifting currents within Protestantism are also a problem. One trend has been the loss of denominational loyalty, the growth of what is termed "voluntarism." The data show that denominational switching has increased, so much so that Alan Wolfe describes his suburban interviewees as "free-agent churchgoers."[41] Robert Bellah and his colleagues write somewhat bitterly that "'Consumer Christians' shop for the denomination that is most convenient for their needs and switch, as casually as they change brands of dishwasher detergent, if they think they can get a better package deal elsewhere."[42] One survey showed that among baby boomers who started off Presbyterian only 29 percent remained in that denomination.[43] Denominational switching, like falling attendance, can pose a problem for the IAF if some of these switchers are leaders whose departure weakens the links between the IAF organization and the congregation they left. However, the more serious difficulty is the rise of evangelical denominations.

Taken as a whole, mainline denominations (Presbyterians, Episcopalians, Methodists, Lutherans, and United Church of Christ) have lost ground to the Southern Baptists, Pentecostals, Assemblies of God, and other evangelical groups. According to a Gallup poll, 45 percent of Protestants reported themselves as evangelical or born again in 2001, up from 41 percent in 1991.[44] Using a different measure (counting denominational membership instead of polling individuals), Robert Wuthnow reports that in 1991, 63 percent of Protestants were evangelical, a substantial increase over 56 percent in 1974.[45]

Just why this has happened is not entirely clear. Robert Bellah and his colleagues argue that the "quasi-therapeutic blandness that has afflicted much of mainline Protestant religion at the parish level for over a century cannot effectively withstand the competition of the more vigorous forms of radical religious individualism, with their claims of dramatic self-realization, or the resurgent religious conservatism that spells out clear, if simple, answers in an increasingly bewildering world."[46] Other students of this trend point to the lack of spiritual energy in mainline religion, the absence of excitement, the failure to have any "good news" to deliver.[47]

To a certain extent (as we saw with Father Alfonso), Catholicism has dealt with this threat by incorporating it. The Catholic Pentecostal movement began at Duquesne University in 1967 and has spread rapidly.[48] The movement is strong in the Rio Grande Valley and has proved to effectively meet the needs of people for a more individualized intense religious experience while keeping them within the structure of the Catholic Church. Of course, the Catholic Church remains vulnerable to the threat. A recent book that has gained a great deal of attention is titled *Is Latin America Turning Protestant?*[49] By one count, 20 percent of United States Hispanic Catholics have left the church and turned to evangelical Protestantism.[50]

Although a substantial fraction of African-Americans are born again or evangelical and still remain committed to progressive politics, there is a clear correlation among whites between being born again and being politically conservative. Born-again whites are the base of the Christian Right, and as my earlier analysis of political attitudes showed, they are the group least likely to support progressive positions.[51] The participation of evangelicals in the Christian Right shows that it is not correct to characterize them as entirely apolitical. Nonetheless, on balance, evangelicals are more likely to practice a privatized form of religion with less civic involvement than are mainstream Protestants. The emphasis is on individual salvation, not social reform. This is the impression of observers, but it is also supported by statistical examinations of the relationship between denominational affiliation and participation in voluntary and civic activities outside of the church.[52]

Given the political conservatism and the weaker civic engagement of evangelicals, it is not surprising that the IAF has not had a great deal of success among evangelical denominations. Whether this can be turned around will depend upon whether the IAF can fashion an appeal to the daily concerns of born-again Christians.

The Limits of Religion

Organizing via congregations is at the core of the IAF model and, as we have seen, is powerful. Congregations provide a stable source of leaders and of financial resources. Religious beliefs and rhetoric provide much of the moral energy and commitment that drive IAF leaders and organizers, and the grounding in religion connects the IAF to the American mainstream.

It is, however, worth asking whether the religious connection also limits the reach of the IAF. In one sense, there is no problem. In any given city with an IAF organization there are plenty of congregations available to be organized. It is not as if the IAF has run out of targets. More dramatically, the surge of immigration has meant that in many cities churches, particularly Catholic parishes, are growing rapidly and offer new opportunities. Nonetheless, from the perspective of building a broad progressive constituency, there is a downside to the religious connection.

One problem is that the Americans who are the least religious are also the most liberal politically. According to a Gallop poll, 76 percent of people who identify themselves as conservatives belong to a church or synagogue, whereas only 52 percent of liberals do so.[53] Another polling organization found that political liberals are far more likely to have a positive opinion of atheists than are any other political persuasion.[54]

The deeper difficulty is that the link between the IAF and organized religion has the potential of limiting access by the IAF to important sources of progressive energy, people, and resources. Given the institutional link between the IAF and churches, particularly the Catholic Church, it is difficult for the IAF to make connections with women's and gay groups. Internally the IAF provides opportunities to people without regard to their gender or sexual preference, but in terms of organizing around issues or public positions there are constraints. Essentially the IAF has made the decision that the advantages of its institutional links to religion outweigh the disadvantages, and all the evidence to date suggests that this is true. How this plays out in the longer run remains to be seen.

Politicians and political movements of all stripes have long understood and drawn upon the power of organized religion. The Christian Right is based in conservative, often evangelical churches. On the other side, in

Pennsylvania, advocates of school finance reform are working through churches by pulling together congregationally based study groups to examine financing inequities and then are traveling to Harrisburgh to lobby. The Progressive Religious Partnership is a group of ten thousand congregations from around the country that has joined an antisweat-shop coalition put together by the garment workers' union UNITE.[55]

Like these efforts, the IAF draws on religion, but it does so in a substantially different way. The IAF has an institutional relationship with churches. From one side, congregations become members of IAF organizations and provide them with people and with funds. From the other side, the IAF works with pastors and with congregations to help reinvigorate their institutions. There is a degree of long-term mutual support that goes far beyond any effort to utilize churches as a vehicle for one-shot mobilizing around a specific cause.

Beyond the simple fact of the institutional relationship, religion plays multiple roles for the IAF. It is a source of belief and inspiration. Many—though not all—of the leaders and organizers take their religion very seriously and draw on it to motivate their work. Churches also provide, as we have seen, effective training grounds for leadership skills. Although the IAF puts great effort into providing its own training, in many instances it begins with people who have been active in their congregation, on one committee or another, and have developed both skills and a following. Churches have other, more subtle advantages. Job insecurity is on the rise, making it harder to reach and organize low-income workers at an identifiable, stable workplace. As a result, organizing efforts (such as the employees' associations I will describe in chapter 5) are often best pursued via contacts made with the targeted employees in churches.

The Religious Right may on occassion seem comical. Speaking of an event called Gay Days at Disney World, Pat Robertson, leader of the Christian Coaltion and televangelist, commented that the event "could bring about earthquakes, tornadoes, and possibly a meteor" and went on to warn "you are right in the way of some serious hurricanes."[56] Nonetheless, it is clear that the Religious Right has tapped into an important current. Most Americans are religious, and many believe that politics would be improved via the infusion of religious values. Progressives have erred by ignoring this impulse. We saw earlier in this chapter that the common equation of religious leanings with political conservatism is wrong. Making this mistake means missing a substantial number of people who are receptive to the progressive message. In addition, ceding the religious high ground makes progressive efforts more vulnerable to attacks from the Right.

Although organizing via congregations has many virtues, it also entails a set of problems. The reach of religion may not be as broad as simple survey evidence suggests. Most Americans do report that religion is important to them, but actual church attendance is, as we saw earlier, much more modest. There may also be a decline over time in Americans' religious commitment. Robert Putnam, in his study of social capital, marshals an array of evidence to suggest that this is the case.[57]

Given the constrained resources of the IAF, the limited and possibly declining religiosity of Americans may not be a problem in the short run. Even in the suburbs there are plenty of healthy congregations yet to be organized, and in many cities the surge of immigration has led to an explosion in the size of many congregations. Nonetheless, as a building block for a national effort, the reach religion does have its limits.

The IAF has responded to these considerations by sticking to its strategy of organizing via institutions but at the same time broadening its affiliations to include schools and unions. Chapter 5 discusses these connections. How successful the IAF is in making these additional linkages will have a great deal to say about its ability to "go national." But for now, the bottom line is that organizing via congregations is a powerful and viable strategy for building broad-based power organizations.

Chapter 4

Practicing a New Politics

The central problem facing progressives is to find a way to mobilize people who have been turned off from politics. People who do not vote are disproportionately drawn from the bottom of the income distribution and are more likely to hold political views that are congruent with the core elements of a progressive platform. Reaching these people requires organizations that connect with them in their neighborhoods and cities. Massaging the message in Washington will not do the trick.

Political participation means more than just voting. A fully engaged citizenry would participate not only in selecting their leaders but also in formulating policy. They would help research issues, be involved in deliberating over the platform and agenda for candidates, and work on learning about their neighbors' needs and preferences. Shaping policy would not be the exclusive province of the experts.

In addition, an engaged citizenry would help ensure that their political leaders were accountable, that they actually did what they had promised once in office. This, indeed, is one of the major sources of cynicism among American citizens. In 2000, only 16 percent of respondents felt that government paid a good deal of attention to what people wanted, whereas 24 percent said that government paid not much attention. The voting patterns reflected these views: 71 percent of the people who felt government listened voted, whereas only 57 percent of the doubters did.[1] After all, if people do not believe that there are mechanisms to ensure that promises are kept, then what is the point of participating in elections?

It is, of course, unreasonable to expect that all people will be fully engaged. Nor is it realistic to expect that all promises will always be kept. What is at stake, however, is the nature of the political culture. If people perceive that they can be involved if they wish, or if they see that some of their friends or neighbors are involved, then this will affect their willingness to connect and, at the least, to vote. Similarly, if people learn that most of the time politicians can be held accountable for their promises, then this too will improve the health of the political culture and enable progressives to mobilize their constituency.

The key, then, is finding ways to mobilize voting, to strengthen other forms of political participation, and to make the results of elections meaningful by enforcing accountability. The social science literature suggests that today we are long way from these goals.

Researchers who study political participation, broadly defined, have found that it is relatively rare in America and very unevenly distributed. The most comprehensive investigation was conducted in 1989 by Sidney Verba, Kay Lehman Schlozman, and Henry Brady, who surveyed a nationally representative sample of adults.[2] Fourteen percent of Americans belonged to political issue organizations, and of these members only 20 percent attended meetings. Just under 10 percent of people reported that they were requested to and agreed to participate in community activities related to politics.[3] Somewhat better numbers were generated in response to a vaguer question about participation in community activities to address local problems (a question that presumably includes the PTA and other similar activities). Here about a third of those surveyed responded affirmatively.[4]

What participation we have is very unevenly distributed. Comparing people who earned (in 1989 dollars) seventy-five thousand dollars or more with those who earned fifteen thousand dollars or less, the wealthier folks were three times more likely to be involved in informal community activities, two and a half times more likely to be affiliated with a political organization, four times more likely to have done campaign work, and (remarkably) more than twice as likely to have engaged in protest activities.[5] Put simply, the richer you are, the more likely you are to be active in politics, and this is true even if campaign contributions are excluded. This is not surprising. People with more income and education have more time and resources to devote to politics, and the political community has a greater self-interest in mobilizing these people because they have more to offer.

In other research, Steven Rosenstone and John Mark Hansen examine participation in twelve different political activities, from signing a petition, attending a local meeting, writing Congress, and attending a rally to attending campaign meetings and working in a campaign and found that better-educated people and people with higher incomes participate at significantly greater rates in all of them.[6] The analysis of participation data does reveal one optimistic finding. In elections in which conflict is higher, and hence in which turnout is greater, the degree of inequality goes down. Apparently when people in the lower end of the income range perceive that there are issues that are relevant to them and for which their votes might make a difference they can be mobilized.[7] However, the bottom line in this research is that participation has declined over time and that it is very unequal. Not a happy story. The picture is even more discouraging because, as we have seen, at least in the case of voting, this inequality has gotten worse over time.[8]

The IAF operates in the face of these national trends and defies them. By building organizations and developing committed leaders who not only work hard on their own but are able to mobilize their personal networks, it has accumulated significant power. As a result the IAF is able to initiate a wide range of social programs ranging from the colonia infrastructure legislation to job training to school reform to numerous local projects such as parks and libraries. But at the end of the day, the IAF's main goal is to change how politics is done in the communities. The goal of the IAF is to build broad-based power organizations. Recall the mantra "power before program." It is because the IAF is ultimately a political organization that the lessons it teaches are so important for the larger canvas of progressive politics in America.

What do IAF politics look like? How does the organization teach its people how to practice politics, and how do the organizations operate politically? These are the questions I will take up in this chapter.

South Texas Politics, Then and Now

South Texas politics is best known as the site of the miracle that delivered, long after the polls had closed, the deciding votes to "Landslide

Lyndon Johnson," in his pivotal 1948 primary race for the U.S. Senate. Had not the boss of Starr Country, George Parr, discovered two hundred votes on the Friday after Tuesday's election, American history in the last half of the twentieth century might have taken a quite different turn.

Through the 1960s the Valley was a classic Jim Crow society dominated by Anglo farmers. A local school superintendent commented, "It is up to the white population to keep the Mexicans on their knees in the onion patch or on new ground."[9] Not only were the schools segregated, but so was daily life: "Mexican women were supposed to shop on the Anglo side of town only on Saturdays, preferably only in the early hours when Anglos were not shopping."[10]

The region was boss ridden and frequently violent. The key was the manipulation of the Mexican-American vote. Lyndon Johnson's biographer, Robert Caro, wrote that the counties in the Valley were run by "men who stalked the streets of the dusty little towns in their domains surrounded by armed, unshaven pistoleros; politics was violent in the Valley. On election day Mexican-Americans were herded to the polls by armed pistoleros."[11] The same pattern was repeated as far north as San Antonio. Caro quotes a local journalist as saying, "The way to play politics in San Antonio is to buy, or try to buy, the Mexican vote, which is decisive."[12] Although the role of guns may have gradually declined, the importance of local bosses and the use of money and favors was much slower to go. When Valley Interfaith began organizing, the mayor of McAllen was a man who was in the midst of twenty-one years of uninterrupted occupation of that office, a term that would only end in 1998.

If politics was crude in the Valley, it was smoother but to much the same effect elsewhere in the state. The central elements of control were local Anglo business-dominated organizations that proposed electoral slates. The business groups introduced a series of "reforms" in the electoral system to assure the slate-makers victory. One of the most important was the use of at-large elections that, by broadening size and geographic scope of the electorate, increased the importance of money in campaigns. Another was the institution of nonpartisan elections, which eliminated the role of parties in mobilizing voters. Other devices, such as obstacles to registration and nonconcurrent elections, also helped the cause. One estimate is that during this period 25 percent of residents of

(Anglo) affluent neighborhoods voted, and 10 percent of residents of poor and working-class communities did so.[13] Overall voter turnout in municipal elections was dismal: an average of 9 percent in Dallas and 14 percent in San Antonio (compared with 54 percent in Chicago and 44 percent in New York City during the same period).[14] It was difficult if not impossible for Mexican-Americans or blacks to elect people to represent their neighborhoods.

In Dallas the dominant organization was the Citizens Charter Association, described by Yale political scientist David Mayhew as "probably as close as anything can get to an executive committee of a ruling class."[15] Like all of the other comparable associations, this one was closed to outsiders. Asked how one got to be a member of this group, one leader replied that "anyone who asks for a place on the Council is never considered."[16] Out of 182 city council members elected between 1931 and 1969, the slate elected 157.[17] The Citizens Charter Association raised all the campaign funds that its candidates expended, and it managed all their publicity.[18] It worked closely with another business organization, the Dallas Citizens Council, whose responsibility was to raise funds to ensure success of campaigns for development bonds.

In San Antonio the business-dominated slate-making organization, the Good Government League, was founded in 1954, and its candidates won seventy-seven of eighty-one city council races between 1955 and 1971.[19] These patterns were replicated throughout the Southwest. In Fort Worth a local reporter wrote in 1976 that "it was taken as the natural order of things that a business elite should run the town."[20] A study of community power in El Paso concluded,

> The strongest political-interest group in El Paso . . . was the City-County Committee. . . . It was composed of some two hundred of the leading businessmen and professionals in the city. Their avowed purpose was to identify and support the best-qualified persons for local public offices.[21]

The combination of the strong business groups, an at-large election system that made it too expensive for any opposition groups to campaign, and a city-manager form of government that removed most decisions from popular control added up to a remarkably closed system. As one political scientist commented with some understatement, "spokesmen for the poor, minorities, working men, neighborhood interests, or any other views that might complicate the business of creating an attractive expansionary climate faced substantial difficulties."[22]

The consequences of the business coalition control of politics were fairly straightforward. The political agenda was growth, and this meant support for infrastructure and development in the growing suburban areas of the cities. Public resources were generously spent on development projects, and very few funds were left for services in neighborhoods where poor people lived. One observer of politics in Albuquerque, which like the other large cities in the Southwest was governed by a business-dominated council that nominated slates, commented that "the expertise many of these persons brought to politics couldn't see their way to bring the least improvements to the center city . . . whereas they were quite eager to extend utilities and other services to the perimeter."[23] Indeed, the first major organizing drive of the IAF in Texas was to fund sewage projects in San Antonio, where neighborhoods were regularly flooded with every heavy rain. In addition, spending on education and social services was stingy, to say the least, and no thought was given to how to raise the wage levels of those people whom the business associations did not represent.

By the time the IAF began organizing in the Southwest, there were already cracks in the dominant political coalition. In the urban areas the Anglo political machines sought to incorporate, or co-opt, a growing Hispanic middle class. Court decisions invalidated the poll tax and forced reapportionment to create legislative districts that better represented minorities. The traditional pattern of outright repression continued much longer in the rural Valley, but it too came under increasing pressure. The echoes of the Civil Rights movement and of the farmworker organizing of Cesar Chavez led to outright challenges to Anglo rule. In the early 1960s and again in 1970, Hispanics voted out the Anglos and took over the government of Crystal City, a small town just north of the Valley. In 1966 a wildcat strike by farmworkers against melon growers in Starr County, on the west side of the Valley, was launched. The strike was broken by Texas rangers and by the importation of replacement workers from Mexico, but it too signaled the demise of Hispanic quiescence.

Remaking Politics in the Valley

In 1983 a major freeze hit the Valley. The freeze, far deeper than earlier ones, killed not only fruit on the trees but the trees themselves. The unemployment rate in the Valley rose from an already high 17 percent to 30 percent.[24] The Reagan administration proposed emergency unemployment insurance, but Valley Interfaith argued instead for a public works program aimed at improving the Valley infrastructure. The organization was able to get the local business community to sign on to this idea and appeared to be making progress in Washington. Very quickly, however, the right wing in the Valley and in Texas counterattacked. Tom Pauken, then the director of ACTION (the domestic Peace Corp), had ties to the conservative wing of the Texas Republican party and had run twice for Congress in Dallas, losing each time. He saw as his mission ensuring that no federal funds be used to finance what he regarded as subversive groups, and he launched what was in effect a red-baiting offensive against Valley Interfaith. He attacked IAF organizer Jim Drake for having worked with the United Farmworkers, calling him an "outsider parachuted in from California," and joined with Othal Brand, the longserving mayor of McAllen, in calling Valley Interfaith "revolutionaries." Pamphlets calling Valley Interfaith "Marxist" began to appear. Pauken also convinced the Reagan administration to back off its support of the public works strategy. One observer of these events attributed them to the desire of the Texas Republican party to suppress the size of the Mexican-American vote, a vote that had received much credit for the 1982 victory of Democrat Mark White in the gubernatorial election.[25]

As a consequence of these attacks, the Valley business community retracted its support of the Valley Interfaith plan and some churches began to leave the organization. Only one Protestant congregation was willing to maintain its affiliation. Valley Interfaith was in danger of being driven down to a base of only poor Catholic parishes. The notion of a broad-based organization was very much at risk.

Now jump ahead to events in the winter and spring of 2000. In February, Valley Interfaith submitted a petition with thirty-one hundred signatures calling for a referendum on changing the McAllen city council from an at-large to a single-member district system. McAllen was, along with Austin, the last large city remaining in Texas to elect its city council at large. This was not the first time that the IAF had fought over this issue. Some twenty years earlier, COPS had benefited from a federal court decree that required San Antonio to adopt a single-member district system in return for permission for the city to annex some outlying areas. This shift had dramatically opened up politics in the city. In the first election in San Antonio after abolition of at-large elections, sixty-nine candidates ran for city council and nine for mayor.[26] But in McAllen the IAF was trying to force through the change on its own with no assistance from the courts.

Valley Interfaith's effort to remake politics in McAllen had its roots in its successful campaign two years before to pass a half-cent increase in the city sales tax. The goal was to fund projects such as the health clinic, local libraries, and VIDA, the Valley Interfaith job-training program. The city leaders also supported this tax increase but had failed in two previous attempts to secure passage. They finally turned to Valley Interfaith for help, and the organization agreed on the condition that its projects would receive a share of the funding. With Valley Interfaith's support, the tax measure finally passed, but the organization was in for a rude surprise. The city board responsible for allocating the funds did not keep its bargain, and Valley Interfaith found itself confronted with the limits of its power in city government. At the same time, complaints increased in Valley Interfaith neighborhoods that phone calls to the city about local issues such as potholes, park cleanups, and the like were not being returned.

The leaders of Valley Interfaith, with Father Jerry Frank in the forefront, began to think about transforming the electoral system. This, like the Milagro clinic, was driven by the leaders, with the organizers going along. In fact, lead organizer Judy Donovan worried about the risks of the campaign. In principle, if Valley Interfaith could put together a large block vote, it could dominate an at-large system. In addition, the effort ran the risk of exposing Valley Interfaith's weakness if it undertook and then lost this campaign. The first step, then, was an internal debate among the Valley Interfaith leaders. It is likely that if the organizers—Judy Donovan backed by Christine Stephens and Ernie Cortes—felt strongly that the campaign was a bad idea, they could have killed it. As always, there was a complicated interaction of leaders and organizers. But the leaders' initiative prevailed. Their argument was straightforward: single-member districts would create a system in which neighborhoods felt that they had their own representation. Furthermore, compared with an expensive citywide campaign, it would be cheaper for candidates to run in a district, and the political system would be opened to a broader range of people.

Valley Interfaith learned quickly that this assessment was correct. Their opponents also saw that a single-member district system would remake power in McAllen, and they reacted accordingly. They were (at least at first) remarkably frank in their statements about what was at stake. One of the at-large city counselors commented to the press that "unless you have a business background how can you run a city where the budget is approaching $50 million. You have to put it in capable hands."[27] A clearer statement in support of elite rule could not be had. Valley Interfaith's opponents raised funds (in a meeting held at a city bank and attended by both the economic and political elite), hired a campaign consulting firm, and launched an attack on the idea, on Valley Interfaith, and on the participation of the church in politics.

At the core of the attack was the argument that a single-member district system would divide the city, pitting one neighborhood against another, and lead to corruption as each counselor sought to use city funds to benefit his or her area. In a more subtle appeal to elite rule, the opponents argued that it was important to have a government that operated on behalf of the common good. They claimed the current system offered (poverty rates, health statistics, and crime rates to the contrary) "a superior quality of life, a clean and orderly city that provides job opportunities to its qualified citizens."[28] The attack on Valley Interfaith was simple. One ad said, "This is not a campaign for power to the people, it is a campaign for power to Valley Interfaith." This line was followed by a barrage of complaints about the role of the church, attributing the effort to the work of "four priests and their attorneys."[29]

Valley Interfaith, caught by surprise by both the ferocity of the attack and the resources of the opponents, scrambled to respond. It lacked the financial resources to match the opposition's ads and its polling, but they participated in debates and obtained statements from the National Conference of Catholic Bishops that it was appropriate for the church to take a stand on public issues. Nelson Wolff, a former Republican mayor of San Antonio, talked favorably about how single-member districts had worked well in his city. Valley Interfaith also worked hard to find allies, ranging from the police officers' association to the Friends of the Library, all of whom had various grievances with city government. At the core of Valley Interfaith's strategy was the gritty work of registering and getting out the vote. The organization set up a system of block and area captains, it organized house meetings, it did neighborhood walks, it signed up voters, and in general it ran a street-level effort.

Rosa Gutierrez was in charge of thirty block captains on the south side, and she and the other leaders spent election day working door-to-door pulling the vote. But opposition members had one last trick. The night before, they had called house meetings at which they asserted that a vote for single-member districts would mean an increase in taxes. Because the Valley Interfaith communities were accustomed to attending house meetings, these events were well attended, and it appeared that the strategy had worked. Voting rates were running below expectations. In response, Valley Interfaith dropped all activities other than pulling votes, and by midday all of the people involved in the campaign were thrown into street work. As the votes came in, it appeared that Valley Interfaith had lost. No media representatives were at Valley Interfaith headquarters, and the opposition was preparing a victory party.

But when the final tallies arrived, the single-member district initiative had passed by 221 votes. People at the Valley Interfaith headquarters prayed and sang *Pueblo Libre*, and the party began. But first, in characteristic IAF fashion, several of the leaders called the city's leading bankers and politicians to begin the process of depolarizing and to make commitments that the IAF would work with them to turn the vote to the entire city's benefit.

The single-member district campaign remade politics in McAllen and, as Judy Donovan described it, "transformed us from being an organization identified with issues to a legitimate power in the city." But, in practical terms, it was only a step along the road, and what happened next was just as significant. Valley Interfaith prepared for the May council elections by organizing a house meeting campaign to define an agenda and then by calling the candidates together for accountability sessions, at which they were asked to state their commitment to that agenda. The candidates who signed on to the IAF agenda won in four out of McAllen's six council districts. The contrast with the early days of red-baiting and boss rule could not be more stark. The days of boss politics were long gone.

Making Citizens

The accomplishments of the single-member district campaign, or of the Milagro Health Clinic, are impressive on their own terms. However, what is of greater significance is the personal transformation of the IAF leaders. Middle-class students are taught in school and by their parents to raise their hands to get attention in school. They are praised from childhood on for any efforts to stand out and to stand up for themselves. By adulthood they may not have any interest in participating in politics, but if they did, they would have no doubt that they were entitled to speak their opinions and that someone would—or at least should—listen.

This confidence is far from the norm among the bulk of the people with whom the IAF works. Many are poor and are not well educated. It comes as no surprise that both traits work against self-confidence and also against any belief that someone will listen on the other end. Many Valley Interfaith leaders are not white, and although there is no necessary correlation between race and self-confidence, the weight of history suggests that nonwhites in this country have good reason to doubt their ability to be heard by the powers that be. Add to this the fact that a good number (though well less than half) do not speak English, and the odds are very much tipped against speaking out about political issues.

Prior to their involvement in the IAF, leaders' attitudes were very much in line with these expectations. Consider these comments typical in virtually all of our interviews:

> Francisca: "When I got to know Valley Interfaith, I was one of those persons who was never involved in anything."

> Tomasita: "When I began to train, I didn't know how to talk."

> Yolanda: "I was a timid person, ashamed. I couldn't talk."

> Elida: "I was more like a shy person. I couldn't talk to other people. I was like in my little shell, not speaking out."

By the same token, the comments were all followed by descriptions of personal transformation. The most common reaction was that the IAF had given people the courage to speak.

Francisca: "It is difficult to change these habits, but in the two years I've been with the organization I have learned a lot and have changed a lot."

Berta: "It gave me the courage to talk."

Joe: "I'm not afraid anymore. Before I thought I'd be afraid to confront a political person of one kind or another."

Yolanda: "I have changed a lot. I'm no longer afraid to talk."

Jaime: "I've learned to lose my fear, to communicate with people, to go to meetings and talk."

Elida, when asked if she speaks out now, replied (laughing), "Now I do," and went on to recount the story of her first experience of public speaking during an accountability session with candidates for school board.

We asked Valley Interfaith leaders how they thought an old friend, who hadn't seen them for some time, would perceive them if they were to meet that person now. Noelia's reply was typical: "[She would] probably say I'm more assertive, That I understand issues a whole lot better." One of Manuela's friends said, "When I first saw Manuela, she was a person very closed up in her house, doing nothing more than taking care of her husband and children. Now she's involved in the problems of the community."

Manuela tells a story about herself:

> Valley Interfaith has brought me a lot of self-esteem. At the beginning, my very first meeting, going to Austin for the water board meeting, I wanted to sit in the back. And the organizer said, "Sit in the front." And I said, "No, no. That's where the mayor and the city manager sit." And she said, "No, you sit in the front because you are the ones that are the taxpayers, and you are the ones that are paying for their salary." I was so embarrassed. But now it is very different. We go there and we sit in the front. I get a paper and pencil, and I don't know how to write, but they don't know I don't know. And I write. I'm using my poor spelling, I spell it out so that I understand it. You won't, but I will. And the meetings that I have with those people, if I have to come up, I write whatever they said and I just look at the word and I say, "You said this." . . . I don't know how to write what they really are say-

ing. But I carry my things and I lift my face. I lift my head. You people are going to have to respect people. Before it was just like, humbling yourself. You know, whatever they said, that's how it is. But it's not that way anymore, and it doesn't have to be that way. And we've learned our rights.

Meetings of city commissioners take place in foreboding courthouses, and it took a great deal of courage for Manuela to move up front at the water board.

Many of the people we talked to described personal changes that went well beyond the purely political. The IAF process almost becomes therapeutic. Manuela says, "I have become a better mother. A good mother. I have become a better wife," and Gilbert comments, "I'm a more peaceful person at some level." Alicia recounted that during a training session she realized that her younger brother's death in a car accident, when she was very young, created a family dynamic in which she was quiet and withdrawn at home. In Alicia's words,

> Well it goes deep into you. I mean, you go deep inside. You just don't go a little bit into the surface. I mean you go deep into the soul, and you really look into yourself. Because often we go through life not knowing who we are. So you get to know yourself better, I think. National training did that to me a lot.

Elida makes a similar point:

> You see, there are so many people that are angry. There are so many people, but there is no one there to help you learn what to do with it. And so part of the whole process of organizing is learning about ourselves and the way we're trained. The process of just learning yourself, developing relationships with others. And I mean relationships that are really profound relationships. I'm talking about relationships among us, the leadership.

Comments of this kind suggest that the boundaries between the political and the personal are sometimes unclear. Evidently the process of developing confidence in one's political efficacy—the ability to speak in public, to research issues, to insist on being taken seriously—spills over into other arenas. Although part of IAF training emphasizes the distinction between the public and the private, with a different set of behavioral norms for each, that distinction loses some force as personal changes in the political realm affect the private. The nature of this connection was made explicit by Joe:

> I don't think that I had any real convictions in my life before. I don't think that I stood for anything. There wasn't any solidity. There wasn't anything solid in my life before I learned about myself through Valley Interfaith. The kind of person that I was. The kind of person that I could be. I was kind of going through the motions. Through not only work, but my marriage. There wasn't anything deep or rooted in my life until I started getting involved with Valley Interfaith and realized that there's more to life than just floating from day to day. And so Valley Interfaith has helped me find conviction, helped me find some roots, helped me find that there is something more important than that. And so, because of that, I have a much better relationship with my wife, my daughter, and my church.

This notion that the IAF leads to broader horizons is also emphasized by Eddie Anaya:

> Well, I think that if it wasn't for Valley Interfaith, I think I would probably be trapped in my own little job, and little world, little family. Not thinking that I could make a difference in anybody's lives and for that matter in my home. I think I've been able to get outside my own family and my own job and been able to get to know other people, help other individuals and grow that way. And by being involved in other people's lives, in other things, it's helped me expand and not lose sight of what's really important. In that respect I think it's kept me really intact as to my community.

Judging from the testimony of the Valley Interfaith leaders, they are different people, in many dimensions, as a result of their involvement in the organization. These changes take place across the educational, social class, and income spectrum. The school dropout who speaks no English tells a story that is similar in all important respects to the college graduate working in a good middle-class job.

Views about Politics

It is often said that Americans are a notoriously nonideological people, that they are deeply resistant to any all-encompassing theory about society or about the economy. This is true if "theory" means the kind of elaborated ideas developed by political theorists and activists, either of the Left or the Right. There are, however, some core ideas that can be fairly said to characterize American political and economic culture.

Probably the most central of these ideas is the notion of individualism: that people are responsible for their own fate and that those who do well deserve or have earned their good fortune and that those who fare poorly have somehow brought their misfortune on themselves. People of course make exceptions to this code: children are not held responsible for the bad behavior of their parents, and some categories of adults— the so-called deserving poor—are also held blameless. But economic individualism pervades American thinking about economic and even political issues.[30]

This theme has been explored by political theorists, but more persuasive evidence comes from interviews with a cross-section of Americans. Given his interviews with suburbanites, Alan Wolfe concludes that "the moral ideal of middle-class Americans revolves around the notion that people are responsible for their own fate."[31] The Californians interviewed by the authors of *Habits of the Heart* defined success "in terms of the outcome of free competition among individuals in an open market. . . . Most of those we talked to emphasized that they had attained their present status in life through their own hard work, seldom emphasizing the part played by family, schooling, or the advantages that came to them from being middle class in the first place."[32]

This view does not necessarily lead to a selfish refusal to help others. The people Alan Wolfe interviewed were active in a wide range of community activities. However, their sense of obligation is modest, as is what they hope to accomplish. Few people Wolfe interviewed felt themselves commanded by God or by any political viewpoint to be very active in righting what is wrong in the world.

The limited sense of moral or political obligation is reflected in another aspect of American political culture that sociologist Seymour Martin Lipset emphasizes in his well-known comparison of U.S. political attitudes with those of other nations: antistatism, or a distrust of government.[33] It is true that the apparatus erected by the New Deal as well as such popular programs as Social Security and Medicare increased people's attachment to government. Nonetheless, popular suspicion of government and politics continues to be a staple of American thinking.

This combination of an individualistic explanation for success and a dislike of politics and government intervention argues against any overall structural perspective on the distribution of economic outcomes. Outcomes are reduced to individual effort, and the role of larger forces or of organized institutions is ignored. Americans—in the accounts of Wolfe, Bellah and his colleagues, and various pollsters—do not have any overarching theory of the economy or society that would point to a political platform or a set of adjustments in how the economy operates as a solution to social or economic inequality.

For an organization such as the IAF, based as it is on a strong sense of social injustice, the foregoing set of ideas would seem to be both uncongenial and a real obstacle. Systematic social inequity presumably calls for broad-scale solutions. The "blaming the victim" emphasis on individual achievement is not very attractive in this context. Furthermore, any solution that has bite would likely need to rely on government action, and hence dislike of government is also a problem.

One would expect, therefore, that IAF leaders would differ from the norm in their views about the roles of government and the individual. However, if the IAF were to stray too far from mainstream American views, it would run the substantial risk of being marginalized. Given that the IAF's aspirations are to create a broad-based organization that encompasses a wide range of people from different backgrounds, it is very important that its views are not too much at variance with those of the people it seeks to incorporate. The trick, therefore, is to hew more or less to the mainstream American perspective but to do so with an edge, an edge that opens the way to a more systematic concern with using politics to press for larger-scale change. It turns out that this is precisely the nature of the political and economic views of the IAF leaders, which should not be surprising given the deep connectedness of the IAF leaders to church, neighborhood, and family.

Consider how Joe, who in his youth thought about blowing up the buildings at his college, responds to a question about what determines who gets ahead in America and who does not: "I think the biggest factor in what determines a lot of the financial or economic side of how people do here in the Valley is education." When he is pressed to think of other factors, he adds, "Ambition. If somebody is ambitious they can do whatever they want."

The IAF does not preach ideology, but it does teach people to become politically active. This has important consequences, because it both creates a political constituency for IAF issues and undermines the assumed authority of politicians. Leaders learn to insist that their voices be heard at every stage of the political process.

Prior to becoming members of the IAF, the leaders shared the dislike and cynicism of politics that are articulated by the suburbanites. Some, such as Berta, simply said that they used to pay no attention at all to politics: "Oh, politics, yes, yes. I never voted. . . . I didn't think that it would really make much of a difference if I voted or not."

Even more common was contempt based on the observation that there was no substance in politics. In Chayo's words, "politics had nothing to do with the issue" but rather was a personalistic favor-based system. Eddie observed that politicians did not fulfill their promises: "Through the years growing up, we were given a lot of hope and a lot of broken promises. And politicians really never came through. They would tell us, well we'll fix the streets, we'll bring water and sewer to our communities. They'd get elected and forget about what they had promised."

The IAF overturns these attitudes. As a first step, and a crucial one, it raises voting rates. Leader after leader testified to the importance of voting. As Yolanda said,

> We still have to put more emphasis on voting, that they don't vote only once but instead that they perceive it as an obligation, as a responsibility that all of us who can do it have, that we have the commitment to go on with a constant voting, because if we just vote once, they will think that we do not show much interest. And now we know that we all have the power to make a difference, as I said, we can do it. And this is what we are working on nowadays. We will work to get organized for voting.

And Rosa Gutierrez, who earlier paid no attention to politics and was involved only in her family, now sounds like a spokesperson for the Advertising Council of America in an ad urging citizens to vote:

I started with my husband. He is a voter, but he didn't use to be.
He didn't care. So once I told him, "We got the taxes and they have
increased." I told him, "Look how expensive taxes are. Each year they
get higher and higher." And I told him, "I will tell you something, you,
since you don't vote. You don't have the right to complain. Your voice
is not important, your voice is neither voice nor vote, because you neither vote nor have a voice. So you are going to pay your taxes and shut
up. When you decide, in case you decide, to vote, then you'll have the
right to talk. And you will be heard."

The IAF leaders have a view of politics in which voting is merely the
first step in a process, but the main effort involves ensuring that elected
officials do what they promise. As Elida comments, "You know, account-
abilities. We need to bring them more accountable for what they do. You
know, my friends say, 'Well, they're already elected. To go ahead and do
their job.' I say, it doesn't work that way. You have to present your needs.
. . . We've got to be in relationship with them. You know, let them know
what's going on." In hindsight, Estela Soza Garza wonders if she almost
became too attached to Henry Cisneros, the popular mayor of San Antonio who was the first Hispanic elected to that position: "I remember being called a groupie for Henry Cisneros, and that was how I was. Now
we recognize what our role is in regard to elected officials. People don't
see elected officials as a God that will dictate, the expert tells us what to
do. Now we're in conversations with them."

Reliance on experts, be they politicians or social scientists, is seen as
a top-down tactic for denying people the opportunity to have a voice in
their communities. In the words of Father Alfonso, "one of the failures
of, I think, politics is because it has denied its capacity to engage the citizen, you know, in a true conversation, because we are in a culture where
we think the expert knows everything. And really when you talk about
the livelihoods of people, you have to ask the people themselves what are
the issues. That's where politics has missed the boat."

Joe's summary captures what many of the IAF leaders told us:

What Valley Interfaith does to bring about these changes is, actually,
let you discover yourself. It makes it easier for you to find out what you
are and take advantage of the talents that you've been given and not to
be afraid of what the circumstances may be as an ordinary citizen.

Someone might say, "I'm not going to get involved. I'm not going to talk to my mayor. I'm afraid of the mayor. He's an important person, so I'm not going to talk to him. I'm not going to talk to my state senator. I'm not going to talk to my representative." But Valley Interfaith has given me the courage to say, "Hey, these guys are human. They are responsible to me because I'm a citizen." So I can go out there and talk to them and tell them what I want, what needs to be done in that area. So, it's given me the courage to do that.

The IAF and the Machine

What kind of political organization is Valley Interfaith? The IAF calls itself a network of "broad-based organizations" and works hard to distinguish itself from movements and civic organizations. We know what protest groups are (the Civil Rights movement) and what civic organizations are (the United Way), but if we want to search for categories that are more familiar in the history of American politics, what are the IAF organizations?

The big city machine comes immediately to mind. From Boss Tweed of New York to Mayor Daley of Chicago and even perhaps to Willie Brown of San Francisco, machines have played a prominent role in American politics and have also fascinated social scientists.

The classic urban machine operates parallel to government. Based in neighborhoods, it organizes people to vote for its candidates in exchange for giving them what they need from government, be that jobs or street repair. Machines make government accessible to people and operate informally to deliver services that would otherwise be hard to attain from large impersonal bureaucracies.

When seen in these terms, it is not hard to believe that the IAF is in the business of building machines. Although the IAF does not endorse candidates, its leaders and followers do vote for those aspirants who agree to support the IAF agenda. The IAF also puts continuous pressure on city government to deliver services to its constituents—ranging from local neighborhood improvements to job training or better schools—and the IAF uses its ability to turn out votes as the weapon to deliver on these efforts. The IAF organizations are decentralized and neighborhood-based, with both the voting effort and many of the services having a strong local character. In short, the IAF looks like a machine.

While at first glance the machine analogy seems right, it is based on an incomplete understanding of both the character of machines and the character of the IAF. Machines do more than simply help people gain access. In his classic analysis of the "latent functions of the machine," sociologist Robert Merton showed that machines help the business community obtain the order and predictability that it needs to conduct its work, that the machines provide an avenue of social mobility (i.e., jobs) for people who would otherwise be excluded, and that machines provide the same services for organized crime—that is, stability and predictability—that they do for the business community.[34] Ira Katznelson more directly argues that machines face in two directions: helping people in the neighborhoods gain services but, out of sight of these constituents, making deals with the powers that be that are inimical to the neighborhood's interests.[35]

When this description is fleshed out, it becomes apparent that the IAF does not fit the model very well. The IAF has nothing to do with organized crime, and the leaders of the IAF and the organizers do not conduct backdoor business with the power elites in their cities. IAF organizations carefully articulate their positions publicly, and these are normally arrived at via open internal discussion. Even when the positions and tactics are decided upon in a relatively closed way (for example, among senior organizers), they are quickly communicated to the membership. It is also the norm in the IAF that when organizers meet with politicians or business executives, leaders also attend. Many a member of the power elite, expecting a quiet meeting with a fellow power broker, has been surprised when four or five leaders arrive with the organizer.

There is little evidence of personal gain to leaders or organizers, and the IAF discourages leaders from utilizing their membership as a source of personal advancement. Stories of such and such a leader who went into politics, trading on the exposure received through work with the IAF, are always recounted with a disapproving tinge, and in fact the examples are relatively rare. If a leader does get actively involved working for a candidate, the leader is asked to take a leave of absence from the organization. Those services that the IAF extracts from government are aimed at neighborhoods or communities and rarely are directed to specific individuals who are part of the organization.

A final distinction centers on how welcome new leaders are. A classic story of the Daley Chicago machine is their reaction to the arrival of a stranger wanting to participate: "We don't want nobody who nobody sent." By contrast, as we saw chapter 2, the IAF is always on the lookout for new leaders and is always trying to broaden its base.

It is indeed true that the IAF does use its abilities to operate in neighborhoods and to gather votes to force the government to be responsive to the needs of its constituents. But the IAF does more than this. As we have seen, it also explicitly and consciously teaches politics to its leaders. It seeks to bridge across divides. Mayor Daley had blacks as well as white ethnics in his machine, but there were separate suborganizations that operated in parallel, with little interaction between them, and that reported up to the mayor.[36] The IAF rejects this model and creates a style of politics that forces people to overcome divisions and to operate in a broad-based manner. Perhaps it would be best to characterize the IAF as the people's machine, as opposed to the bosses' machine.

Practicing Politics

When Valley Interfaith leaders talk about how politics works and what has changed, the word that comes up most often in the interviews is "accountability." The idea of laying out an agenda, asking politicians their views, and then holding them accountable is central to how the IAF thinks about politics. For many Valley Interfaith leaders, attending an accountability session was their first experience with the IAF, and they were struck by how different it was from what they expected or from politics as usual. As Noelia recalled,

> There was an accountability session that I went to, and it was different because it involved the people from the community doing the speaking. The people up there spoke, but it was not like for two hours or for thirty minutes . . . like at times they can go on and on and on. But it was actually the people who had been practicing and everything else. It asked accountability of the governor, accountability at schools and accountability of colonias. That's the first time that I kind of got going.

Accountability sessions are one of the central rituals of the IAF, but they also represent the core of the IAF vision of politics: that organized communities can force politicians to be responsive. An accountability session is a very stylized event. Candidates for office are invited to an assembly that, depending on the city and the offices at stake, might be attended by hundreds or thousands of people from the community. IAF leaders make brief presentations in which they lay out the organization's agenda. Then, one by one, the candidates are called forward and asked whether they support each item on the agenda. The candidates are urged to give yes or no answers. Although they are permitted to explain their answers, they are not allowed to make speeches. If they try to do so, they are politely cut off. If they equivocate, they are pressed until they respond yes or no.

One, not entirely sympathetic, observer likened these sessions to prisoner-of-war rituals in which the captives are asked to denounce their government's policy in a public event. The suggestion is that the content means nothing because the context is so obviously coercive. It is a fair question whether there is substance to these sessions. However, it is not always true that the candidates simply agree to the IAF agenda. At a session in McAllen in preparation for the city council elections, six out of the twenty-six candidates present rejected at least one of Valley Interfaith's planks.[37] The deeper point, however, is that accountability sessions are only the most visible aspect of the IAF's relationship with politicians. There is a substantial amount of interaction and back-and-forth both before and after accountability sessions as IAF leaders research issues and work with politicians and their staffs. Politicians can benefit because it provides them with a clear channel for learning about the interests and concerns of their constituents.

Numerous stories of how accountability is enforced suggest that the process is meaningful. Elizabeth Valdez, for example, recounts the story of a city commissioner who made a commitment to repair roads in a colonia and then reneged. When confronted with his promise, he replied, "I'm going to tell no to five hundred people? Of course I was going to say yes." The organization responded with a large get-out-the-vote effort. As Elizabeth Valdez tells the story,

> Election day comes and the commissioner barely makes it to the run-offs. Then he's the one that gets the least votes of the three in the runoffs. He goes crying to the leader. He says, "I'm very disappointed in you." She says, "Why?" And he says, "Well, because you didn't help me. . . ." She says, "You reneged on your commitment to the leadership. So you should have learned a lesson."

By now every politician in cities where the IAF has a presence is familiar both with the ritual of accountability sessions and with their implications for their prospects of electoral success. These politicians once elected can expect that the IAF will follow up on the issues. Indeed, a remarkable amount of the leaders' time is spent participating in meetings with elected officials and with bureaucrats working to get the agenda implemented. Ernie Cortes has argued that this follow-up is actually good for the politicians. Without it, he says, sympathetic officials would become isolated and cranky, out of touch with their constituency and unable to function effectively with their colleagues. Whether this is actually true, whether the IAF is doing the politicians a favor, is a bit speculative. But what is apparent is that the IAF is doing a favor for the broader cause of rebuilding public confidence in politics by showing how government can be forced to be responsive to its constituents and responsible for keeping its promises.

Working with Allies

Powerful as they may be in their communities, the IAF organizations cannot function alone. Or, to be more accurate, they cannot work in isolation and be effective. They need allies, and they need to be able to work effectively with these allies.

Because its members aspire to be Athenians, and not Melians, the IAF is willing to work with whomever it needs to. Indeed, one of its slogans is "no permanent allies, no permanent enemies," and although this might seem to imply a certain cynicism about the steadfastness of the people or organizations with whom the IAF works today, it also implies a willingness to work tomorrow with current adversaries. The IAF views politics as an ongoing process, not as a war with simple moral absolutes.

The best symbol for IAF cooperation with business is Tom Frost in San Antonio. Frost Bank is one of the oldest independent banks in Texas and was at the core of the San Antonio establishment when Ernie Cortes began organizing there in the early 1970s. When the business elite in San Antonio refused to deal with COPS, the organization made Frost Bank the target and conducted a "change in." Lines of COPS activists queued up at the tellers windows to change pennies into dollars and dollars into pennies. More to the point, COPS was able over time to dominate elections in a majority of city council districts, and this truly got Tom Frost's attention. But although political muscle was the first step, over time COPS found ways to work with Tom Frost, notably by collaborating with him designing a job-training program, Project QUEST. Today the relationship of COPS with Tom Frost is more mature. They are allies on important issues, ranging from job training to working with the state legislature to pass the Human Development fund. At the same time, on other issues (such as efforts by the city to attract a Professional Golf Association tournament to San Antonio) they are opponents.

In Dallas, the IAF organization worked with Ross Perot on school finance reform, and as a result, Christine Stephens explains, Perot's top staff person "credentialed us with the business community." The Dallas establishment was in despair about the state of the city's schools and was looking for allies who would ally with them on reform.

Some deeper dynamics were also at play, both in Dallas and elsewhere. The business community in Texas cities knew that it had to find a way to work with low-income communities. The IAF offered them an effective channel of communication. As Christine Stephens puts it,

> When you have communities that are unorganized, there are people who appoint themselves leaders of the community, and sometimes they're not. And they're very difficult sometimes to deal with, and they're not very reasonable. And they don't understand politics, and they don't want to practice politics. They just want to go in and bludgeon. So to get a group that organizes itself and wants to practice politics, who understands politics, and that there's a difference between being right and being reasonable, is appealing to not only the business community but a number of people in the community.

This argument is similar to a line of thought that explains why on occasion firms may welcome unions, or at least gain some advantage from them. The union provides a way of communicating with the workforce through a mechanism that is credible. If the union is "responsible," then although it will bargain on behalf of its constituency, it will also be willing to sell the deal to the employees. The firm may thus gain from the union's presence relative to the alternative of a suspicious and hostile group of employees who have no one who is able to credibly communicate the firm's viewpoint.

The fact that the business community is not monolithic also creates an opportunity for the IAF. Time and again the IAF has succeeded in identifying a segment of the business community whose interests can be aligned with its own and in some sense splitting these folks off from their more recalcitrant counterparts. Thus, for example, Tom Frost does not find it problematic to support COP's high-wage strategy, whereas San Antonio's tourist and hotel industry are quite unhappy with it.

The politics of the IAF speaks directly to the ills that afflict the political process and, in particular, progressive politics. In most of America, people are turned off from politics, regarding it as either corrupt or just not worth their time. By contrast, the IAF leaders are passionately committed. More to the point, however, is that they were not always this way. The IAF has taught people politics.

This process of teaching politics happens at multiple levels. First, and most basically, the IAF changes people's conceptions of themselves as political actors. Recall Manuela's story. She learned that she had the capacity to master the issues, and she also learned that she had the right to sit in the front of the room and speak as an equal to local authorities. The IAF also teaches the basic techniques of electoral politics, as Rosa Gutierrez demonstrated when she worked as a block captain in the single-member district campaign. IAF leaders learn how to research issues. Think of the story of the Milagro clinic. The leaders learn how to negotiate and compromise. Again, the Milagro clinic is an example, and so are internal debates within IAF organizations as different areas negotiate over the agenda and priorities of the organization. Finally, if necessary, the IAF also teaches confrontation, as demonstrated by Elizabeth Valdez's story of what happened to the commissioner who ignored his promises at the accountability session.

As a result of its success, the IAF has transformed politics in its communities. It has taken the concept of accountability, something that is woefully missing in politics as usual, and put it at the center of how it does business. It has forced politicians and government officials to be more responsive to their constituents. The long-run meaning of this is not simply the benefits that accrue to the IAF communities but rather the message that gets conveyed more generally, namely that it is possible to practice the kind of politics that makes government attractive, not repelling, to ordinary people.

The IAF also speaks to a deeper difficulty that has bedeviled progressive politics. Some time ago Ira Katznelson argued that progressive efforts in the United States have been stymied by the separation of the politics of the workplace from the politics of neighborhoods.[38] The result, Katznelson argued, was that whereas in the factories or offices people might see themselves as workers with a common set of economic and political interests, once at home they thought of themselves in more chopped-up neighborhood or ethnic terms. Because of the disjunction between neighborhood and workplace, people fail to connect their concerns about their neighborhoods and families to any larger political or economic vision. The result has been great difficulty in developing a political perspective in which people whose deep interests are really in common can, in fact, come together.

Katznelson was addressing the long-standing question of why no socialist movement has emerged in America, but while this question has lost interest it remains important to understand why people have been unable to fashion a progressive political response to what bothers them. After all, this is an era in which, on the economic front, prosperity has been very unevenly shared and people in fact realize that this is true.[39] At the same time, in their neighborhoods, schools have failed to come anywhere near to reasonable expectations, and people feel disconnected from the institutions that used to create a real community. Yet most people, and most politicians, do not see how these ills are part of a large problem, and they certainly do not see how to speak to these issues. Despite a set of concerns that should lead to a vibrant progressive politics, very little has happened. By contrast, the IAF by its very nature does bring together neighborhood, community, and workplace concerns. Although the leaders of the IAF are determinedly nonideological, they nonetheless have a more complete view of how the pieces of their lives fit together and how to use politics to address their concerns. It is in this sense that the IAF has the most to teach us about how to practice progressive politics in America.

Chapter 5

Managing Our Economic Destiny

In 1976 the city leaders of San Antonio hired a consulting firm, Fantus, to advise them on the future of the city. Fantus reported that the major advantage of San Antonio relative to its competitors was low wages and that this should be the basis for enticing employers to move in. The report was leaked to COPS, who launched a campaign against the notion of selling its people as low-wage workers. Twenty-five years later, the McAllen Economic Development Commission, in a glitzy PowerPoint presentation about why companies should locate in the Valley, cited low wages as a key drawing card.

How can communities take control of the trajectory of their economy in order to create a fairer set of outcomes? It is clear that the answer to this question is central to any progressive political effort and agenda. Economic security and rising living standards go to the core of what people and their families are entitled to expect and what they look for from politics. The economy also affects the health of community institutions. If people have to work multiple jobs to make ends meet, or if they have no support for taking care of children or elderly relatives, then it is hard to expect them to find the time to participate in churches, community groups, or political organizations.

This is a difficult and discouraging time for addressing economic concerns. The job market is increasingly treacherous, with insecurity on the rise and with wages stagnant for many people.[1] The economic trajectory seems to be increasingly outside the control of ordinary politics, and it is hard to think about what handles we have.

In part this pessimism about the capacity of people to have a voice in economic matters is the creation of the rhetoric of globalization. Thomas Friedman writes that "the world is being tied together into a single globalized marketplace."[2] Newspapers regularly report on the ties that link events in, say, the Japanese stock market to the economic health of America. More directly, Americans are intimately aware of the possibility that their jobs—be they producing automobile parts or keyboarding financial data or writing software—can be shipped overseas. Leaving aside all questions about whether on balance globalization is good or bad for Americans, it clearly creates a sensation that local efforts to shape the course of economic events are, if not futile, certainly swimming against the tide.

The ideology of the economics profession also contributes to this learned helplessness. An unfettered market is seen as the best way to make decisions about the allocation of goods. Any attempt to interfere with that market is an invitation to, if not disaster, then inefficiency and waste. This explains the generalized antipathy in the profession to interventions such as minimum wages and other labor standards. Although not all economists think this way, the general respect for the market and hostility to interference have permeated public discussion and are commonly used by opponents of policy.

Shifts in the balance of power have also complicated efforts to shape a response to labor market concerns. It is true that firms face much greater competitive pressure than they did in the glory days of the post–World War II period (an economic epoch that stretched until the mid-1980s). Not only have domestic industries (such as telecommunications, airlines, banking, and trucking) been deregulated, but in numerous other sectors overseas competition represents a genuine threat. The consequence is that companies need to find new ways of producing more efficiently and utilizing their workforce more effectively.[3] At the same time, the business community has used these changed circumstances as a opening to press their advantage vis-à-vis employees for example, by holding down wages despite the expansion of the 1990s. Voices on the other side are muted. Unions are declining, and other sources of countervailing power are hard to identify. This makes the politics of labor market policy quite difficult.

In the face of these challenges, the IAF has generated initiatives such as job-training programs, school reform, and living wage campaigns. It has tried to block what it regards as wasteful or negative uses of public funds, such as subsidies for sports stadiums or tax abatements for low-wage employers. The IAF jobs strategy has evolved, sometimes in fits and starts, but in the end it has put together the most sophisticated and comprehensive package of community labor market initiatives that exists in the country. The accomplishments, and the limits, of these initiatives say a great deal about how far communities can go in shaping their economic future.

Living Wages

What bothered the IAF leaders and organizers most about the Fantus report and the continued efforts in the Valley to recruit firms looking to pay low wages was the suspicion that the city elite was determined to keep wages low. Valley Interfaith responded with a living wage campaign.

Living wage campaigns are not the only strategy for raising the wages of low-paid workers. There are two standard approaches with a longer history: union organization and improving labor standards, such as the minimum wage. Although historically unions have been effective, in South Texas the going is very rough. There is no deep tradition of unionization in the region, and unions are not well understood. At a meeting of Valley Interfaith, several leaders expressed the standard fears of unions: that they are corrupt, undemocratic, and suck dues from their members. These critiques may be unfair, but they are deeply held and, along with the united opposition of the political and economic establishment, make any unionization drive at the present problematic. Texas is also one of twenty-two so-called right-to-work states, a status permitted by federal labor law that means that even if a union achieves a contract the people who benefit do not have to become members. This creates "free-rider" problems that weaken unions in all such states. The bottom line is that Texas has the fourth-lowest rate of unionization among the fifty states.[4]

Federal labor standards, such as the minimum wage, are a step in the right direction, but they are inadequate. At the time Valley Interfaith began to organize its living wage campaign, the national minimum wage was $5.15 an hour, which translates into just over $10,000 a year for a person who works full-time all year, and it is below the poverty line of $13,290 for a family of three and $17,000 for a family of four. The minimum wage, as important as it is, also suffers from some political vulnerabilities. A nontrivial fraction (roughly a third) of minimum wage workers are teenagers, and the case for raising their wages is weaker than for adults who support families. The political opposition to the minimum wage makes hay over the fact that some beneficiaries of an increase would be comfortable suburban teens in after-school jobs. Although this is not a fair characterization of the bulk of minimum-wage workers, it suggests the need for efforts to establish a higher standard for adults who are working hard to support families.

When Valley Interfaith first considered a living wage campaign, the initial problem the organization faced was not legal or political, but rather intellectual. Most people do not believe that it is either possible or appropriate for them to intervene in the operation of the economy, and certainly the business community works hard to sell this view. Estela describes what Valley firms said when the issue came up: "That we should be grateful that we have a job. That that's the way it has always been. In other words, it can't be different if that's the way that it's always been. With Mexico nearby, it can't be any different. Just a lot of that talk of negative." Gilbert recalls similar admonitions: "Well, we were told by a bank president not to get involved with the wages at all, that Valley Interfaith has no business getting involved with economic kinds of issues. We were in above our heads. We don't know what we're doing, and we're going to make a mess of things. If anything, we're going to scare businesses away and nobody's going to want to come to the Valley."

These warnings are supported by the central message of economic theory. Economists have long argued that the minimum wage is a bad thing. Although it may raise the wages of those people who keep their jobs, the argument is that firms, in the face of higher wages, will reduce employment, and on balance the intended beneficiaries will be worse off. A living wage might have even more deleterious consequences because it is applied to a relatively small geographic area and the affected employers can simply move elsewhere. In fact, the weight of professional economic opinion has shifted to a somewhat more favorable (though still skeptical) stance in the face of substantial research showing that the benefits of minimum wage increases outweigh the costs.[5] However, the core message remains intact: the economy is too complex a mechanism for people to dabble with.

These views exercised a substantial influence on IAF leaders. Leaders felt that it was simply not possible to intervene in the labor market and also feared that any action they took might lead to the loss of jobs. The first challenge, therefore, was to overcome these concerns.

Valley Interfaith had a running start because it could draw on ideas of economic justice that people brought to the table through their religious convictions. Consider the following dialogue with one of the Valley Interfaith leaders:

> Interviewer: Some people say that government should not intervene with the salaries because by doing so they would destroy the economy. Do you agree with that statement?
>
> Lupita: Definitely not.
>
> Interviewer: Why not?
>
> Lupita: Because we have to be conscious that we have dignity, which God gave us and which neither the economy nor the powerful men have the right to take away from us. God gave us that dignity, and we are responsible for disseminating it. This is why the church is responsible for participating in all this and for teaching us all this.

Valley Interfaith organized training workshops in which economists sympathetic to the living wage idea helped the leaders develop an alternative understanding of the job market. First, there is a "zone of indeterminacy" in wage setting within which there is room for discretion and hence for negotiations. That is, a moderate pay increase will either cause firms to find ways to operate more efficiently with the same amount of labor or else simply be absorbed in the form of lower profits. A substantial tradition of research in wage setting supports this.[6] In addition, there is good reason to believe that firms gain some benefits (in the form of greater effort and lower turnover) from paying higher wages, an effect what economists dub "efficiency wages." In the end, leaders came to the view that establishing a wage standard could in fact work to the benefit of low-paid workers in the Valley. Sister Maria Sanchez, a Valley leader, described how this case was made to school districts:

Our point was that if you raised the salaries for the hourly wages then you would get better performance. The turnover would not be as great. You would have happier employees. They would be able to give more output. So we were doing this with the school district. And here their opposition was we would need to raise taxes. And we would say, "Well, are there areas that could be streamlined so that these monies would be there?" And we knew they were there, but they had to come up with it. And so, it was that back and forth with them. I think it was like two or three board meetings when finally it was accepted.

Valley leaders and organizers began to think seriously about a living wage campaign in 1997. Valley Interfaith had just succeeded in passing a bond authorization and small sales tax increase to fund the construction of new schools, libraries, and health facilities. Full of energy from this victory, people began to ask about the wages of the workers who would build the projects. The leaders began researching the construction labor market and found that wages in the Valley were so low that many people traveled north to Houston to find more decent pay. However, they also learned that they faced a legal obstacle in trying to change this: according to the Texas attorney general, it would require state-enabling legislation to give a municipality the authority to set a wage standard for contractors. Although Valley Interfaith would eventually launch a campaign to attain this legislation, as a first step they decided to examine the wage levels of the school district employees themselves.

The living wage campaign was aimed at thirty-two school districts in the Valley. In each of these districts there were food service workers, cleaners, grounds staff, and bus drivers earning the minimum wage or just above. Because each district was independent, Valley Interfaith needed to work on each school board individually. Estela describes what happened in one school district:

We meet with Mr. X and Mr. Y, but basically we knew that the one who makes the decisions was "so and so." So we sat with him, and we knew stories. This person has been here so long and he's still making $5.15. And he was very much aware of it. We had helped him with a bond, and so he's aware that we would like to see some of those monies going towards people getting paid better. That's how that worked.

So then we looked at, okay, it was unrealistic for the budget to go straight to $7.50 because we're talking about hundreds of people. So then we came up with formulas. We'll stagger it. But we knew that within a couple of years they would at least be at that rate. And one of the things that happened was that there was a domino effect, because school districts have to compete. The other school districts started doing that where they had to increase in order to get their workers, and then it just kind of began to happen.

Negotiations of this sort went on for a two-year period. In some cases, Valley Interfaith mobilized large numbers of leaders to attend meetings with school boards and county commissioners, and in other instances small group negotiations worked. In the end, the campaign was a remarkable success. In the summer of 2000 I evaluated the effort by collecting data from the school districts in the Valley. There were three groups of people who benefited from the living wage campaign: people who had their wages raised directly as a result of the campaign, people who were paid above the living wage but who were given an increase in order to maintain customary differentials, and people who worked in districts that were not targets of the campaign but that raised wages in response to the campaign to maintain morale or to avoid losing employees. The campaign increased the wages of seventy-four hundred people by an average of just under ninety cents an hour. Since then, additional school districts have been induced to raise the wages of a thousand more people. Although ninety cents may not seem like much, it is a substantial increase over the base salary of six dollars an hour.

Beyond their direct impact, living wage campaigns have a broader agenda. They aim to change the public discourse around wages by forcing a debate about what is fair. This is important for two reasons. Despite increased inequality there has been little public discussion about fair wages. Advocates of living wages hope to use their campaigns as a vehicle for putting the issue on the table. There is also evidence in the labor economics literature that expectations play a role in wage setting.[7] People enter the job market with a notion of what is fair, what is the "going wage," and employers also have a similar idea in mind. If living wage campaigns can shift these expectations, then there is likely to be at least some impact on actual outcomes.

An example of both processes at work was the living wage campaign that Harvard students waged during the spring of 2001. This effort—

which was aimed at the wages paid to employees who work at firms that receive Harvard subcontracts for jobs such as cleaning and food services—garnered very substantial attention and was highly disruptive to the university. Although very few Harvard jobs were at stake, there is evidence that other universities in the area quietly reconsidered their own wage policies, if only to avoid the embarrassment and disruption that Harvard suffered.[8] In addition, the publicity associated with the campaign involving a university that had a huge endowment but that had employees with poverty-level wages led to a debate about the role of fairness in wage setting.

Living wage campaigns are also an organizing device. The campaigns, and victories, provide community organizations with an issue that they can use to energize their membership. In the Valley, the living wage campaign has been a central focus of the organization for several years, and a substantial number of leaders have been involved in researching wage levels, planning the campaign, and confronting public employers. In addition, some beneficiaries of the campaign have become interested in being active leaders in Valley Interfaith.

Living wage campaigns are also vehicles for forming alliances with unions and with other organizations concerned with economic equity. The nation's first living wage campaign, which took place in Baltimore in 1994, was driven by an alliance between the IAF organization, BUILD, and the public employees' union, AFSCME. The union was concerned about the city government's strategy of outsourcing jobs from city payrolls to private contractors, and BUILD was focused on strategies for raising wages in its communities. These interests came together in the living wage campaign, which set a required wage level for contractors who do business with the city. The success of the campaign led to an ongoing relationship between the two organizations, and in fact, BUILD is now chartered as a local of the union.

Other Strategies to Raise Standards

In addition to living wage campaigns directly aimed at increasing compensation, the IAF has also struggled to ensure that public subsidies to firms are used to attract high-wage employment.

As in many other cities and states, the governments in the Valley and in South Texas deploy a varied set of incentives to attract firms to the area or to enable existing firms to expand. The model that everyone has in the back of their mind is the success of the American South in attracting firms from the North.[9] The professional economics literature tends to be quite critical of these kinds of efforts. From the national perspective they are a zero-sum game in which areas compete with each other by subsidizing companies but only succeed in transferring wealth from taxpayers to companies without generating any net new jobs. Nor is it clear that even from a local perspective these incentive packages make sense. The variations in subsidies from one city to another are typically dwarfed by other location-specific cost differences such as access to markets, labor costs, and transportation and other forms of infrastructure. The best that a recent review of the voluminous research literature could say was that "no definite conclusions can be reached on the basis of published research."[10]

Despite doubts, few political leaders are willing to simply refuse to offer support and then face the political consequence of complaints that they cost their local economy jobs. As a consequence, despite reasons to think that this is bad policy, the incentive game continues at full throttle. A question, however, remains about what kinds of firms should be targeted. A low-road approach still exerts a powerful appeal in South Texas and is exemplified by efforts to attract call centers.

Call centers are essentially large telephone banks (linked to industries such as airlines, credit card companies, entertainment ticket sales, and so on) that either receive calls from customers or call out (apparently always at dinner time) to sell products. These call centers are footloose in the extreme. All it takes to open one is a building with open space, a former department store or warehouse for example, and some telephone lines. The only difficult ingredient is the people who sit at the phones. In the past few years half a dozen call centers have opened in the Valley, and they have received subsidies from public economic development funds. Why did they go there? In a candid moment an executive at Convergys, one of the centers in the Valley that opened to service subscription calls for DirectTV, explained, "We pay the same in Brownsville as in Jacksonville, but the unemployment there reached 14 percent and we were able to hire very good people."[11] The problem is that these are not jobs that can support a family. New hires get two weeks of training and start at $7.00 an hour and move up to $7.50. About half the jobs are held on a part-time basis by college students, the average employee age is twenty-three, and turnover is about 75 percent a year.[12] It is very unclear why public funds should be used to underwrite this employment.

The IAF is equally unhappy with large subsidies to sports facilities. COPS fought, unsuccessfully, against subsidizing the Alamodome, and the IAF network has continued to oppose—sometimes actively and other times via surly silence—other stadium projects in Texas. The economists who have done the most research on this topic report that in the nation as a whole between 1990 and 1998 forty-six stadiums and arenas were built or renovated, with another forty-nine under construction or in the planning stage. A total of $21.7 billion will be spent on these projects, with the public contributing two-thirds of this amount. Despite this subsidy, there is no evidence that cities that make these investments grow any faster than comparable cities that do not, and the fans who do in fact benefit have median incomes 84 percent above the average.[13] Why, the IAF wants to know, should the city spend funds to subsidize the better-off when there are few economic gains and when the funds could be used either to underwrite more evenly distributed economic development projects or to finance human development projects such as education, training, and after-school programs?

Although the IAF was not able to block subsidies of the Alamodome, it has changed the terms of the economic development discussion in its communities. In the Valley, the economic development officials in both Brownsville and McAllen now aver that subsidies will go only to employers who pay living wages. In San Antonio, COPS succeeded in attaching living wage requirements to subsidies to new and expanding hotels in the city. In addition, as I will describe momentarily, the statewide IAF network succeeded during the 2001 legislative season in passing a bill to permit economic development funds that had previously been earmarked only for physical projects to be used also for training and after-school programs.

Preparing People for Work

Educators are offended, and rightly so, when the purposes of schooling are reduced to economic outcomes. Education is about citizenship, learning to think and to enjoy culture, and much else besides work. Nonetheless, education is inextricably linked to economic outcomes. At an IAF education conference in Dallas the central motivating fact was that at the beginning of the new century college graduates earned over 40 percent more than high school graduates, and this gap has grown substantially over the past decade.[14] The federal government projects that although jobs that require an associates degree or more accounted for 25 percent of jobs in 1998, they will account for 40 percent of job growth between 1998 and 2008.[15]

The IAF's first experience with schools was driven by the IAF organization in Fort Worth, Allied Communities of Tarrent (ACT), led by an African-American minister, Nehemiah Davis.[16] Morningside Middle School, in a neighborhood where ACT was active, was a low-performing school, gang and drug ridden. ACT leaders and organizers (lead organizer Sister Mignonne Konecny and Perry Perkins) proceeded in IAF fashion to hold relational meetings with parents and teachers as well as with city leaders. The IAF approach was to find a way to improve the situation by making parents active participants inside the school. Working with a cooperative principal, ACT identified parents who could be strong leaders and organized training sessions and small assemblies on both IAF doctrine regarding leadership and politics and also on education issues.

Over time, the role of the parent community evolved. The goals at first were simply to help parents feel comfortable interacting with school personnel and helping their children with homework. Gradually the parents formed teams to work on school curriculum issues and programs, such as after-school programs. Finally, the parental teams (and teachers) became active in broader community issues, such as traffic and crime, for example, working to shut down a local store selling alcohol, which was located too near the school. Many of the parents and teachers also became active in the larger agenda of ACT and the Texas IAF network.

The Morningside experience was so effective that the IAF began to establish Alliance Schools throughout the state. Although the details vary, the basic story was constant. School reform is viewed as an organizing problem, and teachers and parents are brought together via relational meetings and are trained in leadership skills. They then initiate a variety of reforms in their schools, gradually becoming more ambitious in their objectives both for their schools and for their community.

The story of Berta, a leader in Valley Interfaith, offers a good illustration of both how the Alliance Schools provides the IAF with an institutional base, other than churches, for identifying and organizing leaders and how participation in the effort can help transform the leaders' views of what is possible in working with schools.

Born in the Valley, Berta is a community aide in a local school. Every summer she, along with her husband and three children, worked the harvest in Colorado, Washington, Idaho, and Iowa. Berta connected with Valley Interfaith when her school became an Alliance School:

> And I started going, I got involved. You know, I could see the changes that would come about when the people got organized. When the people worked together for the one same thing. And, you know I saw that it would work.

When we asked Berta what she thought the Alliance Schools effort had accomplished, she gave an example of a walkway that the school needed to protect children from the rain:

> I spoke to the school board, which is something that I had never in my whole life imagined I was capable of doing. But through the association with the other members of the Valley Interfaith, they gave me the courage and they gave me their backing also. I knew that there were some more people there that were behind me. So we went out there, myself, one of the students, and one of the teachers. That was on a Monday evening. Friday afternoon at three o'clock when the bell rang, there was already guys out here digging holes to put the poles for the covered walkway.
>
> I tell a lot of my parents here, okay, maybe you might have one issue and maybe she might have another one and I have something else, but if we work all together and focus on one of them and get that finished and then maybe focus on the next one, you know, and take it like that. Because if one of us is going to pull in a different direction, we're not going to accomplish anything. But if we all work together, it can be done. Because we've seen it. We've seen that it can be done.

In addition to physical improvements, the Alliance School program also emphasizes educational initiatives, such as the expansion of enriched after-school programs, as well as attention to best education practice. It frequently invites educational leaders from around the country to run training sessions for Alliance School leaders.

In the Valley there are now twenty-three Alliance Schools. A flagship of the effort is Sam Houston elementary school in McAllen, the oldest public school in that city, which serves families who attend St. Joseph the Worker.[17] In 1994, the principal and some staff attended a statewide Alliance Schools conference and began serious discussions about the possibility of Sam Houston becoming an Alliance School. Teachers expressed a variety of concerns, most important the fear of losing power to Valley Interfaith and to parents. As the principal commented, "Teachers are afraid that Valley Interfaith is going to come in and tell them what to do . . . [and that parents] could become a monster."[18]

These fears were assuaged in part by conversations between the principal and the teachers, and then teachers were trained in the basics of IAF organizing: how to do one-on-ones with each other and with parents. While working with teachers, Valley Interfaith organized house meetings of parents, during which a variety of issues regarding the neighborhood and the school surfaced, such as unlighted back alleys that students walked through on the way to and from school, abandoned housing, drugs, and crime. Teachers attended these meetings and also began to speak with parents about how they could better work with their children at home, supporting them in their schoolwork. Over time a community of interest developed between the parents and the teachers, in part focusing on neighborhood issues and in part focusing on how to improve what went on inside the school building.

Meetings of parents and teachers were arranged with city officials. The parents and teachers organized a "Kids Action Assembly," which more than three hundred parents attended. The city began to respond: a new police substation was opened near the school, an after-school program was funded, and streets were cleaned up. In addition, parents signed a "parent contract" in which they agreed to ask their children about homework each night at dinner and to insist that it be done. Teachers continued to meet with parents in house meetings to discuss new course material and new curricular ideas.

Boston College Professor of Education Dennis Shirley has analyzed the school's standardized test scores and shows that the school outperformed both district and state averages and that the economically disadvantaged students in the school did better than the comparison group in Texas at each grade level.[19]

After more than a decade of organizing in schools, the IAF Alliance

Schools network today comprises 129 schools in twenty school districts and receives millions of dollars of state funding. Every year an Alliance School education conference attracts more than a thousand parents, teachers, principals, and state officials from throughout Texas. Dennis Shirley found that between 1993 and 1996, for elementary schools, middle schools, and high school students in the tenth grade, the percentage increase in the pass rate for the Alliance Schools far exceeded the statewide percentage increase in pass rates.[20] More recently, according to data provided by the IAF, between 1999 and 2000, the pass rate on the Texas achievement tests increased by 3.6 percent statewide in Alliance Schools, compared with 1.8 percent statewide. Individual success stories are even more dramatic. At Zavala elementary school in Austin, the pass rate on the state writing test increased from 7 percent in 1991 to 93 percent in 1996. At Roosevelt High School in Dallas, the math pass rate went from 15 percent to 70 percent.[21]

The Alliance Schools also provide the IAF with an alternative institutional base for organizing. Now, in addition to religious congregations, the IAF can go into a community and organize through the schools. This maintains the fundamental strategy of organizing via institutions, but it also gives the IAF access to groups of people whom they might not reach through churches.

Job Training and Job Access

School reform is a long-term strategy. It cannot help the adults who are already struggling to find good jobs, and even in the best of all worlds, there will always be adults for whom the schools have failed. For these people, a job-training strategy is important.

The IAF experience with job training began in January 1990, when Levi Strauss closed a plant in San Antonio that had employed more than a thousand people, many of them connected to COPS and Metro Alliance. Following this closure, the two IAF organizations started to investigate the economic situation of their members. In house meetings people told stories of past unsatisfactory experiences with training programs, particularly those in which no recognized certificate or diploma resulted, or in which there were no available jobs after the training period.

In the spring of 1991, a job-training core committee was formed of forty COPS and Metro Alliance leaders. Their work was a classic example of the extent to which leaders are able to become directly involved in formulating policy and programs. The committee met bimonthly for almost two years and worked on three fronts. The first was the design of the training program, Project QUEST. The committee and the IAF organizations then worked to obtain job commitments from the business community. In the end, they were able to generate 650 commitments to hire QUEST graduates. As a result, the people entering the program knew that there were jobs on the other end and that the training itself could be tailored to actual job requirements. Third, the organizations struggled to raise funds. They put considerable pressure on the city via accountability sessions and lobbying. In addition, because the IAF network had played an important role in the election of Ann Richards as governor (she gave a strong performance in accountability sessions and benefited from the IAF get-out-the-vote effort), the organizations were able to tap into state funds.[22]

QUEST was organized as a distinct entity with its own staff. Representatives of IAF organizations, as well as members of the local business community, sit on its board. The IAF organizations play a central role in obtaining continued funding for QUEST and in promoting and protecting it. COPS and Metro have been careful not to treat QUEST as a patronage operation nor as a source of jobs for their members (as has happened with some other efforts organized by community-based groups). The first two directors of QUEST were Anglo ex-military men with no connection to the IAF, and since the beginning of the program the IAF has insisted on entirely merit-based staffing.

To see what makes QUEST special, it is necessary to understand the nature of the typical job-training program: they are quick and dirty. Not only are these programs brief, but they provide no financial support to enrollees. These two features are obviously interrelated: a long-term program is difficult to sustain without some kind of assistance. Short-term programs are also politically appealing. They enable public officials to serve the largest number of people possible, a politically desirable goal even if the results are poor. In addition, most training programs operate "on spec." That is, they train people and hope that jobs will be available. All this adds up to very modest results. The evaluation literature suggests that the gains from typical training programs are not very large and are sometimes zero.[23]

QUEST was very self-conscious about designing a very different model. The program began with a commitment from firms of 650 jobs for the program's graduates. The training could be designed—in cooperation with the employers—for what would be needed upon graduation, and the trainees had a goal that maintained morale throughout the effort. The power of COPS and Metro Alliance was obviously crucial in obtaining these commitments. QUEST training was long term, averaging around eighteen months, and took place in community colleges. The long-term character of the effort meant that real skills were taught. The use of the community colleges relieved the program of the need to invest in costly infrastructure and meant that all training would be done by professional staff. Throughout the program QUEST was able to provide modest financial support to trainees to help them deal with life's emergencies: a rent crisis, medical issues, child care, and the like. Although the trainees provided most of their own financial support, via part-time jobs or family support or welfare, the availability of some emergency funds was crucial and further distinguished QUEST from standard programs.

When I interviewed QUEST participants in several focus groups, many made comments like the following:

"Doors have been opened for me. I'm a lot better off than I was two years ago."

"I see somewhere I'll be instead of moving from job to job."

"Instead of waking up every day and being miserable, I think more about myself."

"I see QUEST as a shaky ladder. It's not the best thing, but I'm climbing out of a hole and moving in the right direction."

More formal evaluation supports these statements. In 1996 I was asked by the Ford Foundation to evaluate Project QUEST. Over the course of a year, I collected preenrollment data on all people who had attended QUEST, whether or not they had completed the program, and did a follow-up survey to learn their postprogram status. The quantitative evaluation showed that QUEST led to substantial gains for its participants, gains that far exceed those of typical training efforts. I estimated the typical annual earnings gain was between forty-nine hundred and seventy-five hundred dollars, with the expected payoff of costs being a very short three years.[24]

Most training programs, no matter how good, are limited in their achievements to the gains (if any) experienced by their clients. This is a problem, because these programs are ultimately small relative to the size of the labor market, and their overall impacts are consequently modest. QUEST has been more ambitious and has had more extensive impacts in three respects: it altered the pay and hiring practices of employers, it improved the community colleges for all of that system's students, and it was linked to the broader organizing goals of COPS and Metro Alliance. QUEST, although superficially designed as a traditional job-training program, acted as an advocate for the people it represented. It is an intermediary that exercised power in the labor market.

QUEST affected wage levels by insisting that employers pay trainees a living wage, and in some instances this led firms to increase the pay for certain categories of jobs. It altered employer hiring patterns by demonstrating that skilled employees can be drawn from pools of workers that the San Antonio employer community had previously ignored. QUEST also led to important changes in how the local community colleges operate, changes that redounded to the benefit of many more students than just the QUEST enrollees. These changes include the creation of a Remediation Institute (which prepared people to pass the entry exam and hence take credit courses), open not only to QUEST trainees but to all people who attend the schools, and various forms of curricular reform that make the programs more accessible. As a consequence of these efforts, the impact of QUEST is greater than simply the gains achieved by clients.

Given the success of QUEST, and the substantial positive publicity it generated, it is surprising but nonetheless true that the program has had difficulty securing a stable funding base. The original funding was a combination of city and state support, with a modest amount of foundation financing, but over time the public resources have fluctuated. This has meant that enrollment levels have not been stable, and the organizations had to engage in an annual or a biannual struggle for resources. In response to this problem, and also as a way of linking the training program to organizing efforts in San Antonio, the state IAF network launched a drive to permit the use of economic development funds for human development programs. The economic development funds were generated as a small fraction of the city sales tax, but state law required that the money be used only for physical projects. The IAF's proposed state legislation permitted their use for training programs, after-school programs, and the like.

Achieving passage of this legislation, dubbed the Human Development Fund, proved to be a major battle, a battle that was waged on two fronts. The mayor of San Antonio supported the idea but wanted the funds to be controlled by an independent public/private corporation. The IAF viewed this as a tactic to remove control of the monies from politics, that is, from the purview of COPS and Metro Alliance. At the state level, economic development officials from various cities, all of whom had plans to use their local sales tax funds for physical projects, opposed the effort. The IAF network mobilized to pass their version of the bill, with COPS and Metro Alliance taking the lead. Elizabeth Valdez, the lead organizer in San Antonio, virtually lived in Austin in the spring of 2001, and every day carloads, and on some occasions busloads, of leaders from around the state traveled to Austin to lobby their legislators. In the end, a compromise was reached with the mayor of San Antonio on how the funds would be managed, and because of vigorous work in Austin, the bill passed through the Republican legislature and was signed by the Republican governor.

The QUEST model has been replicated in the IAF network, although different cities have modified it in various ways. In the Valley Project, VIDA offers shorter-term customized training in cooperation with firms, as well as the standard QUEST model. This works well, provided that the hiring commitments from the firms are very strong and are at acceptable wages. Capital Idea, the program in Austin, also offers the customized option and has a component of the program aimed at high school dropouts that brings them up to the level that permits them to enter the "classic QUEST" track. In Tucson, Job Path requires that its graduates pay the program back either financially or via community service. QUEST-like programs have also been established by IAF organizations in El Paso and Dallas. The IAF network is aggressive in promoting learning across the projects and holds frequent training workshops.

Building Power in the Labor Market

Job training and education reform are worthwhile endeavors. However, they have a certain "pack your own parachute" quality. They place the burden on the individual to make him- or herself more attractive to the labor market, but they do not question how the labor market works. They accept the structure and try to fit people in. A second difficulty leaps out of the occupational projections cited earlier. Although it is true that 40 percent of new jobs will require an associates degree and that this is a higher figure than in the past, it also follows that 60 percent of jobs—more than half—still demand relatively little education. Some of these jobs will be held by young people looking for only casual work, but a surprisingly, and depressingly, large fraction are held by adults who are trying to support families.[25] The realities of the job market are that training is not enough and that it is necessary to address the quality of jobs directly.

Living wage campaigns are a step in this direction, but they do not necessarily build the kind of long-lasting power organizations that are the objective of the IAF. The challenge is to move from living wage campaigns to organization building.

The Southwestern IAF network has already had some experience along these lines. In Omaha, Nebraska (which is considered part of the Southwest for IAF organization chart purposes), the local IAF affiliate held house meetings with employees—mostly immigrants—in the city's meatpacking industry. These house meetings were organized out of the churches, since it was easier, and safer, to contact workers via their congregations than at the workplace. From the house meetings emerged the idea of establishing health clinics to assist with occupational injuries, a frequent problem in the packing industry. The success of the health clinics laid the basis for pressing the governor (a Republican) to investigate health and safety issues in the plants. Not only did he do this, but remarkably, he issued a statement supporting the workers' right to organize. From all this emerged a union drive, in cooperation with the United Food and Commercial Workers, that to date has won two organizing elections.

Valley Interfaith is about to test these lessons in a big way. First it is beginning a drive to push for living wages in the health care sector.

Characteristically, the organization is proceeding on two fronts. The leaders are conducting research on the industry, gathering data on wage levels and on the financing mechanisms and the profitability of the local institutions. Second, the leaders are meeting with CEOs of the large area hospitals. The IAF's approach toward the business community is rarely purely oppositional. It is typically willing to work with the more progressive elements of that community, splitting them off from their more regressive colleagues, and this drive is no exception.

An even more dramatic initiative is also under way in the Valley. Valley Interfaith is beginning to build an employees' association. This drive has proceeded in typical IAF fashion. On a Sunday (termed by Valley Interfaith a "Workers' Sunday"), the pastor preaches on religious social doctrine regarding work. At the end of the service people are asked to attend house meetings if they are interested in discussing work-related issues. At the house meetings people are asked, as Judy Donovan puts it, to "tell a story about how they learned about work values."

The house meetings are followed up with individual one-on-one meetings with organizers. The goal is to identify potential leaders who want to build the association. To date, these efforts have identified about nine hundred people who have an interest in building a workers' association. About half of these had no prior contact with Valley Interfaith. The people who are interested come from disparate parts of the Valley economy. They include low-wage health care workers, public employees, workers who were laid off when the Valley's apparel plants closed and who find themselves trapped in a seemingly endless cycle of training programs that lead nowhere, call center employees, and taxi drivers. When people talk about what is motivating them to participate, the issues that are most commonly mentioned include health insurance, dignity at work, and career ladders.

The next step in this process will be a longer series of training workshops that will include economic education (sessions on how the economy works, labor history, and the like), as well as sessions on IAF principles of organizing. This will be followed by creating an organization and establishing a dues structure. The organization will take its place alongside the churches and Alliance Schools as an institutional member of Valley Interfaith.

As always, the organizing is aimed at surfacing issues and identifying talent, that is, people who have some energy and some anger around the issues and around whom the organization can be built. What is not yet clear is exactly what an employees association will do. It will not be a union that bargains contracts with employers, though over time it might evolve in this direction. It could, however, become an external political force in the labor market, putting pressure on some employers around wages. It might also provide services, such as training, job-finding assistance, or health care, to its members. All this is speculative, but the fact that the effort is under way shows how the IAF has encouraged its labor market strategies to evolve.

The Frontiers and the Boundaries of Community Strategies

The early signature issues of the IAF, protecting poor neighborhoods from flooding in San Antonio and colonias in the Valley, were neighborhood-based. The IAF continues to address neighborhood issues as it works on school reform and improvements such as parks, libraries, health clinics, and housing. Jobs, however, are different. In addressing labor market concerns, the IAF has moved successfully beyond place-based or community organizing and has proved its ability to operate on a larger and more diffuse stage.

In an age of globalization, these strategies have shown that much can be accomplished at the local level. This fits well with a strong new current of thinking about regional economic development. Current interest in regions where clusters of firms seem to innovate and grow in a mixed state of cooperation and competition point to the continued importance of the local.[26] From Silicon Valley in California to Media Alley in New York City to the Research Triangle area in North Carolina to conglomerations of machine tool shops in western Massachusetts, the vitality of the local seems reaffirmed even as the world seems increasingly tied together.

The hard fact, however, is that much of what happens to people in the job market is the result of decisions made at even further remove than the city or the state. Some of these decisions are made by firms as they choose where to locate, where to expand employment, and where to reduce it. Others are decisions made in Washington, as, for example, minimum wages are increased or allowed to stagnate or laws affecting the ease of union organization are passed or rejected. There are also larger trends that diffuse through the business world. An example is the use of contingent employment. Whereas in the past, temporary work was used only to deal with absences or with peak load periods, today firms are increasingly making use of temporary work as part of their ordinary way of doing business.[27] This has implications for job security, benefits coverage, and wage levels.[28]

It is obvious that policies focused on cities or even states, no matter how well conceived, cannot address all of these issues. To an important extent what happens within communities is shaped by forces without. This does not mean, however, that local labor market policies are ineffective. As we have seen, the IAF initiatives have accomplished a great deal both economically and politically. Furthermore, vigorous organizing around the job market provides the basis for moving the arena of action to higher levels. The success of Project QUEST led, for example, to an effective campaign at the state level for the Human Development Fund. Eventually, though not tomorrow, the IAF efforts can move to the national level. This will require coalitions with unions and with other progressive groups, a topic of the next chapter. But for now, it is important to understand the limitations of local action but not to be discouraged by them.

Cutting across these efforts are three broader themes. First, it is important to see how the IAF labor market efforts have evolved and broadened over time. The early training initiatives, though of high quality, were also very traditional in their strategy and aspirations. The workers' association, on the other hand, is cutting edge. Over the years the IAF has engaged in a process of self-reflection and learning, and the evolution of its approach to the labor market shows this.

Second, like everything else it does, the IAF views its labor market programs not as ends in themselves but as vehicles for building broad-based power organizations. The training programs have given the organizations substantial credibility in their communities, both in the neighborhoods and among businesspeople. In addition, the IAF is working to organize the programs' graduates so that over time they can act as a powerful voice in the labor market. In a similar pattern, the success of the Valley's living wage campaign laid the foundation for initiating the employees' association. There is a dynamic relationship between program and power. Good programs provide a foundation for extending organizing, and this in turn provides the basis for creating yet more expansive programs.

Finally, the IAF has not been willing to take labor market outcomes as given and simply try to fit people in. Rather, the organizations have worked hard to improve the structure of the labor market: the quality of jobs, the hiring channels of employers, and the performance of educational institutions. Taken as whole, the IAF has the most sophisticated and comprehensive approach to community labor market issues in the nation.

Chapter 6

Gathering Power

Polls show that far more Americans support progressive positions on the issues than is reflected in politics as it is practiced. This is true among the electorate and even more so among the half of the eligible population that does not vote.[1] The failure of progressives to mobilize their constituency, and to expand it, cannot be explained simply by bad luck or determined adversaries. Certainly these play some role. But at the end of the day progressives will make progress only by rethinking how to organize. The Washington-centric approach is inadequate. Crafting better positions or more persuasive slogans will not capture the long-term loyalty of progressive constituencies. The key to success is finding ways to effectively mobilize people in their communities. Progressives also need to recognize that although Americans share their positions on the issues Americans are also strongly driven by values. Progressives need to find a way to take traditional religious and secular values seriously.

The IAF offers a model of successful mobilization. Its emphasis on developing leaders and transforming people's views of what they can accomplish builds a level of commitment that is absent in the sound-bite strategy that has dominated politics in recent years. The broad-based nature of IAF organizations and their roots in religious communities provide a political foundation that is stronger, more durable, and more consistent with traditional American values than is achieved by any other progressive effort. The importance of the IAF is therefore twofold. Its own efforts do, and will, constitute an important component of any progressive coalition. In addition, the IAF offers an important model—strategies and practices—for efforts by other progressive organizations to grow and expand their influence.

The IAF model also speaks to themes that have emerged in recent work by social scientists regarding the trajectory of American social institutions and politics. Writing from different perspectives, these scholars have reached a common diagnosis that the intermediary institutions supporting effective politics in America have atrophied, that broadly shared community values are less widely respected that in the past, and that American politics has become thin and procedural, focusing too much on formal rights and too little on real citizen participation.

The IAF Model of Politics

The IAF self-consciously reflects on what it does. This self-awareness plays an important organizational role because, as we saw in chapter 2, it enables the IAF to continuously reinforce its culture. It also makes it relatively easy to identify the core elements of the IAF approach toward politics, which are creating agency, politics as community, identifying interests, building broad-based organizations, and incorporating values.

Agency simply means people having the capacity and the opportunity to be political, to have a say in how policies are framed and decisions made. Without agency, we are left with what Benjamin Barber calls "thin democracy," a system from which the best that can be expected is that people elect the elites who do the real work of politics and government.[2] This form of representation alienates its constituents and leads to the falling participation and the tilt toward the top that characterizes modern politics. To create agency, an IAF organizer spends more time identifying and developing leaders than doing any other activity. The leaders are systematically taught how to do politics, and they are pushed to exercise these new skills. They learn and practice concrete skills: how to organize meetings, research issues, confront public officials. More significantly, however, they learn a new mind-set about themselves and about politics.

The notion of "politics as community" stands in contrast to how politics is typically practiced today: isolated individuals on the receiving end of mail and commercials. The idea of a politics as being, at its core, a community of people working on problems has a long provenance in political theory, but it has been lost in modern practice. In his discussion of communities of action (a term taken from philosopher Hannah Arendt, who in turn drew from Aristotle), Michael Piore writes:

> Such communities . . . are created through the interaction among individuals. That interaction is the process through which individuals define themselves, create their identities, and simultaneously define the community and create its identify in the broader social context in which it exists.[3]

The IAF revives this tradition in several ways. At the core of IAF processes is the relational techniques of one-on-one conversations and house meetings. In frequent meetings and assemblies, people come together to read and discuss political and economic writing and to relate it to their day-to-day struggles. These meetings and workshops are extended conversations out of which are created a political agenda. Again, Benjamin Barber: "At the heart of strong democracy is talk."[4] It is through talk that people develop new conceptions of their identities and their interests. The relationships and conversations that the IAF encourages enable people to enlarge their view of themselves and their community. They come to understand that what they had seen as privatized concerns are really social. As they listen to their neighbors' stories, the leaders develop a broader conception of a problem and an appreciation of what it will take to fix it. This new perspective, when combined with the heightened sense of agency, provides the energy that drives the organization and shapes its politics.

Through conversations IAF leaders come to understand their interests, and this brings us to the third core element of IAF political theory. The IAF has a conception of interest that is at once crude and subtle. The IAF has an unapologetic view of what motivates people. Everyone, from an IAF organizer to a rapacious land developer, is driven by self-interest. There is a story about Alinsky in which he, speaking to a group of clergy, cast a biblical conversation between God and Moses as an example of Moses cleverly manipulating God by appealing to his self-interest in "being Number One."[5]

The organization believes that the only reliable way to organize people is to identify and appeal to this self-interest. No other motivation is as durable. The focus on self-interest means that the IAF is very aware that interests can be in conflict with each other. This acceptance of conflict distinguishes the IAF from some of the more utopian views of social reform.

In her study of a New England town meeting and cooperatively run hotline, political scientist Jane Mansbridge distinguished between what she terms "unitary" and "adversarial" democracy.[6] In unitary democracy, the interests of people are the same, and although there may debate, it is about the best way to achieve the goals that everyone shares. In adversarial democracy, interests diverge and decisions have to be made about whose ox gets gored. The IAF view of the world is very much in the adversarial camp. On virtually every issue, from requiring investment in water in the colonias to fighting for living wage ordinances, the IAF will point to what are the interests of "organized money" and what are the interests of "organized people." Even with what appear to be less contentious issues, such as school reform, conflicts emerge. In the 2001 legislative session in Texas, the IAF had to fight to preserve the funding for the Alliance Schools against an effort by a well-connected educational organization that wanted the funds to support its own initiatives.

The IAF's stark view of self-interest and human nature presents serious risks. The IAF appears to accept a radical individualism in which each person is out for him- or herself. People motivated only by their self-interest appear to be very much like classic "economic man," driven only to satisfy their own needs and seeking to maximize their personal utility. This is a perspective that has proved fruitful in a wide range of social sciences but that poses serious difficulties for those interested in communities and in organizing. How, for example, can organizers overcome the free-rider behaviors that are inherent in this view of human motivation? What role can social norms and values and altruism play in such a world? How can the IAF emphasis on relationships and being "relational" be reconciled with such a radical individualism?

The second risk run by the focus on self-interest is that it opens the door to reducing the analysis of what motivates people to crude materialist categories. Combining an "economic man" perspective with the kinds of issues that interest the IAF—living wages, restraining development, health insurance, and so on—makes it a short step to identify an unchanging self-interest of businesspeople as opposition to progressive initiatives. After all, isn't it always in the interest of firms to pay as little as they can get away with and still recruit labor? By the same token, it is tempting to read the self-interest of the poor and working-class IAF constituencies as simply a reflection of their place in the economic hierarchy.

The IAF understanding of how self-interest is formed avoids these twin traps. Ernie Cortes argues that to organize an individual it is crucial to understand that person's story, his or her narrative. This involves learning what people want to do with their life and what is in their long-term, as well as short-term, interest. This understanding takes the concept of self-interest well beyond simple materialistic considerations. The IAF has a slogan, "no permanent allies, no permanent enemies," that reflects a realistic view of the world but that also shields it against a shallow reading of self-interest. As the earlier example of San Antonio banker Tom Frost illustrates, people's understanding of their self-interest can change even though their position in the economic structure is stable. Frost went from being an opponent of COPS to serving on the board of Project QUEST and working with COPS at the state level on various legislative issues.

The deeper point is that in the IAF view self-interest is relational. A person's understanding of his or her self-interest emerges out of interaction with other people—the one-on-ones and house meetings. Organizing, Ernie Cortes argues, "is not what you do, but whom you do it with." An individual might go into a house meeting with one view of what is important to him or her and come out with another. This refined perspective, which reflects the interaction that took place, is also likely to entail an interpretation of self-interest that has a significant other-regarding component. In their introduction to *Democracy in America*, Harvey Mansfield and Delba Winthrop explain that de Tocqueville believed that in associations (such as the IAF) "individuals influence one another, persuade others, and perhaps even change mores. . . . Thus 'the heart is enlarged, and the human mind is developed.'"[7] Summarizing more recent social science thinking on this theme, Jane Mansbridge writes, "People who become active, especially in causes directed at some version of the public interest, sometimes find that they themselves have changed in the course of their activity."[8]

The IAF view is not naïve about the persuasive capacity of conversation and relationships. It also believes that the only two sources of power are "organized people and organized money" and that without power its people will get nowhere in politics. However, with that power in hand, what determines people's self-interest is more complicated than a simple mapping of their economic status would suggest.

It is true that sometimes the IAF view of interest simply turns people off. The advocates of the status quo recognize this and often use the language of "special interests" as a weapon. Recall that in struggles over single-member district campaigns, from San Antonio in the 1970s to McAllen in 2001, the elites claimed to speak for the common interest and attacked the reformers as advocates of more narrow special interests.[9] This line of attack was chosen because it strikes a chord. The authors of *Habits of the Heart*, summarizing the views of the people they interviewed, conclude that "politics connotes something morally unsavory. . . . To the extent that many of those we talked to see politics as meaning the politics of interest, they regard it as not entirely legitimate morally."[10] For these people, and presumably for a broad cross-section of Americans, any organized group that seems able to operate effectively within the political system is seen as a "special interest" and is, if not disliked, viewed with considerable suspicion.

It also has to be recognized that even though we live in an adversarial world the idea of unitary democracy seems more attractive than adversarial democracy. Recall that the suburbanites with whom I spoke did not like the language of power, and my students frequently ask why the IAF seemed so conflictual. In fact, the IAF is always willing to compromise and take half a loaf. Its ability to compromise and engage in a political give-and-take is evident in virtually every issue it deals with. It avoids, in Ernie Cortes's words, "letting the best solution get in the way of a good solution." However, it is also true that the IAF does not believe that simple consensus can be effective in the world as it is. The IAF believes that politics is driven in important measure by power and clashing interests, and the ultimate objective of the organization is to give its people the standing required to be effective given this reality.

The positions that the IAF takes are themselves the result of an internal process of discussion and compromise. The IAF, as we have seen, characterizes itself as a "broad-based" organization. This means that it is neither a civic group, which delivers services, nor a movement, focused on one issue or one interest group. Rather, the IAF seeks to encompass a diverse set of interests within one organization. This structure forces leaders to engage in an internal political process in which they both identify and articulate their own interests and then make compromises with others in order to arrive at common positions. In such a setup the individualistic tendencies of purely self-regarding behavior are managed and muted.

Creating broad-based organizations is in fact the fourth principle of IAF politics. In part this flows from how the IAF goes about organizing through institutions. Because it is an "organization of organizations," and because the constituent organizations are diverse, the IAF by its very nature is broad-based. The broad-based character of the IAF also forces it to search for common interests and issues that cut across its constituent elements. This process also introduces an important measure of realism in debates about issues, since the attention and public resources that the organization believes should be devoted to one topic have to be tempered by the fact that there are other interests sitting around the table. The broad-based character of the organization helps avoid the "mischief of faction" that led James Madison to be wary of organized interests.

Taken together, the IAF's emphasis on agency, power, self-interest, and being broad-based is a recipe for pragmatism. The IAF is nonideological and typically willing to cut a deal. Another IAF slogan urges its members to focus on "the world as it is and not the world as it should be." This lack of ideology has characterized the organization throughout its life, and New Left critics of Alinsky were particularly exercised by the organization's pragmatism.[11] However, although the IAF is not ideological, it is value-based, and this is the final important characteristic of its politics.

In both its organizing and its public presentation of issues the IAF draws from Judeo-Christian religious teaching. These values motivate members and provide a rationale for the positions IAF organizations take. The central place of values within the IAF has several advantages. It is a source of energy and motivation. It enables the IAF to connect with mainstream American concerns about the erosion of values in public and private life, and by the same token it inoculates the organization from charges that it is radical or "un-American." There may be a price to be paid for this focus, because important elements of a potential progressive coalition are suspicious, if not hostile, to ceding a central role to organized religion in politics. On balance, however, the IAF experience clearly suggests that the role it accords to values is a significant source of organizational strength.

The IAF and Social Theory

IAF leaders are not alone in their concerns about the nature of political life in the United States. Social scientists writing from several different perspectives have hit upon a broad set of ideas that they hold in common. At their core is a concern that both politics and society have become attenuated with too few opportunities for membership or participation. On the one hand, civil society—the groups and associations that constitute the fabric of daily life—has declined in recent years. By the same token, politics itself is increasingly procedural and distant, focused more on legal rights and formal representation than on participation. The solution is a revival of community, stronger associations and groups, and a shift in politics toward more opportunities for citizens to deliberate and decide. All of this, of course, is just what the IAF is about. However, at the same time that it is worthwhile to link the IAF to these more abstract concerns, it is also important to avoid homogenizing the IAF model so that it easily accommodates social theory du jour.

Certainly the most well-known analysis along these lines is the argument developed by Robert Putnam regarding the decline of civil society.[12] Putnam amasses an impressive and convincing array of data to show that over the past several decades membership and participation in churches, unions, civic groups, social groups, and political groups have evinced a common downward trend. Alexis de Tocqueville long ago identified the density of these American associations as the distinctive characteristic of our society, and many good things—civic-mindedness, political participation, charity, and even physical health—are thought to flow from these institutions. That they are decaying is surely cause for serious concern.

Interestingly enough, the IAF anticipated by at least a decade the current round of concern with civil society. In the 1978 manifesto *Organizing for Family and Congregation* (a document that is still used in IAF training), Ed Chambers wrote, "Our country is in the kind of crisis that both Madison and de Tocqueville warned us about. The intermediate voluntary institutions —including churches—are ineffectual in a power relationship with the powerful. As a result the middle is collapsing."[13] Clearly the IAF is focused on rebuilding civil society. The IAF organization itself is a de Toquevillian intermediary organization, and the IAF puts substantial resources into what Ernie Cortes terms "reweaving the social fabric," via Congregational Development, Alliance Schools, and the IAF's work with unions.[14]

Although it is attractive and sensible to see the IAF as a piece of a solution to the growing deficit in social capital, there is a significant difference of spirit between the IAF and the social capital story. This difference is hinted at in the Chambers quote above, when he twice uses the term *power*. At its base the IAF wants to alter what it views as an imbalance in power, and it assumes and accepts that as part of its efforts it will encourage and engage in political conflict.

The spirit of the social capital argument is different. Although Putnam and other authors in this tradition certainly are cognizant of and worried about political and social inequality, this is not their core concern. In the hands of social-capitalists, a choral society and a political movement are roughly equivalent. When Putnam discusses politics (in both America and Italy, the scene of his first research on social capital), it is typically in terms of the kind of "good government" issues—efficiency, honesty—that typified the concerns of Progressives at the turn of the last century. Yet, as we saw in chapter 4, these issues are often a mask for elite control. For example, although Putnam is very enthusiastic about the creativity of the early-twentieth-century Progressives in building up a wide variety of social capital institutions, it is also the case that immediately after this period America lived through over a decade of conservative reaction and suppression of immigrant and working-class initiatives. The burst of Progressive creativity was unaccompanied by any success in building political power by those at the bottom. Another illustration of the difference in spirit between the IAF and social capital stories is that when Putnam addresses what changes should occur today in the American workplace, as part of his discussion of how to remedy America's social capital deficit, he offers some important and creative solutions but does not discuss rebuilding the power of the union movement.[15]

A step toward a more political argument is taken by those who dub themselves "communitarian." Etzioni and other communitarians are very much concerned with the importance of values in social life and politics.[16] And the communitarians recognize that unequal economic outcomes can undermine the sense of community that they value.[17] But the communitarians also search for consensus, for a set of beliefs to which all citizens can and should subscribe. The IAF might not deny that these foundational beliefs are valuable, but again the focus is elsewhere. When, for example, it comes to a living wage campaign, the IAF recognizes that there are inevitably conflicting interests at stake and there are also quite different values and ideas in play about the meaning of the "market" and what standing should be accorded to different ideas about wage setting. If a core set of norms or values had to be defined, who is to say whether the norm of the market or the norm of equitable distribution should win out? Conflicts of this nature, which are at the core of what the IAF is about, do not fit comfortably in a communitarian framework.

Along with social capitalists and writers in the communitarian spirit, the IAF shares a deep concern with the vitality of community institutions and with values. It diverges from them because the IAF is fundamentally about politics and power. As such the IAF model has more in common with theories that recognize the importance of community and values but are focused on how politics is done.

Benjamin Barber and Michael Sandel attack a vision of politics grounded in the ideal of isolated autonomous citizens who enjoy a set of legally protected rights but whose politics are not rooted in real participation in self-government.[18] Barber calls this model "thin democracy," whereas Sandel terms it the "procedural republic." The intellectual origins of thin democracy rest on two pillars. The first is a vision of human nature in which everyone is out to maximize their own well-being without regard to anyone else's interest. There is no respect, in this perspective, for community or civil society as a source of values, norms, and constraints on junglelike behavior. This is a perspective that has deep roots in both political theory (think of Hobbes) and that also underlies the classic model of economic man. Combined with this view of human nature is a certain elitism, a disrespect for the capacity of citizens to participate in any real way in their governance. In some hands this elitism is rooted in antidemocratic impulses; in others it emerges from the view that the modern world is too complicated for people to play a substantive role in governance.

The practical consequence of these views is a political system that places heavy emphasis on representative government, in which the only role of the citizen is to vote for someone else who will do the real work. Protections against the depredations of government rest in elaborated legal rights and not in a healthy active citizenry. "Thin democracy," Barber complains, "yields neither the pleasures of participation nor the fellowship of civic association, neither the autonomy and self-governance of continuous political activity nor the enlarging mutuality of . . . deliberation, decision, and work."[19]

There are important virtues to this political model, most important that it seeks to protect people from the tyranny of the majority. It creates a zone of freedom that is precious and that the critics of the model seem to undervalue. But at the same time, defining politics entirely in these terms loses too much. Because it essentially gives up on the idea of community, and because it gives very short shrift to the importance of a common enterprise, this "thin" view of democracy leads to a situation in which people are no longer engaged in politics. As important as elections are, democracy cannot be limited to voting for other people to do the work, because in the end such a truncated view comes "at an enormous cost to participation and citizenship."[20] This view undermines itself by discouraging people from even showing up to vote. The elitism inherent in thin democracy only exacerbates this problem.

The tangent with the concerns of social capitalists and communitarians emerges when we ask what is required to make strong democracy or "republican freedom" work. These political models share the view that vibrant community institutions are essential to a healthy democracy and politics. Sandel observes, "If local government and municipal institutions are no longer adequate arenas for republic citizenship, we must seek such public spaces as may be found amidst the institutions of civil society—in schools and workplaces, churches and synagogues, trade unions, and social movements."[21] It is only via these institutions that people can practice the kind of real politics that strong democracy entails. Such a politics, Barber goes on to argue, is transformational. He quotes Rousseau, who might as well have been describing Manuela or Rosa or Gilbert or Joe: "What is crucial about democratic community is that, as Rousseau understood, it 'produces a remarkable change in man . . . faculties are exercised and developed, his ideas broadened, his feelings ennobled, and his whole sole elevated.'"[22]

It is clear that the IAF vision of politics shares much in common with Barber's "strong democracy" and Sandel's "Republican Freedom." All place heavy emphasis on deliberation and agency. But deliberation and agency are only part of the IAF story. The IAF also has a view about distribution, not simply that the problem lies in a general failure of participation, but that the systematic exclusion of the "bottom third" is the real villain. In addition, the IAF is concerned with power and self-interest, albeit a self-interest modified by deliberation and community. The success of the IAF in obtaining this power and the uses to which it is put are the ultimate test of whether these organizations hold the key to reviving progressive politics.

Gathering Power

Organizing along IAF lines has already attained impressive dimensions. A recent survey examined the diffusion of what the researchers termed "faith-based organizing" and identified 133 organizations in thirty-three states that in total reached somewhere between 1 and 3 million people.[23] (The IAF would not accept the "faith-based" label since it incorporates other institutions in addition to congregations, but the survey did in fact refer to the IAF and similar organizations).

Numbers of this sort are useful, but it is clear, with or without these data, that much still has to happen for the IAF model to have a significant national impact. What will it take for the model to have a broader influence and what are the obstacles that confront it?

One approach to answering this question is to inquire about the expansion of the IAF itself. There are several elements to this. The first is whether IAF organizing can extend to more cities. The second is whether, within a given city, the reach of the organization can become more extensive and thus the organization can become more influential.

Organizing new cities is not complicated in principle. It depends on time, money, and staff. Organizers have to be recruited, trained, and paid, and the recruiting and the paying can be a challenge. Time is a concern because the IAF style of organizing is slow. Typically in a new city the organizers and sponsoring committee (the leaders of the key institutions that have invited the IAF in) spend two or three years in one-on-ones and house meetings before even developing an issues agenda. This pace can be frustrating to allied organizations, such as unions, that move at a more rapid pace. The IAF response is that their organizations are long-lasting precisely because of the early foundational work. However, notwithstanding the natural constraints of time and resources, there is nothing complicated or problematical about extending the model to new locations.

Extending the reach of the IAF within any given city is, on the other hand, a more complex issue. It is true that the IAF is broad-based and includes institutions representing a wide range of economic circumstances, as well as different religious persuasions and racial and ethnic groups. However, the bulk of the IAF power lies, not surprisingly, in poorer communities and among the relatively more religiously committed populations in those communities. The question, then, is how the IAF can reach with greater success beyond this base.

The broad-based nature of the IAF means that the organizing strategy swims against some powerful currents in American political life. One example is the politics of race. As we saw in chapter 2, the IAF is reluctant to organize specifically around race. This is not simply a function of the heavy concentration of Hispanics in the Southwest. Elsewhere in the nation IAF organizations have a very different racial composition, but everywhere the organization is reluctant to make racial issues a centerpiece of organizing.

Recent political events show that this concern is well founded. In the 2001 mayoral race in Houston a conservative Republican almost won because he was Hispanic and drew heavily from Hispanic voters who voted on the grounds of racial identification rather than the issues. Much the same could be said about the 2001 mayoral race in New York, in which the Democratic candidate was perceived as insensitive on racial issues and lost to a Republican in large part because important elements of the Democratic constituency stayed home. Also in 2001 in Los Angeles the mayoral race developed into a contest between Hispanic voters on one side and African-Americans on the other.

Race clearly has much potential for mischief in constructing a progressive coalition, but its power cannot be denied. After all, American politics has been shaped by race since the nation's founding, and African-Americans, Hispanics, and Asians all have good reasons for insisting that racial concerns remain on the political agenda. The IAF may not want to organize around race, but it needs to find an idiom for dealing with it. The idiom not only needs to be theoretically sound (and the IAF can explain persuasively why racially based organizing is a mistake) but must also succeed in making the organizations attractive to people for whom racial concerns are important.

The broad-based strategy also stands against explicitly acknowledging the issues of other identity groups, such as women and gays. This avoidance of identity politics is a strength to the extent that it enables the IAF to avoid expending energy on the kinds of fractional "us versus them" debates that have debilitated the American Left in the past. However, avoiding identity issues can cut the IAF off from a potent source of political energy. In recent years gay groups—as an example—have been willing to deemphasize a political strategy that focuses on differences and instead seek to build power based on what they have in common with mainstream voters. This was true in recent legislative campaigns in Vermont and Oregon.[24]

The final challenge the IAF faces in broadening its reach within any given city or metropolitan area lies in finding issues that can appeal to the suburbs. As we saw in chapter 2, this will not be easy. People in the suburbs are busy, are more oriented to "charity" than to "justice," and are uncomfortable with the language of conflict, power, and interest. At the same time, many suburban residents are notably more sympathetic to the concerns of the IAF than popular clichés would suggest, and these people confront issues—such as transportation and environmental concerns—that require a metropolitan solution. In several cities—Los Angeles, Chicago, and Boston—the IAF is explicitly pursuing a metropolitan strategy. This means that the larger organization (in Chicago, for example, United Power for Action and Justice has three hundred member institutions) is broken into clusters representing particular towns or communities. The clusters address their local issues but also come together on metropolitan ones. Organizing in the suburbs will be much slower work than elsewhere but is by no means impossible.

An important step toward addressing these issues is the rapid pace at which the IAF is working to broaden its base. A particularly hopeful development in this regard is the increasingly close cooperation between the IAF and the union movement, a development that I will take up momentarily. The IAF is working in other ways to broaden its base. The school reform strategy, Alliance Schools, attracts leaders who are not necessarily connected to congregations. In Los Angeles, immigrant rights organizations have joined the IAF. In Chicago, the IAF organization counts as its members a wide range of community service groups such as shelters, AIDS clinics, and senior citizens centers.

Extending the Model

The IAF alone cannot reenergize progressive politics. There are clearly many important players, including some local political parties; unions; other community organizing efforts; identity groups organized around race, gender, or sexual preference; and many others. Taken has a whole, these efforts dwarf what the IAF alone can accomplish. The importance of the IAF is that it provides a model for mobilizing that has proved powerful and effective. The IAF's emphasis on leadership development, broad-based organizing, and incorporation of values offers key insights about how to move ahead. Other progressive elements in American politics should be challenged to take what they can from this model.

The reach of the IAF model can also be extended through its work with allies. In recent years the IAF has, for example, worked hard to develop closer ties to the American union movement. Despite its weakened condition—the fraction of private sector workers who are union members is now less than 10 percent—the union movement still commands far more resources than any other institution. It is unparalleled in its ability to mobilize money and people. Furthermore, at its best, the union movement carries a moral message that goes beyond simple demands for more money and speaks to people's yearnings to have a voice in their workplace and to be treated fairly.

The problem is that the movement is not always at its best. Over the course of its long decline, many unions stopped organizing new employees and limited themselves to managing contracts. In this role they came to be seen as just another special interest asking, like any other, for a larger share for their own particular constituency. The growing dominance of this so-called business unionism cost unions their social movement character and also suppressed internal politics and leadership development.[25] Too many unions became the preserve of middle-aged white men and hence had difficulties connecting with the new workforce as it was developing. At the local level many unions were resistant to working with other community organizations. The unions preferred to hoard their own power and access and also saw community groups as either too flaky or too left-wing. What this added up to was not just a decline in the fraction of the workforce represented by unions but also a growing estrangement between unions and other members of a potential progressive coalition.

Much of this began to change in the 1990s. The Service Employees International Union (SEIU) organized low-wage workers via an imaginative combination of social movement tactics and political action. Its Justice for Janitors campaign obtained contracts in multiple cities for a labor force heavily made up of non-English-speaking (and often undocumented) immigrants. It achieved this by drawing upon the idiom of the Civil Rights movement, obtaining broad community support by emphasizing social justice issues, by identifying points of economic vulnerability of building owners, and by being willing to use nontraditional tactics of marches and demonstrations. The union also organized over sixty thousand home health care workers in California through a combination of traditional organizing and political action in the state legislature. On the east coast, the SEIU has had comparable success in the health care industry, a large employer of low-wage workers. Other unions, such as the Hotel Employees Restaurant Employees (HERE) and the garment workers (UNITE), have also succeeded in new organizing drives that have put new life into the movement. Even in traditional industries, unions seem to have rediscovered their moral voice. For example, the Teamsters strike against United Parcel Service focused on the issues of part-time and contingent employment and obtained surprisingly broad support from the American public. At the national level, the AFL-CIO has reemphasized the importance of new organizing and has pushed locals to spend a larger fraction of their budget on seeking new members.

In a number of cities IAF organizations and unions have begun working together. The nation's first living wage campaign in Baltimore was the product of a joint effort by the IAF organization—BUILD—and the public employees' union. In Los Angeles the IAF works closely with the SEIU and HERE on a number of campaigns. Immigration rights is an issue that resonates powerfully for both the IAF and the unions in that city. In Phoenix and Omaha, the IAF works with the Food and Commercial Workers Union in several new organizing campaigns.

There are, however, significant differences between union and IAF cultures. From the union perspective, the slowness of IAF organizing techniques can be frustrating and even impractical. More fundamental is that even unions that put a great deal of energy into organizing still have to administer contracts and manage workplace relationships, and this kind of service operation is of little interest to the IAF. In politics, unions have a long tradition of endorsing candidates, whereas the IAF refuses to do so.

Leadership development is a potential flash point, depending on the attitudes of the union leaders regarding the role of union members. The heads of local unions are elected by union members, and some heads may fear that if they identify and train new leaders in the IAF fashion, then these people will eventually be rivals for power. In other unions, the style of operation is very top-down, and the only accepted role of members is to pay dues. This can especially be a problem when decisions regarding organizing strategy in a community are made by regional or national union leaders who are completely out of contact with union members.

On the other hand, the case for applying the IAF style of leadership development is captured well by labor historian Nelson Lichtenstein, a very sympathetic observer of the union movement:

> The unions need tens of thousands of new organizers; but the AFL-CIO cannot recruit, train, and deploy such an army, and even if it could, "organizers" who parachute into a campaign are far less effective than those who are part of the community and the workplace. Such a homegrown cadre cannot be recruited in the absence of a democratic, participatory union culture. Unfortunately, thousands of local unions, and not a few national or international organizations, are job trusts that exist to protect the incomes of a strata of long-service officials . . . but without that democratization the union movement will remain a shell.[26]

Some unions might also take the view that although the IAF is effective in the public sector, it has little to offer with respect to private-sector organizing. However, there are at least two important qualifications to this perspective. First, as Justice for Janitors illustrated, private-sector organizing sometimes requires that communities be mobilized, and here the IAF has an important role to play. More fundamentally, the IAF approach of organizing via churches and schools can be very helpful when workplaces are small and scattered and people are in temporary or contingent employment with high turnover rates. In these circumstances, traditional union workplace-based organizing is both difficult and expensive. Workers can more effectively be reached in other settings and subsequently brought together around employment concerns. The emergence of the employees' association in the Rio Grande Valley illustrates this point.

On occasion the IAF and the union movement can morph together. BUILD in Baltimore has established its own local union, and a few other IAF organizations are considering a similar tactic. However, given the differences in organizational structure and mission, the most likely path is one of institutional independence but growing cooperation between the IAF and unions. The vision is not simply an arm's-length alliance but rather a relationship in which both institutions share some functions (e.g., joint organizing campaigns) and work together to define issues and exercise political power. The growing efforts along these lines suggest that this vision is more than plausible.

Political Possibilities

Successful progressive politics will come via local mobilization. The IAF shows that people can be brought into politics if they are given the skills and the opportunity to have a real voice in the issues that concern them. Trying to construct a constituency via clever sound bites and symbolism will not succeed. However, it is important to be realistic about what is possible and what is not. What is a reasonable expectation about what progressive organizations that focus on local mobilization and leadership development can accomplish?

In the short and medium run, these organizations can mobilize a substantial enough bloc of citizens to transform the political discussion and the balance of power. Ironically, a useful analogy is with the Christian Right, which never represented anything more than a small minority, even within the Republican party. Despite this, they have been surprisingly influential within that party. In today's politics, a substantial minority, well organized, can determine platforms and drive elections. This is because the parties and the candidates can typically count on a core of voters who will support them regardless of their positions. The question candidates and parties face is how to add to this core. Identifying narrow slices of swing voters and trying to attract them is what modern politics—with its polling, focus groups, and targeted appeals—is about.

The potential constituency of progressives is much larger than any-thing assembled by the Christian Right. It begins with the people—a quarter to a third of the population—who have simply failed to share in the prosperity of the last decade. Add to this allies such as unions, as well as middle-class citizens who share concerns about schools or the envi-ronment or loss of community. Because of its nonideological pragma-tism and its foundation in broadly shared values, the IAF and other orga-nizations that adopt the model have a chance to include them all among their supporters.

It turns out that it is more than possible that a strong progressive coalition that can drive platforms and tilt elections can be built. The par-ties cannot consider these citizens as part of their "taken for granted" base, because these are people who can be mobilized only through local organizing of the sort the IAF specializes in.

Moving Ahead

Does it even make sense in this era of big government and global econo-mies to talk about the kind of local organizing that the IAF model repre-sents? This is a long-standing question. Progressives have engaged in a century-long dialogue about whether it is best to organize and govern locally or nationally. "The local," wrote John Dewey, "is the ultimate uni-versal and as near an absolute as exists."[27] Set against this was the vision of Herbert Croly, who vigorously argued that the only solution to the growing national power of the trusts and industry was building up the authority of the federal government to regulate and manage.[28] Croly's vision was important to the technocrats who stood with Teddy Roose-velt, and his ideas echoed strongly during Franklin Roosevelt's New Deal. But the vision of the local never disappeared. Ideas about decentraliza-tion and community control remain important in progressive thinking.

It is obvious that important decisions are made at a level above the local and state arenas in which the IAF operates. The federal government establishes the minimum wage, which not only directly affects a large number of low-wage adults but also influences wage setting in the part of the job market that is just above the minimum.[29] Policy makers who set interest rates make their trade-offs between inflation and unemploy-ment in Washington, not in the cities and the towns that benefit or suffer from their decisions. Decisions about where to locate jobs are made in corporate headquarters far removed from the location of the actual plants and offices.

But although the importance of the national is apparent, there is another side to the story. The strongest case for organizing locally is that it is only at this level that politics can be taught. And it is at this level that people are best mobilized. No matter how important the national agenda, the power to achieve it can be generated only through local action. It is also apparent that there is ample scope for local action. From living wages to school reform to job training and local infrastructure, the IAF has shown what can be accomplished.

Moving from communities to states is likely to be the most plausible strategy. The scale of state-level politics is accessible, and the progressive organizations can have an influence and achieve significant success. The success that is attainable at the state level is important because it will energize and reinforce the organizing effort. Furthermore, over time state-level successes will have a national impact. There is a long history in American politics and social policy for innovations to begin in states and to move gradually to the federal level. New Deal innovations such as unemployment insurance were initially implemented in states. More recently, policy experts have characterized states as "laboratories of democracy," and much of the federal devolution of programs and funds is premised on this model.

The reality then is that the local versus national dichotomy is false. Eventually progressive organizations want to build from a local and state base to a national presence. But the kind of careful local organization and mobilization exemplified by the IAF is the right way to begin.

In states and localities where progressive coalitions are influential a positive feedback mechanism is plausible. Local and state government can play important roles in building the power of these local mobilizing organizations. They can help create a virtuous circle in which broad-based organizations build power and the government creates opportunities and resources for them to exercise that power and to build yet more. By repeatedly going back and forth this way in different arenas, it is not hard to imagine that over time the reach and power of these broad-based organizations will grow.

An example is Project QUEST, the job training described in the previous chapter. The IAF created Project QUEST by deploying its political power in San Antonio. The government, local and state, was responsive by providing funds and by legitimizing the role played by QUEST and the IAF organizations in the state's overall labor market strategy. Once in place, QUEST provided the IAF with opportunities: to organize new people (the graduates of the program) and to raise new issues (the use of economic development funds raised through the sales tax). The next step (which is yet to happen) is for the IAF to attain a seat at the table when decisions are made about the allocation of economic development funds. It is not hard to imagine a similar process of broadening out and interaction with government in other arenas of interest such as education reform and water resource planning.

This process of creating space for organizations such as the IAF to play a role and in doing so to build power is similar to what Joshua Cohen and Joel Rogers mean when they refer to associational democracy, in which local groups are given a formal role in developing, coordinating, and enforcing government policy in a number of fields.[30] There is a delicate balance here. IAF organizations do not want to be in the business of providing services or running programs—they insist on remaining political organizations—but they are not averse to sitting at the table. The more opportunities these organizations have to be a player, the more rapidly their power (and that of other progressive organizations that adopt the model) will grow. Government, in this view, not only provides resources and enacts regulations but also creates a governance structure that sets in motion a dynamic leading to greater and greater accumulation of power in the hands of local broad-based political organizations.

Toward a New Politics

In the end, the IAF model aims to reconstruct politics. Politics is not simply about elections every two or four years, but rather about creating space for an engaged citizenry at every step. In the IAF model, issues are identified in house meetings and are aggregated into an agenda via a democratic process of debate and compromise. Politicians are asked their positions on this agenda and depending on their replies receive, or do not receive, the votes of organizational leaders. The organization, and its leaders, stays involved in the implementation and the administration of the programs and policies, and in doing so not only ensures the accountability of politicians to their promises but also enriches the delivery via their own ideas and knowledge. Organized people, and not simply organized money, have a strong voice in government.

At the core of how this works is that people are taught that they have what it takes to play the roles that this political model requires. Rosa Gutierrez says, "We are changing people's mentality," and at the end of the day, this is what it is all about. When people learn what they can accomplish and develop the skills to follow through, then it can be a new political world. Manuela put it well when we asked what she has learned:

> The capacity. The intelligence that we can come up with. The power. The things that I never dreamed that I could do. We're doing them. It's a lot of obligations. A lot of duties. A lot of meetings. It is work. But I can see the accomplishments. That's what's keeping me going.

Notes

1. Reviving Progressive Politics

1. David Brooks, "One Nation, Slightly Divisible," *The Atlantic*, December 1, 2001, pp. 53–65.

2. March 2001, Current Population Survey, Table, FINC-03: Presence of Related Children Under 18 Years Old—All Families by Total Money Income in 2000, http://ferret.bls.census.gov/macro/032001/faminc/new03__001.htm.

3. All of the data in this paragraph are taken from Isaac Shapiro, Robert Greenstein, and Wendell Primus, "Pathbreaking CBO Study Shows Dramatic Increases in Income Disparities in the 1980s and 1990s: An Analysis of CBO Data," Center on Budget and Policy Priorities, Washington, D.C., May 31, 2001.

4. "Hey, What About Us?" *Business Week*, December 27, 1999, pp. 52–55.

5. The data in the remainder of this paragraph are taken from the survey by the Pew Research Center for the People and the Press, "Economic Inequality Seen as Rising, Boom Bypasses the Poor," June 2001, http://www.people-press.org/june01rpt.htm.

6. Quoted in Robert Wiebe, *Self-Rule: A Cultural History of American Democracy* (Chicago: University of Chicago Press, 1995), p. 249.

7. Jack Doppelt and Ellen Shearer, "America's No-Show Non-Voters: Who Are They, Why They Don't Vote," Medill School of Journalism, Northwestern University, September 2001.

8. Alan Wolfe, *Moral Freedom: The Search for Virtue in a World of Choice* (New York: North, 2001), p. 110.

9. National Election Surveys. See http://www.umich.edu/nes/.

10. Richard Freeman, "What, Me Vote?" (paper presented to Harvard Kennedy School Summer Institute on Inequality, June 2001).

11. Steven Rosenstone and John Mark Hansen, *Mobilization, Participation, and Democracy in America* (New York: Macmillan, 1993), pp. 63–67; Robert Putnam, *Bowling Alone: The Collapse and Revival of American Community* (New York: Simon & Schuster, 2000).

12. *The Semi-Sovereign People: A Realist's View of Democracy in America* (New York: Holt, 1960), p. 35.

13. This statistic is based on my analysis of the 2000 National Election Survey. The citation for the 2000 survey is Nancy Burns, Donald R. Kinder, Steven J. Rosenstone, Virginia Sapiro, and the National Election Studies,

National Election Studies, 2000: Pre/Post-Election Study (data set), (Ann Arbor:: University of Michigan, Center for Political Studies [producer and distributor], 2001).

14. Sidney Verba, Kay Lehman Schlozman, and Henry Brady, *Voice and Equality: Civic Voluntarism in America*, (Cambridge: Harvard University Press, 1995). The sample was of adults over the age of eighteen. The survey consisted of a short screener of 15,053 people and a two-hour interview of 2,517. The survey oversampled blacks, Hispanics, and political activists in order to generate adequate numbers for analysis and then was weighted to make it nationally representative.

15. Verba, Schlozman, and Brady, *Voice and Equality,* p. 188.

16. These figures are taken from my analysis of the 1972 and 2000 National Election Survey. The 1972 data are self-weighting, and for the 2000 data I use the weights provided.

17. Theda Skocpol, "Advocates without Members: The Recent Transformation of American Civic Life," in *Civic Engagement in American Democracy,* ed. Theda Skocpol and Morris Fiorina (Washington, D.C.: Brookings; New York: Russell Sage, 1999), p. 497. The data are for 1982.

18. Ibid., p. 500.

19. Alex Keyssar, *The Right to Vote* (New York: Basic Books, 2001), p. xxiv.

20. Skeptics of the gains to be had by mobilizing nonvoters point out that the nonvoting group is heterogeneous (and therefore contains some people who would be hostile to progressive positions). They also argue that any increase in nonvoting turnout, even targeted at likely Democratic party voters, would not have been enough to alter the results of the presidential elections of the 1980s and early 1990s. However, on balance, nonvoters are more friendly than voters to progressive positions. Furthermore, in a world in which progressive politics needs to be rebuilt from the ground up, local and state elections take on as much importance as do presidential elections (and, of course, the 2000 presidential election is one in which turnout differentials clearly made an important difference). Survey data of a representative sample of voters and eligible nonvoters in the three elections between 1996 and 2000 show that the nonvoters are more in favor than the voters of spending on public schools, on child care, and on aid to the poor by a substantial margin. The percentage of voters supporting increased aid to the poor was 41 percent, increased spending on childcare was 51 percent, and increased spending on schools was 67 percent. For nonvoters, the figures were 59 percent, 64 percent, and 77 percent, respectively. These figures are based on my analysis of the combined samples of the National Election Surveys of 1996, 1998, and 2000.

21. Keyssar, *Right to Vote,* p. 315.

22. Ibid.

23. See for example, the debate between Will Marshall, the president of the centrist Democratic Leadership Council's think tank, and Stanley Greenberg, a pollster representing the left of the party, in the *American Prospect*, April 23, 2001.

24. Ruy Teixeira and Joel Rogers, *America's Forgotten Majority: Why the White Working Class Still Matters* (New York: Basic Books, 2000).

25. Sidney Tarrow, *Power in Movement: Social Movements in Contemporary Politics* (Cambridge: Cambridge University Press, 1998), p. 133.

26. Marshall Ganz, "Voters in the Cross-Hairs," *The American Prospect* 5, no. 16 (December 1, 1994).

27. Rosenstone and Hansen, *Mobilization, Participation, and Democracy*; Verba, Schlozman, and Brady, *Voice and Equality*.

28. Rosenstone and Hansen, *Mobilization, Participation, and Democracy*, p. 213.

29. Martin Wattenberg, *The Decline of American Political Parties* (Cambridge: Harvard University Press, 1986), pp. 57–58.

30. Steven Schier, *By Invitation Only: The Rise of Exclusive Politics in the United States* (Pittsburgh: University of Pittsburgh Press, 2000), p. 115.

31. A. James Reichley, *The Life of the Parties: A History of American Political Parties* (New York: Free Press, 1992), pp. 409–10.

32. David Mayhew, *Placing Parties in American Politics* (Princeton, N.J.: Princeton University Press, 1986), p. 200.

33. Ibid., p. 331.

34. In telling this story I have relied heavily on four sources: Keyssar, *Right to Vote;* Wiebe, *Self-Rule;* Francis Fox Piven and Richard Cloward, *Why Americans Still Don't Vote, and Why Politicians Want It That Way* (Boston: Beacon Press, 2000); and Walter Dean Burnham, "The Turnout Problem," in *Elections American Style,* ed. A. James Reichley (Washington, D.C.: Brookings Institution, 1987), pp. 97–133.

35. Piven and Cloward, *Why Americans Still Don't Vote*, p. 48.

36. Amy Bridges, *Morning Glories: Municipal Reform in the Southwest* (Princeton, N.J.: Princeton University Press, 1997), p. 16.

37. Piven and Cloward, *Why Americans Still Don't Vote*, p. 65.

38. Wiebe, *Self-Rule*, p. 206.

39. Aldon Morris, *The Origins of the Civil Rights Movement: Black Communities Organizing for Change* (New York: Free Press, 1984), p. 282.

40. Ibid., p. 53.

41. Ibid., p. 54.

42. Robert Wuthnow, *The Restructuring of American Religion: Society and Faith Since World War II* (Princeton, N.J.: Princeton University Press, 1988), p. 179.

43. Ibid., p. 186.

44. See Eileen Lindner, ed., *Yearbook of American and Canadian Churches* (Nashville: Abingdon Press, 2001).

45. For example, Wuthnow reports that in 1980 Pentecostal Holiness churches had thirty-three clergy and twenty-seven church buildings per thousand members, Nazarenes had sixteen clergy and ten buildings, and Assemblies of God congregations had thirteen clergy and six buildings. In comparison, Methodists had four clergy and four buildings, Episcopalians had five clergy and three buildings, and Presbyterians six clergy and four buildings. Wuthnow, *Restructuring of American Religion*, p. 193.

46. Piven and Cloward, *Why Americans Still Don't Vote*, p. 146.

47. I used data from the 1996 through 2000 National Election Surveys, the same data I used earlier to look at political attitudes. I estimated statistical models that included controls for age, sex, race, region, education, and income. I asked two questions: whether people who have a union member in their household (themselves, a spouse, or a child) are more likely than people without a union connection to vote and, second, whether they are more likely to identify themselves with the Democratic party. Without controls, the fraction of people with union members in their household who voted was 76.6 percent, compared with 64.4 percent without a union connection. Again, without controls, the fraction of people with union members in their household who identified themselves with the Democratic party was 43 percent, compared with 36 percent without a union connection. With the controls included, having a union member in the household raises the rate of voting by 9 percentage points. When I use the same controls and ask about the impact of unions on identification with the Democratic party, the result is that the union connection raises Democratic identification by 8 percentage points.

48. For a description of many of these campaigns, see Mark Warren, *Dry Bones Rattling: Community Building to Revitalize American Democracy* (Princeton, N.J.: Princeton University Press, 2001); and Robert Wilson, ed., *Public Policy and Community: Activism and Government in Texas* (Austin: University of Texas Press, 1997).

49. For a biography of Alinsky, and the source of the material in these paragraphs, see Sanford Horwitt, *Let Them Call Me Rebel: Saul Alinsky, His Life and Legacy* (New York: Vintage Books, 1992).

50. Horwitt, *Let Them Call Me Rebel*, p. 535.

51. Werner Sombart, *Why Is There No Socialism in the United States?* (White Plains, N.Y.: International Arts and Science Press, 1976).

52. Mike Allen and Ceci Connolly, "Nominees Hit Trail as Race Narrows," *Washington Post*, August 19, 2000, p. A1.

53. John Henry and Bennett Roth, "Bush, Gore Let Others Go on Attack," *Houston Chronicle*, August 21, 2000, p. A5.

54. Public Agenda, "For Goodness' Sake: Why So Many Want Religion to Play a Greater Role in American Life" (New York: Public Agenda, 2001). The findings in this report were based on a representative survey of 1,507 adults in November 2000. In response to a question about what would happen were more Americans to become deeply religious, 87 percent would expect an increase in charity and volunteer work, 79 percent would expect crime to decrease, and 85 percent would expect that parents would do a better job of raising their children. At the same time, only between 24 and 33 percent think that politicians should base how they vote on issues such as welfare, abortion, the death penalty, and gay rights on their religious views.

55. I present some evidence on this in chapter 3.

56. Jared Bernstein, Elizabeth C. McNichol, Lawrence Mishel, and Robert Zahradnik, *Pulling Apart: A State-by-State Analysis of Income Trends* (Washington, D.C.: Center on Budget and Policy Priorities and the Economic Policy Institute, January 2000).

57. David Montejano, *Anglos and Mexicans in the Making of Texas, 1836–1986* (Austin: University of Texas Press, 1987).

58. Tech Prep of the Rio Grande Valley, Inc., *Targeting the Future: A Report about the Evolving Labor Market In Texas' Lower Rio Grande Valley* (Edinburg: University of Texas, Pan-Am, 1998), p. 3.

59. "Between Here and There," *The Economist*, July 7, 2001, p. 29.

60. See, for example, Enrique Espinosa and Pedro Noyola, "Emerging Patterns in Mexico-U.S. Trade," in *Coming Together? Mexico–United States Relations*, ed. Barry Bosworth, Susan Collins, and Nora Lustig (Washington, D.C.: Brookings Institution Press, 1977).

61. In a PowerPoint presentation from the year 2000 by the McAllen Economic Development Corporation, one of the slides brags about the cheap labor force.

62. E. J. Dionne Jr., *They Only Look Dead: Why Progressives Will Dominate the Next Political Era* (New York: Simon & Schuster, 1996), p. 13.

63. Wilson Carey McWilliams, *Beyond the Politics of Disappointment: American Elections, 1980–1998* (New York: Chatham House, Seven Bridges Press, 2000), p. 5.

2. Building Organizations

1. Rosenstone and Hansen, *Mobilization, Participation, and Democracy*, p. 43. The data refer to averages for the period 1973–90. Thirty-five percent signed a petition, and 18 percent attended a meeting.

2. Charles M. Payne, *I've Got the Light of Freedom: The Organizing Tradition*

and the Mississippi Freedom Struggle (Berkeley: University of California Press, 1995).

3. Ibid., pp. 336, 364.

4. Ibid., p. 75.

5. Ibid., p. 71.

6. There has been a sharp fall in the number of nuns in America, with fewer women joining orders and with a substantial number leaving. This may make it difficult for the IAF to continue to tap into this source of organizers. See Charles R. Morris, *American Catholic* (New York: Random House, 1997), p. 318.

7. In *Let Them Call Me Rebel*, Sanford Horwitt writes, "Alinsky had a very compartmentalized view of the roles of men and women. Organizing, power, politics, and toughness were all related to manhood . . . and women organizers were a threat to manhood" (p. 289).

8. A more formal academic definition is that an organization's culture is "a pattern of shared basic assumptions that a group learned as it solved its problems of external adaptation and internal integration that has worked well enough to be considered valid and therefore to be taught to new members as the correct way to perceive, think, and feel in relation to those problems" (Edgar H. Schein, *Organizational Culture and Leadership*, 2nd ed. [San Francisco: Jossey-Bass, 1992], p. 12).

9. An example of conflicting organizational cultures is the merger of Morgan Stanley with Dean Witter. There was immediate conflict between the two sides, and in the end, the retail sales side, Dean Witter, came to dominate.

10. Henry Simon, *Administrative Behavior* (New York: McMillian, 1957); Chester Barnard, *The Functions of the Executive* (Cambridge: Harvard University Press, 1938).

11. Horwitt, *Let Them Call Me Rebel*, pp. 359, 472.

12. For a discussion of an exception to the general rule, the lively two-party system of the International Typographical Union, see Seymour Martin Lipset, Martin Grow, and James Coleman, *Union Democracy* (New York: Anchor Books, 1962).

13. Philip Selznick, *The TVA and the Grass Roots: A Study in the Sociology of Formal Organization* (New York: Harper Torchbooks, 1966).

14. Ibid., p. ix

15. See, for example, Jane Mansbridge's study of a crisis center and a town meeting. Jane Mansbridge, *Beyond Adversary Democracy* (Chicago: University of Chicago Press, 1983).

16. William Julius Wilson, *The Declining Significance of Race* (Chicago: University of Chicago Press, 1978), p. 72.

17. Horwitt, *Let Them Call Me Rebel,* p. 359.

18. Ibid., pp. 122, 367.

19. Charles Silberman, *Crisis in Black and White* (New York: Random House, 1964).

20. Lawrence Mishel, Jared Bernstein, and John Schmitt, *The State of Working America, 2000–2001* (Ithaca, N.Y.: Cornell University Press, 2001), p. 366.

21. Alan Wolfe, *One Nation, After All: What Americans Really Think about God, Country, Family, Racism, Welfare, Immigration, Homosexuality, Work, the Right, the Left, and Each Other* (New York: Viking, 1998), pp. 198–99, 237.

22. Robert Bellah, Richard Madsen, William Sullivan, Ann Swidler, and Steven Tipton, *Habits of the Heart: Individualism and Commitment in American Life* (Berkeley: University of California Press, 1985), p. 199.

23. Wolfe, *One Nation, After All,* p. 285.

24. Ibid., p. 251.

25. Bellah et al., *Habits of the Heart,* p. 204.

26. Silberman, *Crisis in Black and White,* p. 347.

3. Faith

1. The data on attendance at religious services and the importance of religion are taken from the Gallup Polls, http://www.gallup.com/poll.indicators/indreligion.asp, and the data on confidence in institutions are taken from http://www.gallup.com/poll.indicators/indconfidence.asp. The data refer to February 2001.

2. This is from my analysis of the National Election Survey 2000. Regular attendees are those who attend religious services one or more times per week.

3. Pew Research Center for the People and the Press, "Religion and Politics: The Ambivalent Majority," June 12, 2001, http://www.people-press.org/relioorpt.htm.

4. For evidence regarding the timing of this shift, see Wuthnow, *Restructuring of American Religion,* p. 237.

5. For a review of some of the literature on the efficacy of these programs, see John DiIulio Jr., "Supporting Black Churches: Faith, Outreach, and the Inner-City Poor," in *What's God Got to Do with the American Experiment?* ed. E. J. Dionne Jr. and John J. DiIulio Jr. (Washington, D.C.: Brookings Institution, 2000), pp. 121–27. For contrary views, see Jim Castelli and John McCarthy, *Religion-Sponsored Social Services: The Not-So-Independent Section* (Washington, D.C.: Aspen Institute Nonprofit

Sector Research Fund, 1998); and Laurie Goodstein, "Church-Based Projects Lack Data on Results," *New York Times*, April 24, 2001, p. A12.

6. Verba, Schlozman, and Brady, *Voice and Equality*.

7. Ibid., p. 329.

8. Fredrick C. Harris, *Something Within: Religion in African-American Political Activism* (New York: Oxford University Press, 1999).

9. This quote, from Autherine Lucy, is taken from Harris, *Something Within*, p. 80.

10. Data on this are provided below.

11. See Wuthnow, *Restructuring of American Religion*, p. 205.

12. Wolfe, *One Nation, After All*, p. 49.

13. I combined the surveys for 1996 and 2000 in order to understand how religion has played out in recent years. For 1996 and 1998, the surveys were conducted in person; in 2000, some were in person and some were on the phone. I have included only the in-person interviews in order to maintain comparability across the years. The results presented are based on analysis using the sampling weights provided. The measures of religiosity that are available include whether religion is important in the person's life (77 percent say yes); whether religion provides a great deal of guidance in the person's life (36 percent say yes); whether the person attends church almost every week or more (37 percent say yes); whether the person prays once a day or more (52 percent say yes); whether the person believes that the Bible is the literal word of God (36 percent say yes); whether the person responds affirmatively to four or five of the above measures (30 percent do). The outcome measures I use are aimed at tapping in various ways into the openness of people to progressive politics. These measures are whether the person identifies him- or herself as a liberal (11 percent say yes); whether the person thinks that the federal budget should be increased in order to add more aid to the poor (48 percent say yes); whether the person thinks the federal budget should be increased in order to spend more on schools (71 percent say yes); whether the person thinks the federal budget should be increased in order to spend more on child care (56 percent say yes).

   There are multiple ways to inquire about a person's degree of religious commitment. As a way of capturing the full range, I use two measures. At one extreme is simply whether or not the person says that religion is important in his or her life. At the other end is whether the person answers affirmatively to four or five of the five different religion indicators cited above (i.e., has a score of four or five on what I call the religion index). I used both of these measures as a way of bracketing the impact of religious commitment on political attitudes. Using these data, I engaged in a statistical exercise that controls for some of the other factors that might influence an individual's political position. These include the person's education, age, income, race, region of the country, and the year of the survey. The results show that all of the clash between religious attachment and progressive politics lies in the attitudes of born-again Christians. It is clear that this group is very conservative. However, the remainder of the religiously committed population is, if anything, friendly to progressive issues. For example, there is strong support for increasing budget outlays to the poor, to schools, and to child care. This leaves very ample scope for progressive organizing, making even clearer what a mistake it is for progressive politicians and organizers to avoid religion and, even worse, to seem indifferent or hostile to it.

14. Horwitt, *Let Them Call Me Rebel*, p. 196.

15. John T. McGreevy, *Parish Boundaries: The Catholic Encounter with Race in the Twentieth-Century Urban North* (Chicago: University of Chicago Press, 1996), pp. 111–13.

16. Ernesto Cortes Jr., "Reweaving the Social Fabric: Faith, Civic Education, and Political Renewal," *Texas Journal* (spring/summer 1995), p. 23.

17. Robert Bellah, *The Broken Covenant: American Civic Religion in a Time of Trial* (New York: Seabury Press, 1975).

18. Pew Research Center for the People and the Press, "Religion and Politics: The Ambivalent Majority," June 12, 2001, http://www.people-press.org/relioorpt.htm. The survey was of two thousand registered voters.

19. Quoted in Harris, *Something Within*, p. 88.

20. Nancy Tatom Ammerman, *Congregation and Community* (New Brunswick, N.J.: Rutgers University Press, 1997).

21. See Robert Wuthnow, *Christianity in the Twenty-first Century* (New York: Oxford University Press, 1993), p. 35.

22. Ammerman, *Congregation and Community*, p. 338.

23. See Andrew Greeley, *The Catholic Experience* (New York: Doubleday, 1967), p. 182; Charles Morris, *American Catholic*, pp. 86–87.

24. My description of these positions is based upon Thad Williamson, "True Prophecy? A Critical Examination of the Sociopolitical Stance of the Mainline Protestant Churches," *Union Seminary Quarterly* 51, nos. 1–2 (1997): 79–116.

25. Quoted in John DiIulio Jr., "Supporting Black Churches: Faith, Outreach, and the Inner-City Poor," in *What's God Got to Do with the American Experiment?* ed. E. J. Dionne Jr. and John J. DiIulio Jr. (Washington, D.C.: Brookings Institution, 2000), p. 121.

26. See, for example, Robert N. Bellah, Richard Madsen, William M. Sullivan, Ann Swidler, and Steven M. Tipton, *The Good Society*, (New York: Knopf, 1991), chapter 6, "The Public Church."

27. Michael Byrd, "'You Will Rebuild Your Ancient Ruins': Religion, the IAF, and Community Organizing in Metropolitan Nashville" (paper

presented at the H-Urban Seminar on the History of Community Organizing and Community-Based Development, http://comm-org.utoledo.edu/papers96/iaf.html).

28. Stephen Hart, *What Does the Lord Require? How American Christians Think about Economic Justice* (New York: Oxford University Press, 1992), pp. 155–61.

29. Will Herberg, *Protestant, Catholic, Jew: An Essay in American Religious Sociology* (New York: Doubleday Anchor, 1960), p. 116.

30. Ibid., p. 120.

31. Jeffrey Burns, "Building the Best: A History of Catholic Parishes in the Pacific States," in *The American Catholic Parish*, ed. Jay P. Dolan (New York: Paulist Press, 1987), p. 44.

32. For an account of Cardinal McIntyre's experience, see Charles Morris, *American Catholic*, pp. 259–61.

33. See Peter Skerry, *Mexican Americans: The Ambivalent Minority* (New York: Free Press, 1993), pp. 193–201, for an account of these problems.

34. Greeley, *Catholic Experience*.

35. Ammerman, *Congregation and Community*, pp. 52, 327.

36. Wuthnow, *Restructuring of American Religion*, chapter 6.

37. Skerry, *Mexican Americans*, p. 192.

38. Bellah et al., *Good Society*, p. 198.

39. Personal interview with J. Bryan Hehir, Harvard Divinity School.

40. The estimates are that actual attendance is half of that reported; see C. Kirk Hadaway, Penny Long Marler, and Mark Chaves, "What the Polls Don't Show: A Closer Look at Church Attendance," *American Sociological Review* 58, no. 2 (December 1993): 741–52. For a series of exchanges with other scholars—some of whom are quite skeptical of this finding—see the February 1998 issue of the *American Sociological Review*. My reading of this evidence is that actual attendance is quite likely significantly below what is reported, though the 50 percent figure is just a rough estimate. The gap between actual and reported attendance is an issue for both Catholics and Protestants, but, this gap notwithstanding, Catholics do attend church at a higher rate than do Protestants.

41. Wolfe, *One Nation, After All*, p. 84.

42. Bellah et al., *Good Society*, p. 183.

43. For the figure on Presbyterians, see Dean R. Hoge, Benton Johnson, and Donald A. Luidens, *Vanishing Boundaries: The Religion of Mainline Protestant Baby Boomers* (Westminster John Knox Press, 1994), chapter 3. For more general data, see Wade Clark Roof and William McKinney, *American Mainline Religion* (New Brunswick, N.J.: Rutgers University Press,

1987). There is less mobility among Catholics in part because of the greater theological difficulty of crossing the Catholic/Protestant boundary and in part because Catholics join churches in their neighborhood and are less likely to travel for a "better deal" elsewhere.

44. http://www.gallup.com/poll/releases/pr010413.asp.

45. Robert Wuthnow, "Mobilizing Civic Engagement: The Changing Impact of Religious Involvement," in *Civic Engagement in American Democracy,* ed. Theda Skocpol and Morris Fiorina (Washington, D.C.: Brookings Institution; New York: Russell Sage, 1999), p. 336.

46. Bellah et al., *Habits of the Heart,* p. 238.

47. For a review of this literature, see Gary Dorrien, *Soul in Society: The Making and Renewal of Social Christianity* (Minneapolis: Fortress Press, 1995),pp. 362–63.

48. Jay Dolan, *The American Catholic Experience* (New York: Doubleday, 1985), p. 432.

49. David Stoll, *Is Latin America Turning Protestant? The Politics of Evangelical Growth* (Berkeley: University of California Press, 1990).

50. Charles Morris, *American Catholic,* p. 403.

51. See also Wuthnow, "Mobilizing Civic Engagement," p. 340.

52. Ibid., pp. 342, 352.

53. The Gallup Organization, "Easter Season Finds a Religious Nation," April 13, 2001, http://www.gallup.org/poll/releases/pr010413.asp.

54. The Pew Research Center for the People and the Press, "Religion and Politics: The Ambivalent Majority," June 12, 2001, http://www.people-press.org/relioorpt.htm. Sixty-five percent of liberals had a favorable opinion of atheists, compared with 32 percent overall.

55. Steven Greenhouse, "Labor Groups Join Coalition to Eliminate Sweatshops," *New York Times,* August 8, 2001, p. A17.

56. Bill Carter, "TV Works in Mysterious Ways for Pat Robertson," *New York Times,* July 30, 2001, p. C1.

57. Putnam, *Bowling Alone,* chapter 4.

4. Practicing a New Politics

1. These data are taken from my analysis of the National Election Survey.

2. Verba, Schlozman, and Brady, *Voice and Equality.*

3. Ibid., p. 135.

4. Ibid., p. 72. Thirty-four percent said they had worked with others on local problems, 34 percent said they were active members in community

problem-solving organizations, and 17 percent said they had formed a group to solve local problems. These data refer to 1987 and are generated from the General Social Survey.

5. Ibid., p. 190.

6. Rosenstone and Hansen, *Mobilization, Participation, and Democracy,* pp. 236–37.

7. Ibid., p. 241.

8. Freeman, "What, Me Vote?"

9. Quoted in Montejano, *Anglos and Mexicans,* p. 193.

10. Ibid., p. 168.

11. Robert Caro, *The Path to Power* (New York: Knopf, 1982), p. 721.

12. Ibid., p. 719.

13. Bridges, *Morning Glories,* p. 148.

14. Ibid., p. 132.

15. Mayhew, *Placing Parties,* p. 241.

16. Quoted in Bridges, *Morning Glories,* p. 122.

17. Ibid.

18. Stephen L. Elkin, *City and Regime in the American Republic* (Chicago: University of Chicago Press, 1987), p. 66.

19. Bridges, *Morning Glories,* p. 149.

20. Quoted in Robert Wilson, *Public Policy and Community,* p. 47.

21. William D'Antonio and William Form, *Influentials in Two Border Cities: A Study in Community Decision Making* (Notre Dame, Ind.: University of Notre Dame Press, 1965), p. 133.

22. Elkin, *City and Regime,* p. 70.

23. D'Antonio and Form, *Influentials in Two Border Cities,* p. 155.

24. Peter Skerry, "Fire in the Valley," *The New Republic* 3, no. 635 (September 17 and 24, 1984): 19–21.

25. Skerry, "Fire in the Valley."

26. Bridges, *Morning Glories,* p. 200.

27. Statement by Jim Schrock, in *Monitor* (McAllen), January 31, 2000.

28. *Monitor* (McAllen), letters to the editor, letter by John DellMaggiora, May 5, 2000.

29. Michael Neary, "District Debate Becomes Heated," *Monitor* (McAllen), April 13, 2000, p. 1.

30. See, for example, Seymour Martin Lipset, *Continental Divide: The Values and Institutions of the United States and Canada* (New York: Routledge, 1990).

31. Wolfe, *One Nation, After All*, p. 267.

32. Robert Bellah et al, *Habits of the Heart*.

33. Lipset, *Continental Divide*.

34. Robert Merton, "The Latent Function of the Machine," in *Social Theory and Social Structure* (Glencoe, Ill.: Free Press, 1957), p. 73.

35. Ira Katznelson, *City Trenches: Urban Politics and the Patterning of Class Conflict in the United States* (Chicago: University of Chicago Press, 1981), p. 113.

36. See Adam Cohen and Elizabeth Taylor, *American Pharaoh: Mayor Richard J. Daley: His Battle for Chicago and the Nation* (Boston: Little Brown, 2000).

37. *McAllen Monitor*, April 23, 2001, p. 1.

38. Katznelson, *City Trenches*.

39. "Hey, What About Us?" *Business Week*, December 27, 1999, pp. 52–55; the Pew Research Center for the People and the Press, "Economic Inequality Seen as Rising, Boom Bypasses the Poor," June 2001, http://www.people-press.org/june01rpt.htm.

5. Managing Our Economic Destiny

1. In its summary of wage trends, the Economic Policy Institute (EPI) reports that "the wages paid at the median of the pay scale . . . declined between 1973 and 1996, but finally began rising in 1997–99. However, this median wage did not surpass the 1989 level until mid-1999 and it remains substantially below the level reached in 1973 when the downturn began." See "Paycheck Economics" on the EPI Web site, http://www.epinet.org. Insecurity is rising as firms increasingly utilize various forms of contingent and temporary employment and as more are willing to engage in layoffs even while profitable. For evidence on this, see Paul Osterman, *Securing Prosperity: How the American Labor Market Has Changed and What to Do about It* (Princeton, N.J.: Princeton University Press, 1999).

2. Thomas Friedman, *The Lexus and the Olive Tree* (New York: Farrar, Straus, and Giroux, 1999), p. xv.

3. For a discussion of these trends in competition and production, see Paul Osterman, Thomas Kochan, Richard Locke, and Michael Piore, *Working in America* (Cambridge: MIT Press, 2001).

4. Data from Barry T. Hirsch and David A. Macpherson, *Union Membership and Earnings Data Book: Compilations from the Current Population*

Survey 1996 Edition (Washington, D.C.: Bureau of National Affairs, 1996), table 8.

5. See David Card and Alan Krueger, *Myth and Measurement: The New Economics of the Minimum Wage* (Princeton, N.J.: Princeton University Press, 1995).

6. In part, these findings come from studies of the impact of unionization on previously nonunion plants. Researchers found a positive "shock effect." See Sumner Slichter, *Union Policies and Industrial* Management (Washington, D.C.: Brookings Institution, 1941); Richard Freeman and James Medoff, *What Do Unions Do?* (New York: Basic Books, 1984).

7. See George Taylor and Frank Pierson, eds., *New Concepts in Wage Determination* (New York: McGraw Hill, 1957).

8. I spoke with personnel officials at other schools.

9. This story is told in James Cobb, *The Selling of the South: The Southern Crusade for Industrial Development, 1936–1980* (Baton Rouge: Louisiana State University Press, 1982).

10. Peter Fisher and Alan Peters, *Industrial Incentives: Competition among American States and Cities* (Kalamazoo, Mich.: W. E. Upjohn Institute, 1998), p. 16.

11. Louis Uchitelle, "Renewed Corporate Wanderlust Puts a Brake on Salaries and Prices," *New York Times,* July 24, 2000, p. A20.

12. These figures are based on interviews I conducted at the Covergys site.

13. The data in this paragraph are taken from John Seigfried and Andrew Zimbalist, "The Economics of Sports Facilities and Their Communities," *Journal of Economic Perspectives* 14, no. 3 (summer 2000): 95–114.

14. Lawrence Mishel, Jared Bernstein, and John Schmitt, *Wage Inequality in the 1990s: Measurement and Trends,* (Washington, D.C.: Economic Policy Institute, December 1998).

15. Douglas Braddock, "Occupational Employment Projections to 2008," *Monthly Labor Review* (November 1999): 51–77.

16. My account of events in Forth Worth is based upon material in Dennis Shirley, *Community Organizing for Urban School Reform* (Austin: University of Texas Press, 1997).

17. The material in this and the following paragraphs is based on Dennis Shirley, *Valley Interfaith and School Reform* (Austin: University of Texas Press, 2002).

18. Ibid., p. 67.

19. Sam Houston is not a perfect scientific experiment designed to capture the impact of Alliance Schools. It is hard to separate out the impact from the fact that midway through the process a new school building was con-

structed in a growing neighborhood and many of the students in the original school moved there.

20. Shirley, *Community Organizing,* pp. 214–15.The percentage passing statewide in 1993 was 46 percent for elementary schools, 45 percent for eighth graders, and 51 percent for tenth graders. By 1996, the figures were 66 percent, 58 percent, and 60 percent, respectively. By contrast, in 1993 in the Alliance Schools, the figures were 21.5 percent, 28.6 percent, and 22.3 percent, whereas in 1996 they were 44.3 percent, 36.2 percent, and 42.3 percent, respectively. In his discussion of these data, Shirley seems to refer to percentage point increases in scores, whereas I am focusing on the percentage increase.

21. Geoff Rips, "Alliances in Public Schools," *Texas Observer,* October 11, 1996, pp. 13–14.

22. A good account of the fund-raising efforts is in Mark Warren, *Dry Bones Rattling,* pp. 170–75.

23. See, for example, Robert Giloth, "Learning from the Field: Economic Growth and Workforce Development in the 1990s," *Economic Development Quarterly* 14, no. 4, (November 2000): 340–59; U.S. Department of Labor, *What's Working (and What's Not): A Summary of Research on the Economic Impacts of Employment and Training Programs* (Washington, D.C.: Government Printing Office, January 1995).

24. At that time, costs were about ten thousand dollars per client, but this has since been reduced to six thousand dollars because of the success of the program in tapping into newly available child care funds from the state. As of December 2000, the program had served 2,345 people. About 60 percent of QUEST placements are in health care, and this percentage has remained stable.

25. In 1998, among adults aged thirty to fifty-nine, 12.4 percent of men and 31.6 percent of women who worked earned less than fifteen thousand dollars. See Anthony Carnevale and Stephen Rose, "Low Earners: Who Are They? Do They Have a Way Out?" in *Low-Wage Workers in the New Economy,* ed. Richard Kazis and Marc Miller (Washington, D.C.: Urban Institute, 2001), p. 47.

26. The initial work along these lines was Michael Piore and Charles Sabel, *The New Industrial Divide: Possibilities for Prosperity* (New York: Basic Books, 1984). Since that work's publication, there has been an outpouring of literature on regional clusters and so-called industrial districts. See Robert P. Giloth, *Jobs and Economic Development: Strategies and Practice* (Thousand Oaks, Calif.: Sage, 1998).

27. See, for example, Susan Houseman, "Why Employers Use Flexible Staffing Arrangements: Evidence from an Establishment Survey" (Kalamazoo, Mich.: W. E. Upjohn Institute Working Paper, October 2000); Osterman, *Securing Prosperity.*

28. For evidence that temporary workers received fewer benefits, see Susan

Houseman, "Flexible Staffing Arrangements: A Report on Temporary Help, On-Call, Direct Hire, Leased, Contract Company, and Independent Contractor Employment in the United States" (Kalamazoo, Mich.: W. E. Upjohn Institute, June 1999).

6. Gathering Power

1. Recall the evidence I presented in the notes to chapter 1.

2. Benjamin Barber, *Strong Democracy: Participatory Politics for a New Age* (Berkeley: University of California Press, 1984).

3. Michael J. Piore, *Beyond Individualism* (Cambridge: Harvard University Press, 1995), p. 137.

4. Barber, *Strong Democracy*, p. 173.

5. Horwitt, *Let Me Call Them Rebel*, p. 382.

6. Mansbridge, *Beyond Adversary Democracy*.

7. Alexis de Tocqueville, *Democracy in America*, translated, edited, and with an introduction by Harvey Mansfield and Delba Winthrop (Chicago: University of Chicago Press, 2000), p. lxxiii.

8. Jane Mansbridge, "A Deliberative Perspective on Neocorporatism," in *Associations and Democracy*, ed. Joshua Cohen and Joel Rogers (London: Verso, 1995), p. 142.

9. These arguments against single-member districts in McAllen were described in chapter 4. In San Antonio, in addition to charges that single-member districts would create a so-called Brown Mafia of Mexican-American politicians, the opponents claimed that "important decisions affecting the entire city [will] be determined by myopic trade-offs for parochial politics." Bridges, *Morning Glories*, p. 198.

10. Bellah, et al., *Habits of the Heart*, pp. 199–200.

11. One critic complained that the IAF has no "transcendent vision of a society worth living in" and that Alinsky's "approach, like the CIO's, can lead only to the integration of insurgent groups into the lower reaches of the political system." These comments by Todd Gitlin are quoted in Horwitt, *Let Them Call Me Rebel*, p. 535.

12. Putnam, *Bowling Alone*, pp. 19–26, provides background on the intellectual history of the idea.

13. Industrial Areas Foundation, "Organizing for Family and Congregation" (Chicago: Industrial Areas Foundation, 1978).

14. Ernesto Cortes Jr., "Reweaving the Social Fabric: Faith, Civic Education, and Political Renewal," *Texas Journal* (spring/summer 1995): 14–23.

15. See the discussion in Putnam, *Bowling Alone*, 406–7.

16. See, for example, Amitai Etzioni, *The New Golden Rule* (New York: Basic Books, 1996).

17. Ibid., p. 81.

18. Barber, *Strong Democracy;* Michael Sandel, *Democracy's Discontent: America in Search of a Public Philosophy* (Cambridge: Harvard University Press, 1996).

19. Barber, *Strong Democracy,* p. 24.

20. Ibid., p. iv.

21. Sandel, *Democracy's Discontent,* p. 348.

22. Barber, *Strong Democracy,* p. 232.

23. Mark R. Warren and Richard L. Wood, "Faith-Based Organizing: The State of the Field" (report to the Interfaith Funders, Jericho, N.Y., 2001; also available at http://comm-org.utoledo.edu/papers2001/faith.htm)

24. Mary Bernstein, "Celebration and Suppression: The Strategic Use of Identity by the Lesbian and Gay Movement," *American Journal of Sociology* 103, no. 3 (November 1997): 531–65.

25. Seymore Martin Lipset, Martin Trow, and James Coleman, *Union Democracy* (New York: Anchor, 1962), p. 456.

26. Nelson Lichtenstein, *State of the Union* (Princeton, N.J.: Princeton University Press, 2002), p. 274.

27. John Dewey, *The People and Its Problems* (New York: 1927), p. 215. Quoted in Wiebe, *Self-Rule,* p. 175.

28. Herbert Croly, *The Promise of American Life* (Indianapolis: Bobbs-Merrill, 1909, 1965).

29. Card and Krueger, *Myth and Measurement.*

30. Joshua Cohen and Joel Rogers, *Associations and Democracy* (London: Verso, 1995).

Acknowledgments

For nearly a decade I have traveled to Texas, Arizona, California, Louisiana, and Nebraska working with IAF organizations. Not only have I learned about politics but I have grown personally. I began with virtually no appreciation of religion and found myself marveling at its impact on others and on myself. I have also learned how to practice politics, on the scale of cities and states but perhaps more important at the level of interactions between individuals.

Financial support for much of my initial work helping the IAF think through their job market strategies was provided by the Ford Foundation, and I am grateful to it and my program officer, Mara Manus. When it came to writing this book, I needed support for research, travel, and writing. The Annie E. Casey Foundation was more than generous in providing this, and I thank the foundation and my program officer, Bob Giloth. Needless to say, neither foundation bears any responsibility for the arguments I make in this book or necessarily agrees with them.

The middle chapters of the book include stories of IAF campaigns and introduce many people who are active in the organizations. In part, these stories and portraits draw from my years of work with the organizations, but they are also based on more formal interviews with many participants. Natasha Freidus, then a graduate student (now a graduate) at MIT, conducted many of these interviews. Natasha is a remarkably sensitive and perceptive interviewer. She also knows a great deal about the subject and our conversations were always instructive. It was a pleasure working with her.

Several other people helped me with research and transcriptions. On the research side, I thank Aziza Agia, Jen Schuetz, and Cathy Shaw, all of whom made important contributions. For careful and accurate work with transcriptions, I am grateful to Susan Cass, Carmen Garcia, and Jaime Fantas.

My colleagues and friends were very generous in reading book drafts and giving me comments. For this, I thank Rose Batt, Susan Eckstein, Natasha Freidus, Tom Kochan, Joel Lamstein, Rick Locke, and Mike Piore.

My agent, Lisa Adams, of the Garamond Agency, did a wonderful job of helping me think through the shape of the book. She also went beyond the call of duty by commenting extensively and perceptively on the draft manuscript. I thank my editors at Beacon—Joanne Wyckoff and Brian Halley—and my first editor, Deb Chasman, for the care they have given this book.

Obviously this book could not have been written without the cooperation of the leaders and organizers of the IAF in the Southwest. However, my debt to them goes beyond this. Working with them has been a transforming experience for me, and I am deeply grateful for the opportunity. There are too many people to thank by name, but many (though not all) appear in this book.

The book is dedicated to my family. The people I live with, Susan, Rachel, and Michelle, have been a constant source of motivation because I believe that the politics I describe will make the world a better place for them. Both of my parents died while I was writing this book, and I want to acknowledge how much I learned from them and how grateful I am to them.

Index

accountability, 12, 14, 22, 32, 122, 123, 139, 191
accountability sessions, 5–6, 33, 131, 142–144, 146
  Alvarez on, 48
  leaders and, 52
  organizers and, 54
  religion and, 98
  Richards and, 162
ACTION (domestic Peace Corp), 128
AFL-CIO, 186, 187
African-Americans
  churches and, 19, 76, 79–80, 91, 106–107
  at conferences, 6, 76
  COPS program and, 76
  Dallas Area Interfaith (DAI) and, 77, 78
  evangelicals and, 118
  IAF organizations and, 78, 79
  labor strikes and, 75
  racial concerns and, 183
  Temporary Woodlawn Organization and, 23, 76
  See also Civil Rights movement
AFSCME (public employees' union), 155, 186
agency, 34, 172, 177, 181–182
Alabama Christian Movement for Human Rights (in Birmingham), 19
Alamodome, 157
Albuquerque, 127
Alfonso, Father, 71, 103, 113, 116, 118, 139
Alinsky, Saul
  background of, 23–24
  churches and, 93, 109
  IAF culture and, 66–67
  on organizing, 55
  pragmatism and, 177
  racial issues and, 75–76
  on self-interest, 49, 173
Alliance School program, 2, 4–5, 22–23, 157–161, 174, 179, 184
Allied Communities of Tarrent (ACT), 158
allies, 144–147, 185
Alvarado, Yolanda, 50–51, 132–133, 138
Alvarez, Alicia, 48, 134
American Jewish World Service, 106
Ammerman, Nancy Tatom, 105, 110
Amos (prophet), 3
Anaya, Carmen, 52, 76, 101

Anaya, Eddie, 135, 138
anger, 45–46, 48–49, 82, 103, 134
antistatism, 137
apparel industry, 29
Arendt, Hannah, 173
Aristotle, 173
Asians, 183
Association of Catholic Trade Unionists, 105
authority, 63

Back of the Yards (BOY) organization, 23, 75–76, 93
balanced capitalism, 81
Baldwin, Carissa, 53
Baptists, 20, 79
Barber, Benjamin, 172, 173, 180, 181
Bart, Father, 71–72, 113, 116
Bellah, Robert, 82, 83, 94, 99, 113, 117–118, 137
Bennett, Willie, 55
Berman, Howard, 16
Board of Global Ministries of United Methodist Church, 107
Boden, Rosa, 4, 6
Boston, 184
boycotts, 19
Brady, Henry, 10, 123
Brand, Othal, 128
Bridges, Amy, 17
Britt, Gerald, 77, 80
Brooks, David, 7, 8
Brothers Karamazov (Dostoyevsky), 63–64
Bryan, William Jennings, 16–17
BUILD, 155, 186, 188
Burnham, Walter Dean, 9
Bush, George W., 26, 89, 101
business unionism, 185
Business Week, 8

California, 23, 29, 107, 109, 128, 168
  See also Los Angeles
call centers, 156–157
Capital Idea, 165
Caro, Robert, 125
Catholic Campaign for Human Development, 107
Catholic Church, 92, 99, 106, 107–109, 112, 119
  See also Catholics

Catholic Pentecostal movement, 118
Catholics
  African-Americans and, 79
  Alinsky and, 23
  El Paso IAF organization and, 27
  evangelicals and, 118
  immigration and, 119
  organizers and, 56
  Protestants and, 106
  social justice and, 105
  Virgin of Guadalupe and, 103–104
  See also Catholic Church
Catholic Worker movement, 105
caucus church, 99
Ceasar, Sister Pearl, 55–56, 70, 114
Chambers, Ed, 24, 93, 178, 179
charitable choice, 101
Chavez, Cesar, 23, 127
Chicago, 126, 184
China, 29
CHIP program (for uninsured children), 5
Christian Coalition, 120
Christian Right, 18, 20, 92, 118, 119, 188, 189
Christ the King Church, 98, 99, 104, 116
church(es), 14, 31, 32, 40–41, 93, 104–114
  African-Americans and, 19, 76, 79–80, 91,
    106–107
  attendance, 117, 121
  caucus, 99
  Christ the King, 98, 99, 104, 116
  denominational dilemmas, 116–121
  Holy Spirit, 110
  learning political skills and, 90–91
  Local Movement Centers and, 19
  mobilization and, 19
  Our Lady of Queen of Angels parish, 115
  Saint Joseph the Worker Church, 98, 104,
    160
  social justice and, 89–90
  St. Elizabeth Ann Seton, 107
  See also Christian Right; religion
CIO Packing Workers Organizing Commit-
  tee, 75
Cisneros, Henry, 139
Citicorp, 65
Citizens Charter Association, 126
Citizenship School, 53–54
City-County Committee, 126
civil religion, 94
Civil Rights movement
  churches and, 89, 91, 104, 109
  mobilization and, 14–15, 18–19, 20
  risk and, 47
  South Texas politics and, 127

unions and, 186
  See also Mexican-American Civil Rights
    movement
civil society, 178–182
Clark, Septima, 53–54, 104
class warfare, 25, 26
Clinton, Bill, 13, 81, 89
Cohen, Joshua, 191
colonias, 27, 30–31, 37, 64, 71, 96, 115
Common Cause, 11
communidades de base (base communities),
  96–97, 98, 99
communitarian(s), 179–180, 181
communities of action, 173
Communities Organized for Public Service
  (COPS)
  economic issues and, 148, 157
  evolution of program, 73–74
  founding of, 22, 99, 162–165
  organizers and, 55
  as political machine, 73
  race and, 76
  religion and, 99, 112–113, 114
  Sarabia as president of, 48, 175
  school finance and, 71
  single-member district system and, 129
  working with allies and, 144–145, 146
community, 7, 23, 34, 83–84, 168–170, 172–
  173, 180–182, 185
Community Development Block Grant
  funds, 74
compromise, 176–177
Congregational Development, 41, 96,
  114–116, 179
Consumer Christians, 117
contingent employment, 168–169, 186
Convergys, 157
COPS program. *See* Communities Organized for Public Service (COPS)
Cortes, Ernesto, Jr. (Ernie)
  accountability and, 144
  anger and, 48
  churches and, 93
  compromise and, 176
  decision-making process and, 71
  on organizing, 42, 69–70
  racial issues and, 76
  on "reweaving the social fabric," 179
  self-interest and, 175
  speech by, 2–4
  on suburbs, 83
  transforming the electoral system and, 129
  Valdez and, 36–37
Coughlin, Father, 109

Crisis in Black and White (Silberman), 76
Croly, Herbert, 189
Crystal City, 127
culture, organizational, 59–67
Cushing, Cardinal, 113
cynicism. *See* political cynicism

Daley, Mayor Richard J. (Chicago), 141–142
Dallas Area Interfaith (DAI), 2, 77–78
Dallas Citizens Council, 126
Dallas Independent School District, 78
Dallas Theological Seminary, 20
Davis, Nehemiah, 158
Day, Dorothy, 105
democracy
    associational, 191
    states as laboratories of, 190
    strong, 181
    thin, 172, 180, 181
    unitary vs. adversarial, 174, 176
Democracy in America, 175
Democratic Leadership Council, 13
Democratic party, 6, 12, 13, 21
    See also political parties
Democrats, 1, 9, 13, 16–17, 89
de Tocqueville, Alexis, 175, 178
Dewey, John, 189
Dionne, E. J., 33
Donovan, Sister Judy
    on anger, 49
    on labor market issues, 167
    leadership and, 44, 52–53
    religion and, 95, 109, 116
    on remaking politics, 129, 130
Dostoyevsky, Fyodor, 63–64
Drake, Jim, 37, 71, 128
DuBois, W. E. B., 106
Duquesne University, 118

economic issues, 1, 8, 26, 28, 32, 148–149
    attitudes, 7
    disconnect between politics and economics, 8
    equity/inequality, 7–8, 32, 106, 137
    individualism, 136
    justice, 89, 105
    regional economic development, 168
    See also labor market issues
education. *See* schools
efficiency wages, 152
electoral system, transforming, 129–131
employees' association, 167–168, 169, 188
employment. *See* contingent employment;
job-training programs; labor market
issues
environmental causes, 15
Episcopal Church, 106
Episcopal Diocese of Tennessee, 107
EPISO (in El Paso), 2
Espinoza, Noelia, 51, 72, 110, 133, 142
ethnic diversity, 28
evaluation ritual, 65
evangelical movement, 20, 117–118, 119

Falwell, Jerry, 20
Fantus consulting firm, 148, 150
First Unitarian Universalist Church, 107
Fitzpatrick, Bishop, 113
Flaat, Father Bart, 35, 96
Flores, Archbishop Patricio, 112–113
Florida, 29, 30
Food and Commercial Workers Union, 186
Ford Foundation, 163
Francisca, Camacho, 132–133
Frank, Father Jerry, 110, 129
free-agent churchgoers, 117
Freedom Rides, 19
free-riders, 38, 150, 174
Freidus, Natasha, 27
Freire, Paulo, 54
Friedman, Thomas, 149
Frost Bank, 144–146
Frost, Tom, 144–146, 175
Fuller Theological Seminary, 20

Gallup poll, 117, 119
Galvan, Tomasita, 102, 132–133
Ganz, Marshall, 14
Garcia, Gilbert, 23, 52–53; 102, 151
Garza, Estela Soza, 84–87, 110, 139, 151,
    153–154
General Assembly of the Presbyterian
    Church USA, 106
General Convention of the Episcopal
    Church, 106
German Social-Democratic party, 67
Germany, 1
globalization, 1, 149
God, 102, 103
Gonzalez, Berta, 133, 138, 158–159
Good Government League, 126
Gore, Al, 8, 13, 25–26, 89, 101
Graf, Arnie, 56
Greeley, Andrew, 109
Guevara, Father Alfonso, 6, 47, 98–100
Gutierrez, Rosa
    background of, 35–36

Bart and, 96
communidades de base (base communi-
    ties) and, 97
health care issues and, 85–87
religion and, 103–104
self-interest and, 50
single-member district campaign and, 131
teaching politics and, 146, 192
on voting, 138–139

Habits of the Heart, 82, 136, 176
Haiti, 29
Hansen, John Mark, 15, 124
Harvard University, 154–155
health issues, 5–6, 13, 23, 46, 84–87, 167, 186
Herberg, Will, 108
Herrera, Elida, 132–133, 134, 139
Higgins, Monsignor George, 109
Higgs, Joe, 55
Highlander citizenship schools, 104
Highlander Folk School, 20, 53
High School Evangelical Fellowship, 20
Hinojosa, Joe, 48–49, 53, 110, 135, 137–138,
    139–140
Hispanic(s)
    churches and, 107, 109, 118
    Cisneros as, 139
    at conference, 6
    COPS program and, 76
    Dallas Area Interfaith (DAI) and, 77, 78
    education issue and, 80
    in IAF, 78–79
    Mexican-American Youth Movement
        (MAYO) and, 98
    race issue and, 183
    South Texas politics and, 127
    St. Joseph the Worker Church and, 95–96
History of the Peloponnesian War (Thu-
    cydides), 61
Hobbes, Thomas, 180
Holy Spirit Church, 110
Horton, Myles, 53, 54
Hotel Employees Restaurant Employees
    (HERE), 186
house meetings
    decision-making and, 72–73
    expansion of IAF and, 182
    functions of, 47
    IAF model and, 191
    IAF organization building and, 46–47
    institutional development and, 66
    job-training programs and, 161
    labor market and, 166, 167
    Milagro Health Clinic and, 85–86

organizational structure of IAF and,
    42–43
organizers/leaders and, 70–71
on organizing, 35–36
on relational techniques of, 173
religion and, 96, 115, 116
schools and, 160
single-member district system/campaign
    and, 130, 131
training for, 37
Hughes, Karen, 26
Human Development Fund, 165, 169
Human Development Fund and Alliance
    Schools conference, 2–5

IBM (International Business Machines), 59
identity politics, 42, 184, 185
immigrants, 10, 17, 108, 166, 179, 184, 186
immigration, 28, 31, 119, 121
incentive packages, 156
individualism, 136–137, 174
Industrial Areas Foundation (IAF)
    Alliance School program, 2, 4–5, 22–23,
        157–161, 174, 179, 184
    as broad-based, 106–107, 124, 140, 176–177
    Catholic Church and, 106, 107–109
    Chambers and, 24
    as coalition, 33
    Congregational Development and, 114–116
    Cortes and, 24
    culture of, 60–67
    decision-making in, 72–73
    described, 2, 22, 24–25, 26–27
    doing good and, 51–52
    faith-based character of, 26
    Human Development Fund and Alliance
        Schools conference, 2–5, 22, 24
    institutional development, 66
    iron law of oligarchy and, 69
    leaders/leadership development, 35–37,
        43–45, 47–54, 69, 70–73, 132–135, 187,
        188
    legislation and, 23
    multiple issues of, 25
    one-on-ones, 45–46, 160, 167, 173, 182
    organizers, 43, 45, 54–58, 69, 70–73
    political machines and, 140–142
    political views and, 137–139
    racial issues and, 75–81
    rally, 5–6
    social theory and, 178–182
    South Texas politics and, 124–127
    suburbs and, 81–84
    teaching politics at multiple levels, 146

working with allies, 144–147
See also accountability sessions; Alinsky, Saul; Communities Organized for Public Service (COPS); house meetings; Industrial Areas Foundation (IAF) model; labor market issues; organization building; organizing; religion; Rio Grande Valley; union(s); Valley Interfaith
Industrial Areas Foundation (IAF) model
on advantages of, 25
church and, 93, 119
on core of, 31
extending the, 32, 182–183, 185–188
importance of, 39
of politics, 171–177, 191
for progressive politics, 34, 39
institutional development, 66
Inter Civic Council (in Tallahassee), 19
Internal Revenue Service, 8
international trade, 28
See also NAFTA (North American Free Trade Agreement)
iron law of oligarchy, 67–69, 73
iron rule, 64–65, 67
Is Latin America Turning Protestant?, 118
isolation, 50–51, 83

Japan, 1
Jesus Christ, 102, 103, 106
Jewish Fund for Justice, 107
Jewish traditions/congregations, 105–107, 109
Jim Crow laws, 19, 29
Job Path, 165
job-training programs, 129, 161–165
Johnson, Lyndon, 125
Justice for Janitors campaign, 186, 187

Katznelson, Ira, 141, 147
Kevers, Bill, 78
Keyssar, Alex, 11
Kids Action Assembly, 160
King, Dr. Martin Luther, 53
Knights of Columbus, 11
Knights of Labor, 105
Konecny, Sister Mignonne, 158
Kress, Sandy, 78

labor market issues, 148–170
Alliance School program, 157–161
community strategies and, 168–170
high-wage employment issue, 155–157
job-training programs, 129, 161–165

living wage campaigns, 150–155, 166, 169, 180
organization building and, 166–168
See also economic issues
labor movement, 67
LA Metro, 40
La Milipas, 64
La Raza, 109
Latin America, 96, 97, 118
leaders/leadership development, 35–37, 43–45, 47–54, 67, 69, 70–73, 132–135, 187, 188
Leo XIII, Pope, 105
Levine, Mel, 16
Levi Strauss, 161
liberation theology, 96
Lichtenstein, Nelson, 187
Lilienthal, David, 68
Lipset, Seymour Martin, 136–137
living wage campaigns, 150–155, 166, 169, 180
Local Movement Centers, 19–20
Lopez, Maria, 45, 46, 48
Los Angeles, 40, 183, 184, 186
See also California
Lucio, Eduardo, 5–6

Madison, James, 177, 178
Manning, Archbishop Timothy, 109
Mansbridge, Jane, 174, 175
Mansfield, Harvey, 175
Maryland (Montgomery County), 7
Massachusetts, 168
Mayhew, David, 16, 126
McAllen
Alliance Schools and, 160
business community and Valley Interfaith, 64
economic development and, 148, 157
Holy Spirit Church in, 110
on mayor of, 125
Mexico and city leaders in, 30
Milagro Clinic in, 85, 86–87
Rio Grande Valley and, 29
Saint Joseph the Worker Church in, 95–96, 104
single-member district system and, 128–129, 130
McAllen Economic Development Commission, 148
McCluskey, Tim, 96
McIntyre, Cardinal, 109
McKinley, William, 16–17
McWilliams, Wilson Carey, 34

meatpacking industry, 166
Medicaid, 5–6, 30
Melian Debate, 61–64, 67
Merton, Robert, 141
Metro Alliance, 73, 74, 76, 162–165
Mexican-American Civil Rights movement,
    24
Mexican-Americans, 28, 29, 96, 99, 112–113,
    125, 126, 128
Mexican American Youth Movement
    (MAYO), 98
Mexicans, 29, 125
Mexico, 27, 28, 29, 30, 98, 103–104, 127, 151
Michels, Robert, 67
Milagro Health Clinic, 84–87, 96, 146
minimum wage, 150–151, 189
Mississippi, 53
mobilization, 14–18
    Christian Right and, 18, 20
    churches and, 19
    Civil Rights movement and, 18–19
    Cortes on, 42
    IAF model for, 171, 185
    on institutions for, 33–34
    local, 6, 9, 188
    requirements for effective, 12
    unions and, 18, 20–21
Montgomery Bus Boycott, 19
Montgomery Improvement Association
    (MIA), 19
Moody Bible Institute, 20
Moral Majority, 26
Morningside Middle School, 158
Morris, Aldon, 18–19
Moses, Mike, 78
motor voter bill, 11

NAFTA (North American Free Trade Agree-
    ment), 29, 30, 31
Nashville Christian Leadership Council, 19
National Association for the Advancement
    of Colored People (NAACP), 19
National Association of Evangelicals, 20
National Conference of Catholic Bishops,
    130
National Conference of Catholic Charities,
    93
National Council of Churches, 106
National Election Surveys, 26, 92
National Voter Registration Act, 11
New Deal, 12, 68, 105, 109, 137, 189, 190
New York, 23, 24
New York City, 23, 126, 168
North Carolina, 168

Omaha, Nebraska, 166, 186
one-on-ones, 45–46, 160, 167, 173, 182
organization building, 35–87
    culture and, 59–67
    dilemmas of, 67–73
    keeping to original mission in, 73–74
    labor market initiatives and, 166–168
    leadership and, 47–54
    Milagro Health Clinic and, 84–87
    organizers and, 54–58
    race and, 75–81
    suburbs and, 81–84
organizers, 43, 45, 54–58, 69, 70–73
organizing, 3–4, 31–32, 34, 54–58, 69–70
    community, 23
    Cortes on, 42
    faith-based, 182
    living wage campaign as device for, 155
    on process of, 85
    as professional career, 55
    suburban, 82–83
    in wealthy congregations, 109–110
Organizing for Family and Congregation, 178
Ortega, Linda, 74
Our Lady of Queen of Angels parish, 115

parent contract, 160
Parks, Rosa, 19
Parr, George, 125
pastors, 95–100, 110–112
Pauken, Tom, 128
Payne, Charles, 53, 54
Pedagogy of the Oppressed (Freire), 54
Pennsylvania, 7, 120
Perkins, Perry, 158
Perot, Ross, 145
Philadelphia Interfatih Action, 109
Phoenix, 186
Piore, Michael, 173
political attitudes, 9
political cynicism, 6–7, 12, 14, 33, 47, 122, 138
political machines, 17, 73, 127, 140–142
political participation, 10–12, 15, 37–38, 122,
    123–124
political parties, 9, 14, 15–17, 22, 34, 41, 81,
    185
    See also Democratic party; Republican
    party
political pragmatism, 62–63, 67, 177
political views, 136–140
politics
    decline in, 1–2
    disconnect between economics and, 9
    general contempt for, 9–10

national vs. local, 189–190
of workplace vs. neighborhoods, 147
Populists, 16–17
poverty, 28, 81
power, 32, 177, 179, 182, 183
    Dostoyevsky story and, 64
    forms of, 3–4, 67
    leaders and, 67
    Melian Debate and, 61–62
    political organizations and, 38
    public relationships and, 65
    sources of, 175–176
    suburbs and, 81–83
pragmatism. See political pragmatism
Presbyterian Church USA, 106, 107
procedural republic, 180
Progressive Religious Partnership, 120
Project QUEST, 22, 145, 162–165, 169, 175,
    190–191
"Pronouncement on Christian Faith: Eco-
    nomic Life and Justice" (United
    Church of Christ), 106
Protestants, 105–109, 117
Putnam, Robert, 121, 178, 179

QUEST. See Project QUEST

racial issues, 25, 27, 75–81, 183
Rauschenbusch, Walter, 105–107
Reagan administration, 128
realpolitik, 62–63
red-baiting, 27, 128
Reed, John, 65
Reichley, A. James, 16
relationships, public vs. private, 65–66
religion, 88–121
    charitable choice and, 101
    civil, 94
    Congregational Development and, 41, 96,
        114–116, 179
    denominational dilemmas, 116–121
    "faith-based" social policy, 89
    on mixing politics and, 101–102
    organizing and, 31–32
    pastors and, 95–100, 110–112
    progressive potential of, 90–92
    relationship between voting patterns
        and, 89
    social justice and, 89–90, 105, 105–107
    social movements and, 104
    See also Christian Right; church(es)
Religious Right, 89, 120
Remediation Institute, 164
representative government, 180

republican freedom, 181
Republican party, 26, 27, 128, 188
    See also political parties
Republicans, 9, 13, 17, 89
Rerum Novarum (Pope Leo XIII), 105
retirement security, 13
Richards, Ann, 162
Rio Grande Valley, 4–6, 23, 27–31, 35–36,
    76–77, 118, 188
Robertson, Pat, 20, 120
Rogers, Joel, 13, 191
Roosevelt, Franklin, 189
Roosevelt High School, 161
Roosevelt, Teddy, 189
Rosenstone, Steven, 15, 124
Rousseau, Jean-Jacques, 181
Rubio, Joe, 55
Ryan, John Augustine, 109

Saint Joseph the Worker Church, 95–96, 98,
    104, 160
Sam Houston elementary school, 160
San Antonio
    Cisneros as mayor of, 139
    Fantus consulting firm and, 148
    Frost and, 144, 146
    introduction to, 28
    job-training programs and, 161, 164–165,
        190–191
    Valdez as leader in, 37
    on voting in, 125, 126
Sanchez, Joaquin, 45, 46, 48
Sanchez, Sister Maria, 87, 152
Sandel, Michael, 180, 181
Sarabia, Andy, 48
Schattschneider, E. E., 10
Schlozman, Kay Lehman, 10, 123
schools, 93, 121, 147, 153–155
    See also Alliance School program
self-interest
    doing good vs., 51
    IAF focus on, 173–175, 176, 177, 182
    Melian Debate and, 61, 62
    power of, 49–50
    public vs. private relationships and, 65
    racial issues and, 80
    religion and, 107, 109, 110, 113, 115
    suburbs and, 82
Selznick, Philip, 68, 73, 74
Semi-Sovereign People, The (Schatt-
    schneider), 10
Service Employees International Union
    (SEIU), 69, 186
Sheil, Auxiliary Bishop Bernard J., 93

Shirley, Dennis, 160, 161
Silberman, Charles, 76
Sinclair, Upton, 75
single-member district system/campaign, 129, 130–131, 176
Skocpol, Theda, 11
slam-dunk group, 78
social capital, 179, 181
Social Gospel, doctrine of the, 105
social justice, 105–107, 137
social movements, 14–15
Social Principles of the United Methodist Church, 106
social theory, 178–182
Sombart, Werner, 25
South America, 29, 97
Southeast Conference of United Church of Christ, 107
Southern Christian Leadership Conference, 20, 53
South Padre Island, 30
special interests, 176
stadiums, 157
Starr County, 127
St. Elizabeth Ann Seton Church, 107
Stephens, Sister Christine, 49, 55–56, 58, 73, 74, 77–78, 129, 145
Student Nonviolent Coordinating Committee (SNCC), 19, 53
suburbs, 81–84, 117, 121, 138, 184

Tarrow, Sidney, 14
Teamsters, 186
Teixeira, Ruy, 13
Temporary Woodlawn Organization, 23, 76, 87
Tennessee Valley Authority (TVA), 68
Texas
    Austin, 165
    Brownsville, 29, 30, 43, 71, 98, 104, 157
    Crystal City, 127
    Dallas, 27, 28, 78, 84, 126, 145, 161, 165
    El Paso, 27, 37, 55, 126, 165
    Fort Worth, 55, 126, 158
    Houston, 28
    IAF conference in, 2–5
    living wage campaign and, 150
    Plano, 107
    Republican party, 128
    Rio Grande Valley in, 4–6, 23, 27–31, 35–36, 76–77, 118, 188
    South, 124–127, 155–156
    Starr County, 127
    See also McAllen; San Antonio

Thucydides (Greek historian), 61
tikkun olam, 106
TNT (Tying Nashville Together), 107
tough love, 64, 65
Tucson, 165
TVA and the Grass Roots, The (Selznick), 68

union(s), 1, 22, 93, 121, 168, 179, 182, 184, 188, 189
    AFL-CIO, 186, 187
    AFSCME (public employees' union), 155, 186
    Alinsky and, 23
    allies and, 145
    American Catholic Church and, 105
    Association of Catholic Trade Unionists, 105
    as broad-based organizations, 41
    business unionism, 185–186
    CIO Packing Workers Organizing Committee, 75
    decline of, 149
    differences between union and IAF cultures, 186–187
    as element of progressive coalition, 34
    Food and Commercial Workers Union, 186
    Higgins and, 109
    Hotel Employees Restaurant Employees (HERE), 186
    labor market initiatives and, 166
    living wage campaigns and, 155
    maintaining organizations and, 58
    mobilization and, 14, 18, 20–21
    NAFTA and, 29
    organizing, 47
    race and, 75
    Service Employees International Union (SEIU), 69, 186
    Teamsters, 186
    United Farm Workers, 24, 128
    UNITE (garment workers' union), 120, 186
    Valdez as president of, 36–37
United Christian Movement (in Shreveport, La.), 19–20
United Church of Christ, 106, 107
United Farm Workers, 24, 128
United Food and Commercial Workers, 166
United Methodist Church, 106, 107
United Parcel Service, 186
United Power for Action and Justice, 40, 184
UNITE (garment workers' union), 120, 186
University of Alabama, 91
urban reformers, 17

Vaello, Chayo, 103, 138
Valdez, Elizabeth, 35, 36–37, 73–74, 143, 146,
    165
Valley Interfaith
    accountability and, 142–144
    attendance at conference and rally, 2, 6
    budget goals of, 41
    COPS program and, 74
    decision-making and, 71–72
    doing good and, 52
    Donovan and, 95
    Gutierrez and, 35–36
    health care and, 84
    Hinojosa and, 110, 135, 139–140
    institutional development and, 66
    iron law of oligarchy and, 69
    issues and, 43
    labor market initiatives and, 167
    leaders, 43–47, 49–50, 71, 132–135
    living wage campaign, 150–155
    members of, 40
    Milagro Health Clinic and, 87
    organizational culture and, 64
    organizers and, 55, 71
    religion and, 96, 97–98, 99, 101, 102, 104,
        110, 113, 115–116
    remaking politics in the Valley, 128–131
    South Texas politics and, 125
    Valdez and, 37
values issue, 26, 177–178, 180
Verba, Sidney, 10, 90, 91, 123
Veterans of Foreign Wars, 11
VIDA (job-training program), 129, 165
Virgin of Guadalupe, 103–104
Voice of Christian Youth, 20
voluntarism, 117
Von Hoffman, Nicholas, 76

voting
    churches and registration for, 20
    class bias in, 11–12
    importance of, 138–139
    income and, 10–11
    political involvement and, 37
    rates, 16
    registration for, 94
    relationship between religion and pat-
        terns of, 89
    secular decline in, 17–18
    in South Texas politics, 125–126
    turnout for, 9–10, 11–12, 17, 122–123
    unions and, 21

Washington, D.C., 1, 2, 7, 14, 19, 42, 168, 189
Waxman, Henry, 16
Weil, Sandy, 65
welfare reform, 89
White, Mark, 128
Why Is There No Socialism in the United
    States? (Sombart), 25
Wiebe, Robert, 18
Wilson, William Julius, 75
Winthrop, Delba, 175
Wolfe, Alan, 9, 81, 83, 92, 117, 136, 137
Wolff, Nelson, 130
Women's Political Council, 19
workers' association. See employees'
    association
World Trade Organization, 2
Wuthnow, Robert, 20, 92, 111, 117

Youth for Christ, 20

Zavala elementary school, 161
zone of indeterminancy, 152